ENVIRONMENTAL POLICYMAKING AND STAKEHOLDER COLLABORATION

Theory and Practice

American Society for Public Administration
Series in Public Administration & Public Policy

David H. Rosenbloom, Ph.D.
Editor-in-Chief

Mission: Throughout its history, ASPA has sought to be true to its founding principles of promoting scholarship and professionalism within the public service. The ASPA Book Series on Public Administration and Public Policy publishes books that increase national and international interest for public administration and which discuss practical or cutting edge topics in engaging ways of interest to practitioners, policy makers, and those concerned with bringing scholarship to the practice of public administration.

RECENT PUBLICATIONS

**Environmental Policymaking and Stakeholder Collaboration:
Theory and Practice**
by Shannon K. Orr

Organizational Assessment and Improvement in the Public Sector Workbook
by Kathleen M. Immordino

Challenges in City Management: A Case Study Approach
by Becky J. Starnes

**Local Economic Development and the Environment:
Finding Common Ground**
by Susan M. Opp and Jeffery L. Osgood, Jr.

Case Studies in Disaster Response and Emergency Management
by Nicolas A. Valcik and Paul E. Tracy

**Debating Public Administration:
Management Challenges, Choices, and Opportunities**
by Robert F. Durant and Jennifer R.S. Durant

Effective Non-Profit Management: Context, Concepts, and Competencies
by Shamima Ahmed

Environmental Decision-Making in Context: A Toolbox
by Chad J. McGuire

American Society for Public Administration
Series in Public Administration and Public Policy

ENVIRONMENTAL POLICYMAKING AND STAKEHOLDER COLLABORATION

Theory and Practice

SHANNON K. ORR

CRC Press
Taylor & Francis Group
Boca Raton   London   New York

CRC Press is an imprint of the
Taylor & Francis Group, an **Informa** business

CRC Press
Taylor & Francis Group
6000 Broken Sound Parkway NW, Suite 300
Boca Raton, FL 33487-2742

© 2014 by Taylor & Francis Group, LLC
CRC Press is an imprint of Taylor & Francis Group, an Informa business

No claim to original U.S. Government works

Printed on acid-free paper
Version Date: 20131203

International Standard Book Number-13: 978-1-4822-0638-8 (Hardback)

Library of Congress Cataloging-in-Publication Data

Orr, Shannon K.
    Environmental policymaking and stakeholder collaboration : theory and practice / Shannon K. Orr.
        pages cm. -- (American society for public administration)
    Includes bibliographical references and index.
    ISBN 978-1-4822-0638-8 (hardcover : alk. paper) 1. Environmental policy--United States--History. 2. Environmental policy--History. I. Title.

GE180.O77 2014
333.70973--dc23   2013038222

Visit the Taylor & Francis Web site at
http://www.taylorandfrancis.com

and the CRC Press Web site at
http://www.crcpress.com

To my daughter Bella,
whose long naps made this book possible.

Contents

List of Figures xiii
List of Tables xv
Preface...xvii
Acknowledgments xix
About the Author xxi

1   Introduction 1
    Introduction 1
    Central Concepts.. 3
        Stakeholders.. 3
        Public Policy 7
    Stakeholder Collaboration Planning 8
    Overview 11
    References 12

2   Stakeholders: Theoretical Foundations 15
    Introduction 15
    Stakeholder Theories.. 18
        Stakeholder Definitions 18
        Stakeholders and Policy Theory 19
        Approaches to Stakeholder Analysis....................................... 23
    Interest-Based Typology... 26
    Identifying Stakeholders 29
    Stakeholder Interests 31
        Sources of Interests 32
        Conflict and Participation 33
        Changing Interests.. 36
    Stakeholder Participation 37
        Nonparticipation 37
        Levels of Stakeholder Involvement... 38
        Successful Collaboration... 39

Counterarguments to Participation..41
Conclusion..44
References...46

3 Stakeholders and Decision Making..49
Introduction 49
Stakeholders and Public Policymaking 50
    Problem Definition..50
    Agenda Setting 51
    Policy Formulation 52
    Policy Legitimation..54
    Implementation 54
    Evaluation..55
Importance of Stakeholders for Policymaking...........................55
    Expertise and Resource Sharing...56
    Policy Relevance 57
    Fostering Innovation...59
    Anticipate Reactions 59
    Trust and Legitimacy..61
Stakeholder and Agency Roles 63
    Agency Responsibilities 64
    Stakeholder Burnout...64
Inclusivity and Working with Marginalized Groups................65
    Theoretical Considerations 65
    Practical Considerations 65
    Helping Stakeholders Feel Valued..68
Conflict Management...69
    Sources of Conflict 69
    Intervention 70
Measuring Effectiveness of Stakeholder Collaboration...........72
Working with Stakeholders in Policymaking.............................73
    Initial Assessment 73
    Stages of Participation 74
    Information-Sharing Considerations 75
Promoting Good Communication..75
    Dealing with Threats 76
    Managing Technical Complexity..77
Stakeholder Participation Ideas in Practice 79
    United Nations Conference on Sustainable Development
    (Rio+20) 79
    Dialogue on Public Involvement in EPA's Decisions.......81
    Citizen Science 82
    Online Gaming 83

      Mobile Apps 83
   Conclusion...84
   References...86

4 Case Study: Yellowstone National Park...............................**91**
   Introduction 91
   Yellowstone National Park 92
   Bear Management..93
       Policy Background...93
       Policy and Stakeholder Analysis................................95
   Wolf Reintroduction...96
       Policy Background...96
       Policy and Stakeholder Analysis................................97
   Snowmobiles..98
       Policy Background...98
       Policy and Stakeholder Analysis..............................101
   Bioprospecting and Benefits Sharing................................101
       Policy Background...101
       Policy and Stakeholder Analysis..............................105
   Wildfires..105
       Policy Background...105
       Policy and Stakeholder Analysis..............................107
   Conclusion..107
   References...110

5 Stakeholder Collaboration Tools......................................**111**
   Introduction 111
   Planning 111
   Recruitment Tools 114
       Networking 114
       The *Federal Register*...114
       Sampling 125
       Public Notices 125
       Social Media 127
   Identifying Stakeholder Interests 127
       Stakeholder Analysis..127
       Proximity and Power Diagram 127
       Fishbowl..129
       Electoral Process 130
       Imbizo 130
       Focus Group 131
       Dot Poster..133
       Mobility Map 133

Village Walk 134
Seasonal Calendar 135
Participatory Cost/Benefit Analysis 136
Surveys 137
Public Comments 138
Experimental Auction 139
Engagement Tools...140
Road Show...140
Community-Directed Visual Images 140
Listserv 141
Retreat...141
Town Hall Meeting 142
Historical Mapping 142
Kitchen Table Discussion..143
Mobile Apps 143
Field Trip 144
Citizen Jury 144
Partnership Grants..145
Public Forum...145
Social Media..147
Strategic Thinking Tools...150
Impact/Effort Matrix 150
Charrette 151
Force Field Analysis 152
Ranking and Sorting 152
Problem Tree 153
Consensus Workshop 154
Social Audit 155
Citizen Report Card and Community Scorecard..........................156
Delphi Study 157
Concentric Circles 158
Risk Chart 159
Open-Ended Stories..161
Advisory Committee..161
Residents' Panel 162
SWOT Analysis...163
Brainstorming...164
Education 167
Public Exhibition..167
Speakers' Bureau 167
Website 168
Storefront..169
Deliberative Polling 170

Workshop 170
Conference 171
Technical Reports 171
Press Conference 171
Radio/Talk Shows 172
Telephone Hotline 172
Brochure 173
Agency Open House 173
Mailouts 173
Public Speaking 174
Featured Media Stories 174
Inserts and Advertisements in Newspapers 174
Newsletters 176
Project Management Tools for Stakeholder Collaboration 176
Meeting Planning Tools 176
Project Scope Chart 177
Gantt Chart 177
Logical Framework 180
Communication and Teamwork Tools 181
Communication Needs Assessment 181
Active Listening 181
Stakeholder Introductions 181
Team-Building Exercises 184
Conclusion 185
References 186

Index **189**

List of Figures

Figure 3.1   EPA stakeholder involvement continuum. 63

Figure 3.2   Agency roles. 64

Figure 5.1   Steps to organize stakeholder initiatives. 112

Figure 5.2   Proximity and power diagram for stakeholder analysis. 129

Figure 5.3   Mobility map of city nature preserve. 134

Figure 5.4   Impact/effort matrix. 151

Figure 5.5   Force Field Analysis. 152

Figure 5.6   Problem tree construction. 153

Figure 5.7   Sample problem tree—lack of clean water. 154

Figure 5.8   Concentric circles for public park amenities. 159

Figure 5.9   Risk chart. 160

Figure 5.10   Risk chart of threats to the Komodo dragon. 160

Figure 5.11   Starburst brainstorming. 166

List of Tables

Table 1.1   Environmental Stakeholders by Interests 4

Table 2.1   Stakeholder Models in Public Policy 24

Table 2.2   Stakeholder Typology 28

Table 2.3   Policy Stakes and Interests 34

Table 2.4   Sources of Conflict in Stakeholder Collaboration 36

Table 2.5   Stakeholders in Key Policy Issues....................................45

Table 3.1   Challenge.gov Challenges 60

Table 3.2   Sources of Stakeholder Conflict 70

Table 4.1   Winter Use Policy History 102

Table 4.2   Stakeholders and National Parks Policy in Yellowstone..............108

Table 5.1   Stakeholder Tools Summary.. 115

Table 5.2   Questions to Consider When Choosing a Collaboration Tool 126

Table 5.3   Stakeholder Analysis 128

Table 5.4   Threats to Local Agriculture 135

Table 5.5   Seasonal Calendar for Local Nature Preserve Activities 136

Table 5.6   Floor Plan Options for a Public Event................................146

Table 5.7   SWOT Strategies 164

Table 5.8   Writing a Press Release..175

Table 5.9   Action Notes Template...177

Table 5.10 Project Scope Chart...178

Table 5.11 Basic Gantt Chart with Prioritizing.................................179

Table 5.12 Gantt Chart with Assigned Tasks...179

Table 5.13 The Logical Framework...180

Table 5.14 Logical Framework for Stakeholder Collaboration in Local
Watershed Issues...180

Table 5.15 Communication Needs of Stakeholders.......................................181

Table 5.16 Active Listening Techniques..182

Preface

The history of environmental policy is characterized by challenges and controversy. From the failure to develop a policy to effectively address greenhouse gas emissions in the United States, to the rising number of species on endangered lists, environmental policy formation is a complex proposition. While causes of failure are numerous, conflict between interests or stakeholders has in many ways become a defining characteristic of environmental policymaking.

The idea for this book first came to me in 2002 when I was at the United Nations Framework Convention on Climate Change (UNFCCC) negotiations in New Delhi, India. I was there doing research on nongovernmental organizations, spending most of my days chasing people down for interviews and finding out what they hoped to achieve at the negotiations. Toward the end of the two-week negotiations a young man approached me and introduced himself as the director of a small NGO in India that was working to bring wells to rural communities in India. He asked me how he could talk to the government delegates about his project, because no one was listening to his ideas and he was not sure what to do next. In that moment it struck me how fundamentally challenging it is, in a world with so many diverse and competing voices, for those with good ideas but little experience to be heard. The established NGOs knew what they wanted to accomplish and how to make it happen. They knew how to network with each other and with delegates, how to capture the attention of the media, and how to make sure their voices were heard by those in power. But so many stakeholders lack the sophistication, experience, knowledge, and capacity to know how to achieve those goals, or even how to get just one government delegate to listen to what they have to say.

This book is intended not just to assist government agencies but also to encourage organizations and individuals to think more constructively about collaborating with other interests, particularly those representing marginalized groups. The first half of this book is focused on theories of stakeholder collaboration, on understanding why stakeholder collaboration is simultaneously critical for effective policymaking and so challenging. The second half of this book is a collection of practical and applied tools that government and stakeholders can use to actually make collaboration work in a meaningful way. While the focus of this book is on environmental policymaking, the theories and tools can be applied to any issue area. Government cannot be expected to solve our public problems in isolation; we must ensure that diverse interests are heard and represented in the policymaking process.

Acknowledgments

I would like to thank the many people who have supported me throughout this project. I thank Dr. Charles Elder of Wayne State University, who helped me to work through many of the early ideas that are now in the book. He continues to inspire me to take on new challenges in academia. I would also like to thank my graduate research assistant Briana Walsh, who handled a series of research disasters with laughter and a positive spirit and was an immense help with this book. This book would not have been possible without the graduate students in my Environmental Management and Program Evaluation classes, who helped me develop and test many of these tools and whose spirited discussions of stakeholders helped me to develop many of the ideas discussed in this book. Lenore McMillan took being a supportive friend to a new level by creating the figures for this book, a poor use for her incredible artistic skills, but highly appreciated nonetheless. Thanks to the Bowling Green State University Institute for the Study of Culture and Society for their funding support; portions of this book were written while I was a Scholar in Residence at the Institute. I thank also my colleagues in the Political Science Department; I am privileged to work with people who strive for excellence in teaching and research.

I extend much gratitude to my entire family, who are enthusiastic supporters of all that I do. A special thank-you to my parents, who had the good sense to never say the words "Are you done yet?" My father taught me to pursue a career that brings happiness and fulfillment, a gift for which I am thankful every day. My stepmother Ann has instilled in me the importance of balance and being open to new opportunities. Thank you to my husband, Marco, who brings so much laughter to my life, and whose boundless support makes anything possible. I'm glad we're on this journey together. And to my daughter Bella, a special thank-you for reminding me of the importance of naps, snacks, and finding joy in the simple pleasures of life.

About the Author

Shannon K. Orr is Associate Professor of Political Science at Bowling Green State University. Shannon has written extensively on the role of competing interests in the policymaking process. Her research combines an institutionalist framework with a pluralist orientation to study policymaking at both the domestic and international levels. Her research has been funded by the Canadian Embassy in Ottawa, the Social Science and Humanities Research Council (SSHRC), Hosted Survey, the American Political Science Association, and Bowling Green State University. The research for this book was funded in part by a fellowship through the Bowling Green State University Institute for the Study of Culture and Society.

Chapter 1

Introduction

Introduction

Manatees are one of the enigmas of the seas: great, lumbering creatures endowed with docile and curious natures. Currently classified as endangered by both the federal and state governments, and predicted to eventually face extinction, manatees have become the center of a contentious battle between divisive interests. In Crystal River, Florida, manatees have started congregating at the warm water outflows near power plants, rather than migrating south, raising conservation concerns both for their dependence on the continued operation of the power plants and for their year-round residency in highly developed areas. Neither sought after for hunting nor prey to a larger predator, the main threat facing manatees is usually boat propellers, often causing dismemberment or disfiguring gashes along their bodies. The issues at stake are both complicated and emotional: boating regulations, property rights, tourism money, and of course conservation of a species that is both curious and awe-inspiring (White 2013).

The Crystal River issue highlights the challenges of making environmental policy today. While ultimately it is the responsibility of governments to make the decisions that become law, the process through which that happens occurs in an arena crowded with diverse interests or stakeholders, including interest groups, the private sector, scientists, the media, political officials, and local citizens, among others. These stakeholders exert power and influence at every stage of the decision-making process. There is growing recognition of the importance of integrating multiple viewpoints in environmental policymaking and the value of expanding the use of more inclusive and participatory processes involving multiple stakeholders in decision making at all levels of government (Koontz 2005; McGurk, Sinclair, et al. 2006; Santos, Antunes, et al. 2006; Mangun, Throgmorton, et al. 2007; Watson and Foster-Fishman 2013). While many applaud these efforts, there is still much to understand both theoretically and practically about how to integrate inclusive stakeholder practices into the policy process. Public information forums and token advisory groups that rarely meet, while often preferred by decision makers for their ease of use, are insufficient. Public and stakeholder participation in environmental issues requires the development of new ground rules and new expectations in order to facilitate efficient and effective policymaking.

Environmental Policymaking and Stakeholder Collaboration is a critical appraisal of why environmental policies fail or succeed from the perspective of stakeholder collaboration. At the heart of the argument of this book is the idea that stakeholders matter. Too often in management decision making we ignore the voices of dissent. This book argues that principles of stakeholder collaboration are key to navigating complicated decisions and negotiations. In addition to an examination of policy and stakeholder theory, the book also provides a series of resources to guide the implementation of inclusive approaches to stakeholder collaboration to be used by both governments and organizations to improve decision making.

The argument of this book is that the role of stakeholders, along with the frequent reluctance of decision makers and stakeholders to work with each other, is a key factor for policy failure, and conversely, that appropriate stakeholder collaboration techniques can both improve policy outcomes, and in many cases facilitate the policymaking process. There is a fundamental difference here between simple stakeholder input, such as an online comment form or an inactive Facebook page, and true partnership/collaboration, which may be more complicated, but creates opportunities for dialogue, innovation, and bridging differences to forge a common understanding. This book focuses on the challenges and opportunities for integrating stakeholders into environmental policymaking.

This book is important because in an era of heightened demand for accountability, stakeholder participation must be a key component of the policy process. Stakeholder collaboration increases the likelihood of successful policymaking because it promotes policymaking that is culturally sensitive (Gilliam, Davis, et al. 2002), is based on partnership models rather than adversarial relations (McDaniel and Miskel 2002), increases innovation by tapping into diverse expertise and resources (Burroughs 1999; Olden 2003; Dedual, Sague Pla, et al. 2013), promotes higher levels of trust in decision makers and policymaking (Selin, Schuett, et al. 2000), helps establish credibility (Gilliam, Davis, et al. 2002), and ensures more efficient implementation of policies and programs (Jonsson 2005).

The Malpai Borderland Group is an example of how stakeholder collaboration can provide meaningful improvements to policy problems. Ranchers in the Malpai region of New Mexico and Arizona face a number of challenges: erosion, development threats, and water shortages that are difficult to address alone. Policy issues related to water management such as water quality, fish and wildlife habitat, and flood management have traditionally been managed through government agencies operating under technocratic decision-making processes. Public participation in water management was limited to public hearings and comment periods that simply refined or fine-tuned agency policy proposals or informed participants about decisions.

The Malpai Borderlands Group was formed as a collaborative arrangement between ranchers, the Nature Conservancy, the Bureau of Land Management, and the Department of the Interior's Fish and Wildlife Service to try to address these challenges and create a new model for policymaking and ecosystem management. Together the group has developed a joint fire management policy to try to improve wildlife habitat, reseeding programs, and additional cooperative arrangements with universities and other government agencies to try to improve the watershed. One of the most innovative projects the group has developed is a 300,000-acre conservation easement, or "grass bank" set aside in perpetuity for grass and prairie conservation. In periods of drought, the provisions of the easement allow ranchers to move their cattle onto the grass bank when the forage available on their own lands is too sparse. Inclusive approaches such as the Malpai Borderlands Group improve the abilities of policymakers and public managers to make decisions that reflect the needs and wants of their diverse constituencies and help them to anticipate reactions before they become stumbling blocks to project success (Carmin, Darnall, et al. 2003).

While focused on government policymaking, the theoretical discussions and practical applications explored in this book pertain equally to government agencies, non-governmental organizations (NGOs), and private industry. This work integrates theory across a number of subfields, including studies of interest groups in American government and NGOs in global environmental politics, and also applies to issue areas beyond just the environment: "collaborative initiative effectiveness, however, will depend on an enlightened set of policies and management systems that ensure that the public interest is being served through collaboration and to justify organizational investments in collaborative activity. Social science research can illuminate this managerial path" (Selin, Schuett, et al. 2000, p. 745).

Central Concepts

Stakeholders

The publication of Freeman's (1984) *Strategic Management: A Stakeholder Approach* inspired a body of literature on stakeholders relating to both the private and public sector. "Stakeholder collaboration is more flexible, open, inclusive, trusting, and based on collegiality whereas stakeholder management is more inflexible, closed, exclusive, wary, and based on control. Thus, the collaborative approach can better obtain stakeholder commitment, develop effective stakeholder relationships, balance power and control, use knowledge and resources, and solve complex problems" (Olden 2003, p. 44). Stakeholders in environmental policymaking are by

Table 1.1   Environmental Stakeholders by Interests

Private industry
Tribal organizations
Government agencies
Elected officials
Bureaucrats
Tourists/recreationists
NGOs/interest groups
Trade associations
Local communities
Businesses
Trade unions
Academics
Scientists
General public
Youth
Individual private actors
Grantors

their very nature a diverse collection of interests and may include some or all of the interests listed in Table 1.1.

While environmental groups have much in common, these groups have also splintered into factions; competition for funding, political access, and media attention as well as disagreements about tactics and strategies have created a number of significant divides that continue to plague the environmental movement (Bosso and Collins 2002; Orr 2006). Ideological differences are a divisive reality within the environmental movement. There is also a divide in terms of size, sophistication, and relative power; critics of these large mainstream environmental organizations charge that they have become government insiders who have lost touch with the environmental movement and distanced themselves from the grassroots of the movement. Standing on particular issues such as the use of nuclear power is a major dividing issue for many environmental organizations, as is the use of more extreme tactics to influence policymaking. Organizations that favor more academic tactics such as researching and preparing policy briefs may be at odds with groups that orchestrate public demonstrations or engage in radical practices.

The rise of wise-use groups in recent years has changed the policy landscape to a certain extent. Wise-use organizations such as the American Land Rights Association and the Blue Ribbon Coalition support private property rights and increased use of and access to public lands. They have organized against government policies, for example, to protect wetlands or to extend habitat protection as part of the Endangered Species Act. Members in these umbrella groups often include representatives from property owners, land development companies, resource extraction industries, loggers, mill workers, farmers, miners, off-road vehicle users, and ranchers. From a policy perspective they have developed into a well-organized counterpoint to environmental groups, usually positioned in opposition to stakeholders favoring environmental preservation policies.

While business and industry are also key stakeholders in environmental policymaking, one must be cautious in making sweeping assumptions about their intentions. Like environmental organizations, these stakeholders represent a full continuum of interests and power, with most falling somewhere in between the extremes, as highlighted by the climate change issue. Alternative energy industries such as solar and wind power have emerged with a strong interest in environmental issues by promoting their products as solutions to climate change problems. In contrast, the fossil fuel sector has devoted significant resources to disproving climate change, out of concerns that climate change policies will negatively impact their business practices and profits. Meanwhile, industries dependent on particular weather conditions, such as ski resorts, wineries, and maple syrup producers are increasingly active in lobbying for climate change policies to reduce warming. Blanket statements about business and industry stakeholders are clearly problematic.

With the development of the twenty-four-hour news cycle, the media has emerged as an influential stakeholder, particularly in terms of setting the agenda or increasing salience of an issue. While motivations of the media may at times be subject to debate—such as "creating" news versus reporting, or pandering for viewership in the highly competitive market—the media nonetheless has emerged as a stakeholder with the power to set the agenda, define problems, and marshal others.

The general public is an increasingly important stakeholder in environmental policymaking, in terms of their influence over elected officials, the ability of concerned citizens to mobilize around issues, and the growing realization that they must have input into the issues and policies that affect them. The general public can be an important stakeholder in policymaking at every stage of the policy process. The publication of Rachel Carson's *Silent Spring* (1962) raised public concern about the possible environmental effects of DDT such as eggshell thinning, bird poisoning, and chick mortality among birds of prey such as peregrine falcons and bald eagles, and the public response was a major factor in the government decision in 1972 to eliminate agricultural use of DDT in the United States.

The scientific community also plays an important role as stakeholders in policymaking, often serving as advisors or consultants, although they may also act as advocates for particular policy solutions. In many regions, aboriginal people are also critical stakeholders, particularly in issues dealing with land use.

Why do stakeholders participate in policymaking? The most obvious reason of course is to try to influence policy outcomes. However, stakeholder motivations are usually more complicated and nuanced, and agency decision makers will be ill served by working from such a basic assumption. In fact, as is argued in this book, stakeholders may be motivated by much more complex interests and will participate for a variety of reasons entirely separate from public policy such as personal or financial gain, networking, curiosity, boredom, academic interests, or the desire to make a name for oneself.

While conducting interviews at the United Nations climate change treaty negotiations in New Delhi, India in 2002, I was astounded by the frankness with which stakeholders would admit that they were participating in the treaty negotiations because they wanted to see India, because they were hoping to make employment connections, because it would look good on a resume, and because "it sounded cool."* Those comments have stayed with me ever since, and as I've continued to study stakeholders and interview both government decision makers and stakeholders in the United States, Canada, and around the world, I've come to realize how challenging it is to work with disparate interests, and yet how very important stakeholder collaboration is for the development of coherent and effective public policy. One of the biggest challenges is figuring out how to work with stakeholders who may not have the best interests of policymaking at heart, and who in fact may be more interested in conflict than in collaboration. This is where this book comes in. This research does not presuppose that stakeholder collaboration is easy, or in fact that it always works. It does, however, assume that an informed and committed attempt is critically important.

What is in it for decision makers? Why should decision makers open themselves up to criticism and frustration and spend valuable time and money to do so? The benefits of such activities are numerous. Effective stakeholder collaboration has the potential to improve both the integrity and functioning of the policy process, as well as the final outcomes. Stakeholder collaboration can lead to the pooling of resources, better information/data sources, integration of multiple perspectives, fostering of innovation, and anticipation of reactions and can give credibility to final decisions. "Stakeholders bring unique information, resources, agendas, power, interests, interrelationships, experience, capabilities, support, credibility, and access to target groups" (Olden 2003, p. 44). Meaningful stakeholder participation can also be a way to share responsibility, which is vital when policy problems are beyond the risk tolerance of a single organization or agency. In such a way, the web of

---

* Interviews conducted at the United Nations Framework Convention on Climate Change in New Delhi, India, 2002.

stakeholders can be important for providing support and stability to policymakers and can also help to provide legitimacy.

Stakeholder collaboration is a partnership between administrators and stakeholders (Graci 2013). Administrators must be willing to share power, and at the same time stakeholders must be willing to participate constructively (Burroughs 1999). If stakeholders perceive that a particular transaction is imposed on them unilaterally, then they may withdraw commitment and support; "whether serving on a committee or receiving a survey, being involved with management of a public resource and realizing that managers care enough to ask may enhance stakeholder appreciation of the resource and their image of managers" (Lafon, McMullin, et al. 2004, p. 228).

This book also proposes a new typology of stakeholders to help decision makers plan collaboration strategies. In the typology, stakeholders can be divided into five different types based on their assumed roles: players, would-be players, monitors, opportunists, and the curious. *Players* are those who are actively involved in policymaking and have the most access to decision makers. *Would-be players* are those who aspire to participate, or have something valuable to offer decision makers, but do not actually participate because of either barriers to access or internal limitations such as competing time demands. *Defensive monitors* are those who engage in defensive surveillance of government policymaking but are not actively involved in the decision-making process itself; for example, they may be observing government behavior to report back to their constituents. *Opportunists* are those who use the policymaking venue as a way to pursue their own outside interests such as networking, negotiating business contracts, engaging in research activities, or trying to raise the profile of their organization. *The curious* are those who are inquiring about policymaking or exploring avenues for participation but have not yet committed to being involved. The typology is used in Chapter 4 to highlight the challenges of stakeholder collaboration in Yellowstone National Park.

Public Policy

For environmental policy to be effective, it must include cooperation with a range of groups. The literature is rife with examples of governments or industry "fighting fires" (i.e., dealing with stakeholder anger to policies or projects) and causing additional expenditures of time and money that could have been prevented. Environmental concerns have a high likelihood of becoming public disputes because they affect a wide range of stakeholders and a broad scope of issue areas. The purpose of stakeholder participation is to prevent that from happening: to save decision makers' money, court costs, time, and negative publicity by preventing conflict and crises. Learning is an important part of the collaboration process because environmental problems involve significant uncertainty and complexity. Throughout the following chapters real-life case studies will be profiled to highlight how theory has been, and could be, translated into practice. For example, in the Henry's Fork Watershed of eastern Idaho and western Wyoming a group of non-profit organizations, local citizens, government agencies, and scientists have formed the Henry's Fork Watershed Council to try to address controversial and uncertain watershed management issues. Through consensus-building initiatives this group of former adversaries has been able to collaborate on research and restoration of the watershed resource in meaningful ways that were not possible previously.*

One challenge in working with stakeholders is trying to establish a balance between competing interests, particularly when there are varying levels of interest and stake. According to Blair, Stanley, et al. (1992), effective managers "do not try either to minimize costs or maximize quality. Nor do they try to meet the demands of all stakeholders. Rather, they minimally satisfy the needs of marginal stakeholders while they attempt to maximize satisfaction of the needs of key stakeholders. Achieving given levels of efficiency and effectiveness are only a means to achieve what policymakers, leaders, and managers really desire: satisfaction of key stakeholders" (Blair, Stanley, et al. 1992). The tools section of this book (Chapter 5) includes ideas to help decision makers to identify interests and power in different ways and put these ideas into practice.

Stakeholder Collaboration Planning

Stakeholder collaboration is not simply an academic enterprise. Policymaking occurs at every level of government (local, state, and federal), within every government agency charged with decision making, and within international organizations such as the United Nations that are themselves composed of countries vested with the authority to make decisions. As such, there is a bewildering array of opportunities for stakeholders to be involved in policymaking. Furthermore, laws such as "open public meetings laws" and the Administrative Procedure Act and the Freedom of Information Act have opened up the government to significantly more scrutiny and outside participation than in the past, further expanding entry points for stakeholders.

In recognition of the importance of stakeholder interests, a number of agencies have formalized partnership plans to both facilitate and control participation. The Environmental Protection Agency (EPA) has made extensive use of stakeholder collaboration; many of the laws and regulations that govern the agency suggest or require that the EPA provide certain outreach or public input activities such as notification, open comment periods, or access to information. Many of the EPA program offices regularly go beyond these legal requirements, providing additional opportunities for collaboration and input, although it has not always been so.

---

* Henry's Fork Watershed Council, http://www.henrysfork.com/watershedcouncil/council. htm.

In February 1979 the EPA announced regulations supporting public participation in the Clean Water Act, Safe Drinking Water Act, and Resource Conservation and Recovery Act. Later that year, the EPA began work on the Agency's first Public Participation Policy, including publishing a preliminary draft in the *Federal Register* in April 1980 for comments, and ten public meetings to solicit feedback. The final Public Participation Policy was issued on January 19, 1981; however, plans to publicize and implement the policy, including training staff, were never carried out. In July 1999, the EPA Innovations Task Force issued "Aiming for Excellence: Actions to Encourage Stewardship and Accelerate Environmental Progress," which included a pledge to evaluate public participation policies and regulations. In October of that year, the EPA convened a cross-agency workgroup to evaluate prevailing participation requirements and practices and to develop recommendations. On November 30, 1999, the EPA republished the 1991 Public Participation Policy in the *Federal Register* to solicit feedback. Based on those comments and internal reviews, the workgroup published "Engaging the American People" and recommended overhauling the 1981 policy, including public involvement training for staff, sharing public involvement information across the agency, and tracking/evaluating the effectiveness of public involvement activities. A revised draft policy was released for public comments on December 28, 2000, and the final Public Involvement Policy and accompanying framework for implementation were released in May/June 2003 (EPA 2003).

The Department of Energy Public Participation Policy is another example of a formal stakeholder collaboration plan: "The Department recognizes the many benefits to be derived from public participation, for both stakeholders and DOE. Public participation provides a means for the Department to gather the most diverse collection of opinions, perspectives and values from the broadest spectrum of the public enabling the Department to make better, more informed decisions. Public participation benefits stakeholders by creating an opportunity to provide input and influence decisions" (Department of Energy 1999). The core values of the DOE participation policy include the following: accessibility, accountability, accuracy, communication, consistency, fairness, honesty, innovation, openness, peer review, respect, responsiveness, scientific credibility, sincerity, and time/timeliness (Department of Energy 1999).

Participation plans are not unique to the United States or to domestic politics. Agenda 21, the United Nations action plan for sustainable development, states that stakeholder participation is vital to sustainable development planning:

> One of the fundamental prerequisites for the achievement of sustainable development is broad public participation in decision-making. Furthermore, in the more specific context of environment and development, the need for new forms of participation has emerged. This includes the need of individuals, groups and organizations to participate in environmental impact assessment procedures and to know

about and participate in decisions, particularly those that potentially affect the communities in which they live and work. Individuals, groups and organizations should have access to information relevant to environment and development held by national authorities, including information on products and activities that have or are likely to have a significant impact on the environment, and information on environmental protection measures (Agenda 21, Chapter 23.2, 1992).

Stakeholder participation is not just important for environmental policy, and in fact is a formal part of policy planning in many other policy areas. For example, according to the World Bank, stakeholder participation is an important element of many projects:

Participation is the process through which stakeholders influence and share control over priority setting, policy-making, resource allocations and access to public goods and services. Stakeholder participation in World Bank-funded projects and programs can be key for ensuring their long-term sustainability. Promoting participation helps build ownership and enhances transparency and accountability, and in doing so enhances effectiveness of development projects and policies (The World Bank 2009).

Stakeholder collaboration processes have their strengths and weaknesses and must be used appropriately. Unique situations call for unique techniques. For example, while public forums may be appropriate for educating local residents about water conservation strategies to deal with drought conditions, they would be inappropriate for highly technical issues such as choosing industrial designs for a groundwater remediation system. On the Yakutat Ranger District in Alaska, a stakeholder collaboration initiative including the Forest Service, the University of Alaska at Fairbanks, the Bureau of Indian Affairs, and the Alaska Department of Fish and Game is working together on a Participating Agreement to study moose habitat and population in an effort to improve moose management in the north. Given the complexities of moose management issues and the potential for conflict among interests, a formal partnership arrangement increases the likelihood of policies being developed that both integrate multiple interests and are acceptable to those most affected.

Of course, not all stakeholder collaboration is rooted in conflict, as highlighted by the story of the Whooping Crane Eastern Partnership. For many people, mention of the endangered whooping crane calls to mind the image of a majestic white bird following an ultralight plane piloted by a volunteer in a white bird costume. This quirky image is the result of an imaginative and innovative partnership to save the species from extinction. The whooping crane, one of North America's rarest birds, was reduced to just 15 birds in one migrating flock in 1941 due to hunting and habitat loss. The only naturally occurring wild population of whooping cranes in the world wintered near the Aransas National Wildlife Refuge on the Gulf Coast of Texas and in spring migrated to Wood Buffalo National Park near the Northwest Territories in Canada. Because the flock was so small and concentrated, scientists became concerned about the vulnerability of the flock to habitat changes, weather, or disease; long-term survival of the species would require multiple and separated populations. As part of a recovery plan for the whooping cranes, as mandated by the Endangered Species Act, specialists from Canada and the United States determined that a minimum of two additional flocks of 24 breeding pairs each were crucial to improve population health to the point that the species could be down-listed from endangered to threatened. The Whooping Crane Eastern Partnership, a unique collaboration between nonprofit organizations, individuals, state agencies, the U.S. Fish and Wildlife Service, the U.S. Geological Survey, and corporate sponsors, was formed to pool resources and ideas to save the species. The result was a plan to breed cranes from captive flocks that would then be reintroduced to the wild. Newly hatched cranes are taken to a release site for acclimation to the wild, where costumed human "parents" teach them survival skills such as foraging and roosting. The birds are then trained to follow a costumed guide in an ultralight aircraft along predetermined migration routes. Despite a number of challenges, including predators and the 2007 Central Florida tornadoes, which almost entirely wiped out a group of 18 yearlings, as of April 2013 there were 108 surviving whooping cranes in the eastern migratory population due in large part to the innovative stakeholder partnership.[*]

Overview

While there are competing viewpoints about how policymaking works and who the key actors are, the assumption in this research is that policymaking occurs in arenas filled with competing interests. In some issue areas those interests are highly trained specialists, either in science or politics; in others, those interests encompass a much broader range of expertise including the general public, or some combination of the two. Not every policy needs public input, and in some cases such input may actually be a liability. Foreign policy and homeland security, for example, are most often closed policymaking milieus, limited to a few highly trained stakeholders with high security clearance. This book is focused on areas of policymaking where stakeholder participation is meaningful and possible.

Stakeholder participation is certainly not unique to environmental policymaking. For example, concerns about the lack of awareness of immigrant and Latino issues in Jackson Hole, Wyoming, a major tourist destination with a high

---

[*] For more information see the Whooping Crane Eastern Partnership, http://www.bringback-thecranes.org/.

proportion of Latino workers in the service industry, led to a series of study circles called "Changing Faces, Changing Community" to discover ways to improve the community and promote intercultural communication between community leaders, residents, tourists, and seasonal employees. The study circles then presented their findings, and small groups were formed to develop and implement action plans to address the most pressing concerns (Fanselow 2007). The theories and tools in this book can be broadly applied to almost any issue area.

The rest of the book proceeds as follows. Chapter 2 is a theoretical review of stakeholders, including consideration of interests and participation. Chapter 3 is an integration of stakeholder and policy theories, analyzing the relationship between stakeholders and the policy process, with particular attention to collaboration throughout the policy process. Chapter 4 is a series of case studies of Yellowstone National Park, demonstrating how stakeholders have played both pivotal and frustrating roles in policymaking. Finally, Chapter 5 provides a series of practical tools for organizing and implementing effective stakeholder collaboration.

References

Blair, J. D., J. Stanley, et al. (1992). "A Stakeholder Management Perspective on Military Health Care." *Armed Forces & Society (Transaction Publishers)* 18(4): 548–575.

Bosso, C. J. and M. T. Collins (2002). "Just Another Tool? How Environmental Groups Use the Internet." *Interest Group Politics.* A. J. Cigler and B. A. Loomis. Washington, DC, CQ Press.

Burroughs, R. (1999). "When Stakeholders Choose: Process, Knowledge, and Motivation in Water Quality Decisions." *Society & Natural Resources* 12(8): 797–809.

Carmin, J., N. Darnall, et al. (2003). "Stakeholder Involvement in the Design of U.S. Voluntary Environmental Programs: Does Sponsorship Matter?" *Policy Studies Journal* 31(4): 527.

Carson, R. (1962). *Silent Spring.* New York, First Mariner Books.

Dedual, M., O. Sague Pla, et al. (2013). "Communication Between Scientists, Fishery Managers and Recreational Fishers: Lessons Learned from a Comparative Analysis of International Case Studies." *Fisheries Management & Ecology* 20(2/3): 234–246.

Department of Energy (1999). Public Participation Policy. Department of Energy—Office of Congressional and Intergovernmental Affairs. Washington, DC.

EPA (2003). Framework for Implementing EPA's Public Involvement Policy.

Fanselow, J. (2007). "Jackson Hole, Wyo., Residents Work Together on Immigration." Retrieved February 8, 2009 from http://www.everyday-democracy.org/en/Article.527.aspx.

Freeman, R. E. (1984). *Strategic Management: A Stakeholder Approach.* Boston, Pitman.

Gilliam, A., D. Davis, et al. (2002). "The Value of Engaging Stakeholders in Planning and Implementing Evaluations." *AIDS Education & Prevention* 14: 5.

Graci, S. (2013). "Collaboration and Partnership Development for Sustainable Tourism." *Tourism Geographies* 15(1): 25–42.

Jonsson, A. (2005). "Public Participation in Water Resources Management: Stakeholder Voices on Degree, Scale, Potential, and Methods in Future Water Management." *AMBIO—A Journal of the Human Environment* 34(7): 495–500.

Koontz, T. M. (2005). "We Finished the Plan, So Now What? Impacts of Collaborative Stakeholder Participation on Land Use Policy." *Policy Studies Journal* 33(3): 459–481.

Lafon, N. W., S. L. McMullin, et al. (2004). "Improving Stakeholder Knowledge and Agency Image through Collaborative Planning." *Wildlife Society Bulletin* 32(1): 220–231.

Mangun, J. C., K. W. Throgmorton, et al. (2007). "Assessing Stakeholder Perceptions: Listening to Avid Hunters of Western Kentucky." *Human Dimensions of Wildlife* 12(3): 157–168.

McDaniel, J. E. and C. G. Miskel (2002). "Stakeholder Salience: Business and Educational Policy." *Teachers College Record* 104(2): 325.

McGurk, B., A. J. Sinclair, et al. (2006). "An Assessment of Stakeholder Advisory Committees in Forest Management: Case Studies from Manitoba, Canada." *Society & Natural Resources* 19(9): 809–826.

Olden, P. C. (2003). "Hospital and Community Health: Going from Stakeholder Management to Stakeholder Collaboration." *Journal of Health & Human Services Administration* 26(1): 35–57.

Orr, S. K. (2006). "Policy Subsystems and Regimes: Organized Interests and Climate Change Policy." *Policy Studies Journal* 34(2): 147–169.

Santos, R., P. Antunes, et al. (2006). "Stakeholder Participation in the Design of Environmental Policy Mixes." *Ecological Economics* 60(1): 100–110.

Selin, S. W., M. A. Schuett, et al. (2000). "Modeling Stakeholder Perceptions of Collaborative Initiative Effectiveness." *Society & Natural Resources* 13(8): 735–745.

The World Bank. (2009). "Participation at Project, Program & Policy Level." Retrieved April 1, 2013, from http://go.worldbank.org/1S57LH08E0.

United Nations. (1992). Agenda 21, UN Doc A/Conf.151/26.

Watson, E. and P. Foster-Fishman (2013). "The Exchange Boundary Framework: Understanding the Evolution of Power within Collaborative Decision-Making Settings." *American Journal of Community Psychology* 51(1/2): 151–163.

White, M. (2013). "I Love You, Manatee." *National Geographic* 223: 82–97.

Chapter 2

Stakeholders: Theoretical Foundations

Introduction

In 1994 the Ministry of Canadian Heritage convened the Banff–Bow Valley Task Force to assess the use and development of the Bow River watershed within Banff National Park (Alberta, Canada).* The two-year, $2 million Banff–Bow Valley Study identified ways to "integrate environmental, social and economic considerations in order to develop management and land-use strategies that are sustainable and meet the objectives of the *National Parks Act*" (Banff–Bow Valley Study 1996, p. 2).

The task force was composed of five experts from the academic and private sectors with expertise in public policy, ecological sciences, management, and tourism. In addition, a round table was convened of representatives of fourteen stakeholder sectors with an interest in the valley: culture/heritage, natural environment, local environment, municipal government, federal government, First Nations Siksika, First Nations Wesley, park users, the task force, infrastructure/transportation,

---

* Banff National Park, established in 1885 in the Canadian Rocky Mountains, is Canada's oldest national park. The Bow Valley is the most developed area of Banff National Park, with a permanent population of around 7,500 residents. Development in the valley includes the Trans-Canada Highway, the Canadian Pacific Railway, the Bow Valley Parkway, the Icefields Parkway, the Banff-Radium Highway, three peripheral ski hills, one golf course, the resort town of Banff, and the resort hamlet of Lake Louise. The Town of Banff has a densely developed small downtown core featuring retail and restaurants. More than three million tourists visit Banff National Park every year.

social/health/education, commercial outdoor recreation, commercial visitor services, and tourism/marketing. The mandate of the round table was expansive: "we should endeavor to break away from a pattern of confrontation of opposite views, to a common vision of the future. A vision based on our best scientific knowledge and a shared determination to keep the unique quality of the park for future generations" (Banff–Bow Valley Study 1996, p. 6).

The study objectives were (1) to develop a vision and set of goals for the Bow Valley in Banff National Park that encompasses ecological, social, and economic values; (2) to both analyze available data and provide direction as to future data collection and analytic needs; and (3) to guide management of human use and development in such a way as to maintain the ecological integrity of the Banff–Bow Valley, and at the same time provide for sustainable use and tourism.

In recognition of the importance of the general public as a stakeholder group, the task force developed a public involvement plan by first soliciting public input on how people would like to be involved. The task force received more than 261 submissions and 11 deputations as a result. The public was kept informed about the process through regular newsletters, public forums, news releases, community television, web updates and workshops. Round table meetings were open to the public and were held across Canada to expand public input beyond the Bow Valley. A storefront office in downtown Banff was opened to facilitate outreach and engagement with the local public and to provide additional resources to interested visitors. A number of complementary studies were also commissioned to improve understanding of the environmental, economic, and social issues in the Banff–Bow Valley.

In October 1996 the Banff–Bow Valley Task Force submitted more than 500 management recommendations to the minister responsible for the Parks Canada agency. A government advisory group was then appointed to assess how the department would address the recommendations and incorporate them into the park management plan. While far more extensive than most stakeholder collaborations, the Banff–Bow Valley Study remains noteworthy for its commitment to inclusive participation and provides insight into the broad scope of possibilities for integrating stakeholder concerns into policymaking.

As highlighted by the Banff case study, there is growing recognition within environmental policy that stakeholder collaboration is a valuable tool for decision-making processes (Selin, Schuett, et al. 2000; Kloprogge and van der Sluijs 2006; Mangun, Throgmorton, et al. 2007; Bryner 2008; Jarman 2011; Davies and White 2012; Graci 2013). Such collaboration of course depends on a number of key factors: correctly identifying stakeholders, developing appropriate and effective participation venues, fostering their capacity to participate effectively, and using the output in a meaningful way. Participation and collaboration may include simple strategies such as newsletters informing stakeholders of decisions, Listserv discussions, requests for comments through an online web form, or more extensive activities such as workshops, web conferences, public forums, and advisory boards.

For policymakers, stakeholder collaboration is about manipulating the complex relationships between organizations and political processes to create a functional system to support policymaking. Rather than closing off policymaking and making decisions in isolation, stakeholder collaboration is an attempt to build relationships with affected and interested stakeholders (Blair, Stanley, et al. 1992). While traditional policymaking and decision-making approaches may have been based on an "announce and defend" framework, such tactics are no longer tenable given increased demands for transparency, accountability, and public participation. Instead, collaboration is promoted as both an ideology and a prescriptive tool for policymaking. Collaboration can be described as diverse stakeholders working together to try to develop and advance a common vision or resolve conflict (Eschenbach and Eschenbach 1996; Selin, Schuett, et al. 2000; Sabatier, Focht, et al. 2005; Graci 2013).

While many decision makers in environmental policy have come to recognize the value of stakeholder collaboration, it is a particularly timely approach for a number of reasons. For one, growing interest in measures of accountability and performance can be accommodated through participatory measures in which stakeholders serve as ongoing checks for legitimacy. These initiatives help to protect the integrity of transparent decision making. Increasing complexity in decision-making procedures brought about both by the expansion of the scope of government and by the intricacies of environmental issues means that integrating diverse perspectives and views has never been so important. Access to information via the Internet has led to a corresponding rise in the self-identification of stakeholders. Facebook, Twitter, web conferences, e-mail, texting, Listservs, and message boards have all dramatically increased opportunities and expectations regarding participation. Finally, the severity of the environmental issues facing the world—climate change, natural disasters, access to clean water, resource depletion, and endangered species, to name a few—means that policymakers are facing pressing challenges with looming deadlines and must take advantage of all the expertise and knowledge that is available, even if it exists outside the public sector.

This urgency for stakeholder collaboration is not unique to environmental policymaking:

> Stakeholder analyses are arguably more important than ever because of the increasingly interconnected nature of the world. Choose any public problem—economic development, poor educational performance, natural resources management, crime, AIDS, global warming, terrorism—and it is clear that "the problem" encompasses or affects numerous people, groups, and organizations. No one is fully in charge; no organization "contains" the problem. Instead, many individuals, groups, and organizations are involved, or affected, or have some partial responsibility to act. Figuring out what the problem is and what solutions might work are actually part of the problem. (Bryson 2003, p. 6)

Stakeholder Theories

Stakeholder theory in business is an attempt to expand the scope of a manager's attention beyond simply profit maximization, to also include the interests and claims of non-stockholders such as the financial community, unions, trade associations, competitors, and suppliers (Mitroff 1983; Wallace 1995; Eschenbach and Eschenbach 1996). The next section reviews how scholars have attempted to answer the question of who is a stakeholder and what constitutes a stake, and highlights a number of typologies/frameworks that circumscribe the range of participants. A new typology based on interests is also proposed.

Stakeholder Definitions

Most understandings of stakeholders embrace an inclusive approach suggesting that any organization or individual can be a stakeholder:

- "Stakeholders are all those interest groups, parties, actors, claimants, and institutions—both internal and external to the corporation—that exert a hold on it. That is, stakeholders are all those parties who either affect or who are affected by a corporation's actions, behavior, and policies" (Mitroff 1983, p. 4).
- "On the question of who is a stakeholder, generally the trend in environmental conflict literature seems to be inclusive in nature, trying to accept a large number of individuals and organizations as stakeholders" (Elias, Jackson, et al. 2004, p. 89).
- Clarkson (1995, p. 106) defines stakeholders as "persons or groups that have, or claim ownership rights, or interests in a corporation and its activities, past, present, or future. Such claimed rights or interests are the result of transactions with, or actions taken by the corporation, and may be legal or moral, individual or collective."
- According to Freeman (1984, p. 46) "A stakeholder in an organization is (by definition) any group or individual who can affect or is affected by the achievement of the organization's objectives."
- Bryson argues that the nominally powerless also deserve consideration: a stakeholder is "any person, group or organization that can place a claim on the organization's attention, resources or output, or is affected by that output" (Bryson 2003, p. 27).

A second, less common approach is to consider stakeholders based on their ability to influence or exercise power. By such reasoning, marginalized groups lacking the resources to influence decision making cannot be considered stakeholders. For example, Eden and Ackerman (1998) propose that stakeholders are "people or small groups with the power to respond to, negotiate with, and change the strategic future of the organization" (p. 117). More narrow definitions take into account the notion that managers have limited attention and resources and cannot give credence to all actual or potential claims.

The trend in environmental policy is to embrace more inclusive approaches to stakeholder collaboration (Graci 2013), a position supported in this book. One example of successful inclusive collaboration is management of the Em River Basin in southeast Sweden. The program is based on a watershed cooperation model involving local municipalities, regional administrative boards, the Farmers' Union, NGOs, fishing interests, and local history associations. The Em River is one of the most valuable rivers in the country, home to 32 species of fish, the freshwater pearl mussel, the kingfisher, the otter, and other wildlife. The area includes rich pasture flora, old-growth forests, and swamp forests. Stakeholder cooperation was seen as central to creating an economically and environmentally sustainable society in the region. Representatives of the stakeholder groups sit on the board of directors, and working groups carry out specialized projects. Throughout planning decision making, stakeholder input is solicited, and actions are only implemented with common agreement from a large majority of the stakeholders. They have agreed that planning documents must be accessible to the general public and that there must be opportunities for all individuals and organizations to express their opinions about river basin management plans. "Active dissemination of information" to stakeholders and the public was identified as a key method to engage the public and to promote responsible water behavior (Jonsson 2005). This approach represents an inclusive model of stakeholder participation.

Stakeholders and Policy Theory

Public policy analysis tends to embrace a relatively broad view of stakeholders, including not just decision makers and interests but also beneficiaries and payers, as well as future generations (Weimer and Vining 2010). While much of the stakeholder literature highlights the operations of stakeholders largely in isolation or as individuals, in studying the policy process specifically, policy research has generally focused on stakeholders within a larger context, comprising both competing and allied groups, institutions, and governmental actors.

One of the early theories of participation in the policy process was based on the "iron triangle." Iron triangles are made up of interest groups, congressional committees, and government agencies that exercise "iron-clad" control over the policy process. Iron triangles develop around areas of public policy dealing with complicated matters of concern, and the participants administer public policy within its narrow realm without significant opposition from elsewhere in the governmental or economic system (Cater 1964). They are essentially closed arenas made up of a limited number of participants with stable relations. Iron triangles have been criticized for capturing the policy process and being self-serving, thereby circumventing the principles of democracy (Hanks 2000).

By the late 1970s and early 1980s, several authors began to question the adequacy of the iron-triangle concept in representing the true nature of public policy making in the United States. Heclo (1978) developed an alternative approach based on the idea that much of contemporary American politics took place in environments that were ad hoc, open, and unstable rather than regular, closed, and stable. Heclo referred to these policymaking milieus as issue networks. Issue networks have disaggregated power and many participants with varying levels of commitment and dependence on others flowing in and out of decision making. These are fluctuating networks with no one group or participant setting the agenda or controlling the policy process (Heclo 1978).

The issue network is a more amorphous relationship than an iron triangle. Participants become involved in the policy process until they achieve their goals, which typically involves victory over those with an opposing agenda. Coalitions will form within the policy area and dissolve either when the coalitions feel that there has been a resolution or when it is felt that their actions are no longer worthwhile (Berry 1989). Issue networks can be an effective means of transmitting information quickly, serving as a means for research and for advocacy for both policymakers and interest group participants. The flow of information allows for alliances to develop within the issue network composed of those working toward a common outcome. Issue networks as a result are characterized by both a high degree of conflict and a high degree of cooperation (Berry 1989).

A refinement of the issue network idea that has gained traction in policy studies is the policy subsystem. The policy process can be thought of as operating within partially segmented "policy subsystems," which are made up of institutions and actors that are directly involved in the policymaking process in a specialized policy area. These actors may include interest groups, think tanks, academics, government representatives, and government agency personnel. Central to the subsystem concept is the recognition that policymakers do not operate in isolation; rather they formulate and implement policy in conjunction with stakeholders, recognizing their interests as a necessary component of policymaking (Heclo 1978; Cobb and Elder 1981; Kingdon 1995; Sabatier 1999).

The core assumption of the subsystem model is that through the subsystem, the participants themselves bring some kind of expertise to the policy process, either directly or peripherally related to the issue at hand. For example, within the climate change subsystem, experts come not just from climate change science but also from diverse fields such as sustainable development, public transportation, and manufacturing. The pooling of knowledge from these experts can help to make policy more comprehensive, and presumably more effective. Participation within the subsystem may be fluid, as participants move in and out of the subsystem depending on their interest and priorities and the level of activity within the issue domain; or it may be more stable with less fluid movement. As a whole, the subsystem is usually quite stable, with a core group of participants that is highly involved in the policy process.

Within the policy process, subsystem activities may include bringing issues to the agenda, developing and helping to pass legislation, formulating rules and regulations, preparing and passing budgets, administering and implementing programs, and evaluating/revising programs (Thurber 1991). Policy subsystems may be particularly important in providing expertise that is beyond that of government representatives:

> The number of policy issues that can actively be considered and acted upon constitute a small portion of the range of possible issues demanding attention. Policy subsystems serve to structure the agenda of government to focus the attention of policymakers through a routinized division of labor. As products of past decisions, they represent legitimated formulae for accommodating established interests. By structuring participation and by providing preexisting decisional premises, subsystems serve to limit the conflicts and uncertainties that must be dealt with at any one time, therein facilitating the development of the type of consensus necessary for decision. (Cobb and Elder 1981)

One of the most important characteristics of subsystems is their diversity. Subsystems may vary in terms of size, degree of connectedness, conflict, longevity, commitment, degree of formal/informal participation, and scope of activities. There is no one subsystem design; rather the structure and activities are reflective of the policy domain and environment in which they exist. The larger policymaking milieu in which subsystems operate can be a complex environment. Factors such as public salience, catastrophic events, changing government priorities, elections, media coverage, modifications to the problem definition, involvement of policy entrepreneurs promoting new policies, changes in economic or social conditions, or decisions in other policy domains may impact the structure and activities of the subsystem itself (Cobb and Elder 1981; Kingdon 1995; Hanks 2000).

Thurber's typology of subsystems highlights the fact that subsystem structure and activities can vary significantly. According to Thurber, dominant policy subsystems exhibit stable communications and a small number of participants, which control the issue or demonstrate significant influence over the policy area. These subsystems tend to be found in the area of distributive policies. There are long-standing lines of communication among actors who have developed trust and who share interests and policy preferences. This results in stable relationships, which in turn reduce uncertainty, information costs, and opportunistic behavior. Dominant subsystems tend to be based on cooperation, compromise, and bargaining, with only a narrow scope of conflict. There is an active effort to control competition and to keep the decision-making process closed (Thurber 1991).

The actors involved in dominant subsystems are not usually high-profile participants but instead have significant experience in the area. Participants tend to be territorial, resisting pressure both from those in power who do not have formal jurisdiction in their issue area and from interest groups that are not regular participants. Competition introduces costs and uncertainty, which are to be avoided. Similarly, dominant subsystem participants may try to limit the involvement of the media unless it is beneficial to their cause (Thurber 1991).

In contrast to the dominant subsystem, a competitive subsystem is composed of participants in a constant state of competition, and the system as a whole is more open and complex. There tend to be more participants, but those participants are still typically experts in the field. What distinguishes participants here is their claim to expertise rather than their material interests. Relationships between actors are usually less stable than in dominant subsystems. Within a competitive subsystem, the participants on both sides of the issue tend to be well known to each other. Competition may result from external events that affect the subsystem or from challenges to power. Competition may then create new relationships and patterns of interaction and eventually result in a new dominating coalition. Over time the competition itself may become institutionalized—for example, in the case of the long-standing conflict between environmentalists and industry in the area of clean air policy (Thurber 1991).

Disintegrated subsystems are the rarest but may develop as a result of intense competition or a shift to a macro political style of decision making. It is difficult to bring rationality to a disintegrated subsystem because there is a lack of authority. Policy change may occur, however, through a jurisdictional change, through the introduction of new actors, or by moving the issue to a higher level of government.

Advocacy coalitions, one of the most recent theoretical advancements in the area of stakeholder participation in policymaking, further refine the notion of alliances to look at the role of belief systems in coalition formation (Sabatier 1999). Within subsystems, members tend to cluster into competing advocacy coalitions that promote distinct policy perspectives and that share a set of normative and causal beliefs (Sabatier 1999). The advocacy coalition framework (ACF) is based on the idea that there is a hierarchy of belief systems within each of these coalitions:

■ At the highest level are the *deep core beliefs*, which include fundamental general beliefs such as the relative value of individual freedom versus social equality. With respect to climate change, these beliefs would be expressed in opinions about the role of the international community in solving environmental problems.

■ At the next level are *policy core beliefs*, which represent a coalition's basic beliefs regarding a particular policy domain. These include fundamental value priorities such as economic development versus environmental protection and beliefs regarding the basic causes of the problem of climate change as a result of human factors or a natural process.

■ Finally, the *secondary aspects* of a coalition's belief system are made up of a large set of narrower beliefs centered on the specifics of a policy domain. These beliefs include the level of severity of the problem, the relative importance of various causal factors, preference for particular institutional design, and the particular distribution of costs and benefits.

Table 2.1 provides a comparative summary of these different theories of stakeholder participation in policymaking.

Approaches to Stakeholder Analysis

Moving beyond definitions of stakeholders and the aggregated analysis of behavior, Mitchell et al. proposed an analysis of stakeholders based on socially constructed attributes that are *internal* to an organization (Mitchell, Agle, et al. 1999). They proposed that classes of stakeholders can be identified based on which of three, if any, attributes stakeholders possess: (1) power to influence, (2) the legitimacy of a relationship to the firm, and (3) the urgency of the stakeholder's claim. Power is about the ability of a stakeholder to influence decision makers and can be manifested through force, material resources such as money, and symbolic resources such as prestige. Political savvy, group cohesion, financial resources, membership size, broad-based support, and long-term commitment may influence power. Legitimacy is the moral right or interest of stakeholders, "a generalized perception or assumption that the actions of an entity are desirable, proper, or appropriate within some socially constructed system of norms, values, beliefs, definitions" (Mitchell, Agle, et al. 1999, p. 869). Legitimate stakeholders are assumed to be operating in a desirable way. The third attribute is urgency, or the extent to which a stakeholder claim requires immediate attention. The bases for urgency include time sensitivity, or the degree to which the stakeholder requires immediate attention, as well as the level of importance of the claim or the stakeholder (Mitchell, Agle, et al. 1999).

These three attributes can then be used to categorize stakeholders as definitive (possess all three), expectant (possess two), latent (possess one), and non-stakeholders (possessing no attributes). Expectant and latent can be further categorized based on the combination of attributes they possess. While non-stakeholders may often be ignored, changes to the policy environment or priorities may change their status. Latent stakeholders have policy claims of low priority—they have a high degree of one attribute, but low degrees of others. Within that category dormant actors have power, discretionary stakeholders have legitimacy, and demanding groups claim urgency. Latent stakeholders may have the potential to exert influence, but by and large they are passive whether unable to act or deliberately choosing not to. Expectant stakeholders are more active in policymaking than latent stakeholders. They have two of the listed attributes, giving them moderate salience. As such they do exert some influence over policy. The definitive stakeholder has high degrees

Table 2.1   Stakeholder Models in Public Policy

Concept	Definition	Decision Making	Participation
Iron triangle	Iron triangles are made up of interest groups, congressional committees, and government agencies that exercise "iron-clad" control over the policy process.	Closed (regular meetings and a system of rules)	Restricted
Sub-government	A stable group of a limited number of interest groups, legislators and their aides, and agency personnel who interact regularly and dominate policymaking in a particular issue area.	Closed	Limited
Issue network	Issue networks have disaggregated power and many participants with varying levels of commitment and dependence on others flowing in and out of decision making. These are fluctuating networks with no one group or participant setting the agenda or controlling the problem definition process.	Open (lack of common rules and hierarchy)	Boundless
Policy subsystem	Subsystems are made up of institutions and actors that are directly involved in a specialized policy area.	Variable	Fluid
Issue niches	Each group works within a particular issue niche or set of issues. Groups are isolated into narrow constellations.	Restricted	Limited

(Continued)

Table 2.1   Stakeholder Models in Public Policy (Continued)

Concept	Definition	Decision Making	Participation
Policy community	There is a common view of the rules of operation, frequent interaction between a limited number of participants, with a few groups or individuals consciously excluded. The community is characterized by bargaining over resources between members, and the ability of policy leaders to bring others to agreement.	Closed hierarchy	Limited
Policy monopoly	Decisions are dominated by a limited number of participants who develop a common understanding of the issues in the subsystem. Participants share policy goals and are largely removed from public scrutiny.	Closed	Limited
Advocacy coalition	Participants share a particular belief system (basic values, causal assumptions, problem perceptions) and have a fair degree of coordinated activity.	Restricted	Limited

of all three attributes and the highest level of salience. These stakeholders make explicit claims on policymakers (Mitchell, Agle, et al. 1999).

Blair, Stanley, et al. (1992) posit a different analysis of stakeholders based on their *relationship* to decision makers. Types of stakeholders identified by these scholars include supportive, mixed, nonsupportive, and marginal. Supportive stakeholders support the missions, goals, and actions. These are low threat, with high potential for cooperation. Nonsupportive stakeholders have a high likelihood of threat and low potential for cooperation. Mixed-blessing stakeholders have potential for both threat and cooperation. Marginal stakeholders have low threat/cooperation potential and are not relevant for most issues. Mixed-blessing stakeholders should be managed through collaborative efforts in order to maximize the likelihood for cooperation and make it more difficult for them to oppose the organization (Blair, Stanley, et al. 1992).

Interest-Based Typology

Although a broad definition of stakeholders is useful from the standpoint of ensuring that no one is overlooked, its utility is somewhat limited from an applied perspective. The reality is that governments have almost endless competing demands on their time and resources, and attempting to embrace every possible stakeholder is an exercise in futility. While inclusivity reduces the likelihood that someone is missed, it also increases the complexity of the policy process. As such, a typology that delineates *interests* such as the one proposed here can be of value in these cases, as a way to provide some structure and limits. Such structure can facilitate managers in balancing competing claims and interests and prioritizing needs.

Stakeholders become involved in policymaking for a number of intersecting reasons. Genuine concern for the policy issue may be a motivating factor; however, less altruistic motivations such as seeking prestige, institutional legitimacy, competitive advantage, individual goals, and self-esteem also come into play. This typology is based on recognition that stakeholders have varying levels of interest and at the same time have various levels of expertise and access to resources, elements that have been overlooked in other stakeholder analyses but are intrinsic to policy studies. These categories —players, would-be players, the curious, opportunists, and monitors—can be applied to any policy issue area.* This typology was developed based on surveys and interviews with stakeholders in national parks policy and United Nations climate change negotiations. The missions, goals, and activities of these stakeholders were coded and analyzed into these categories.

Players are stakeholders who participate in order to specifically influence the policymaking process, often through lobbying. As highlighted in the interest group literature (Berry 1989; Salisbury 1990; Baumgartner and Leech 1998; Hula 1999) lobbying activities are usually twofold: first, obtaining access to decision makers, and second, influencing decisions. Access may be direct (face-to-face) or indirect (through political aides, mass media, or appeals to public opinion). Negotiating access is the first step in lobbying. Access may depend on the resources available to a group, including financial, physical, organizational, political, and motivational resources.

---

* This typology is discussed in greater detail in Orr, S. K. (2006). "Policy Subsystems and Regimes: Organized Interests and Climate Change Policy." *Policy Studies Journal* 34(2): 147–169; Orr, S. K. (2007). "The Evolution of Climate Policy—Business and Environmental Organizations: Between Alliance Building and Entrenchment." *Global Policy Arrangements: Business and the Countervailing Powers of Civil Society.* K. Ronit. London, Routledge.

Players can serve as an intermediary link between citizens and governments, providing the means through which members can voice their opinions and influence the policy process. The means to do so may include meeting with government representatives, providing policy analysis, protesting, distributing petitions, using the media, and disseminating information on the stakeholder opinions (Baumgartner and Leech 1998; Bloodgood 2001).

Trying to influence government officials by organizing and directing public opinion has become a familiar strategy and is often used by players, particularly those with less direct access to decision makers. Such grassroots efforts may include public rallies, attendance at public meetings, letter writing campaigns, and use of the Internet. Today grassroots efforts may be structured more like political campaigns, involving mass marketing, high technology, and public relations ploys. Through advocacy efforts, publications, and publicity campaigns, stakeholders can make people more aware of issues and the range of solutions as well as encourage individuals to contact their elected representatives to make their views known. This can be a key tactic for developing public support for a policy issue (Baumgartner and Leech 1998).

Players may also be active in policymaking by providing information to policymakers as discussed earlier. Because environmental policymaking can be so technically complex, decision makers may lack the knowledge and understanding to develop policy. As such, players may serve a valuable and supporting role by providing credible information and analysis to decision makers

Would-be players are those stakeholders who want to participate in policymaking but do not. There may be a lack of time, resources, connections, or knowledge, which prevents their participation. They may also be waiting to be asked to be involved. Marginalized groups who lack the power or resources to navigate the policy process may also fall into this category. Studies have found that in domestic politics groups often are granted access only to members of Congress who already agree with their positions or with whom they have preestablished relationships, thereby making it difficult for many stakeholders to gain access (Baumgartner and Leech 1998). Would-be players are often those stakeholders who complain that government will not listen to them.

Barriers to participation in policymaking for would-be players include the following:

- Access to technology
- Language barriers
- Too much competition from other groups for access
- Lack of sophistication
- Poor reputation
- Lack of organizational resources
- Lack of time/money to foster relationships
- Political challenges

Table 2.2 Stakeholder Typology

	Interests	Power and Influence	Primary Activities
Players	Influencing policy	Exercising high power and influence	Lobbying
Would-Be Players	Influencing policy	Low power and influence	Trying to lobby and network Studying policy issue Attending policy related events Networking Research Media
Curious	Observing what is going on Trying to identify if participation is worthwhile	Not yet exercising power and influence	Attending policy related events Studying policy issue
Monitors	Tracking policy debate	No power, varying degrees of influence	Following policy publications Networking for information
Opportunists	Self-interest	Varying degrees of power and influence	Networking Research Media

- Too many access points to navigate
- Uncertain of how the process works
- Unaware of what policymakers need

Overcoming these barriers may help would-be players transition to full player status. As illustrated in Table 2.2, would-be players may be actively trying to become players, by lobbying and networking and the like, or they may be less politically sophisticated and aware and be uncertain how to proceed.

The curious are those stakeholders who are considering participating but have not yet committed to doing so. For example, they may be scoping out the situation or internally debating whether it is worthwhile. They may be uncertain of the benefits of participation, or they may be trying to figure out if this would be an appropriate use of their resources. They may also be researching alternative venues for participating such as local, federal, or international policymaking. Curious stakeholders may have done some preliminary participation—for example, attending policy issue conferences—but have not fully committed to doing more. Curious stakeholders can be problematic for policymakers who are uncertain of their status and thus unclear as to how much attention they should be given or how much power they may wield in the future.

Monitors are observing the policymaking process but are not trying to exercise influence. They may change roles at any time, however—for example, if they feel that their interests are unexpectedly threatened. While other categories of stakeholders such as players may also be engaged in monitoring, this is the primary intent of monitors. Monitors may be trying to keep track of what is happening in the policy process, tracking developments, alerting others about the status of policies, or doing background preparation on responses and strategies. Other monitoring activities include reading government publications and notices, attending policy discussions and conferences, meeting with decision makers to assess the status of policies, conducting research, networking, and collaborating with other stakeholders to tap into other perspectives. As part of their monitoring, stakeholders may be marshaling resources, waiting for the right time to become a player, or simply taking a wait-and-see approach to the policy process.

Opportunists use participation in policymaking primarily to further their own outside interests such as networking, negotiating business contracts, conducting research, or raising the profile of their organization. For example, academics studying a policy issue may be actively participating in negotiations and policy events, but their primary interest is not in a particular outcome. Opportunists may be only peripherally interested in influencing policy, if at all, although they may try to hide that fact in order to maximize their own self-interest. Opportunists present a unique challenge for policymakers, who may not have a clear understanding of why they are participating and involved. One interesting note about opportunists is that they may appear at both the organizational and individual level. For example, individual representatives from an environmental interest group may participate in a policy conference out of their own personal self-interest to find new employment. Opportunists can be problematic as they may take up scarce resources, creating a drain on government resources.

Identifying Stakeholders

Deciding who should be involved in policy decision making is an important strategic choice. Successful leaders need to recruit a broad range of participants, inspire and motivate them by clearly articulating goals and the mutual benefits of collaboration, empower participants to support decision makers, help participants develop positive relationships with one another, encourage them to synthesize different ideas and resources, and develop meaningful and useful results (Lasker and Weiss 2003; Elias, Jackson, et al. 2004; West and Clark 2006). No easy task.

Identifying all stakeholders is essential for understanding the scope of the problem at hand, its causes, the range of solutions, foreseeable impacts, and the resources that are available (West and Clark 2006). Particularly when other stakeholders will be involved in the implementation of a policy, or in promoting a program, or will be affected in some way by the change, it is critical that the initiating organizations be aware of the resources available from stakeholders.

Policymakers must look beyond their allies to seek out stakeholders who can contribute meaningfully to decision making. While identifying stakeholders is usually based on two elements—the interest of an actor in the issue, and the resources or strengths that he or she can bring to the process (West and Clark 2006)—practically identifying stakeholders can be a challenge. The logical first step is to identify and list all possible stakeholders in a policy issue including who will be directly affected (e.g., local businesses that have to change their practices), who will be indirectly affected (e.g., local authorities that have to enforce a new regulation), who has expertise in the area (e.g., academics), and who might have an interest in a successful or unsuccessful conclusion (e.g., environmental organizations active in the issue). It is up to the initiating partner to determine who has a significant enough interest to be contacted (Economic and Social Commission for Asia and the Pacific 2001).

It is often in the best interest of the decision makers to bring a diverse array of stakeholders into the process. In a critique of a stakeholder engagement project between The Nature Conservancy (TNC) and the La Amistad Biosphere Initiative in Panama/Costa Rica and one of the oldest transboundary projects in Central America, the authors argue that

> TNC utilized criteria for stakeholder identification that limited the list to those participants with whom TNC could easily forge beneficial relationships or those that benefited from a TNC partnership. This was an overly selective contextual map; it was not comprehensive enough. For example, other stakeholders such as industrial, agricultural or private sector interests clearly dependent upon La Amistad resources and affected by policy management were overlooked. Instead certain nongovernmental organizations (NGOs), governmental organizations, and scientific institutions were included as stakeholders. This overly selective list of participants shows that a more contextual approach is needed. (West and Clark 2006, p. 37)

The stakeholders were almost exclusively environmental NGOs and government agencies. West and Clark argue that because La Amistad is a binational biosphere and World Heritage Site, international actors should have been involved, as well as those who were potential adversaries such as industrial, agricultural, or private-sector interests.

According to Mitroff (1983) stakeholders can be identified in seven different ways. The *imperative* approach identifies those who have reacted strongly to an agency's activities or policies, for example, those organizing protest campaigns. The *positional* approach is a list of those who hold formal positions in a policymaking capacity such as government. The *reputational* approach is based on a snowball sampling approach whereby stakeholders identify others who may have an interest. The *social-participation* approach includes those who participate in relevant activities such as attend meetings and serve on committees. The *opinion-leadership* approach identifies those in position to influence the opinions of other stakeholders such as newspaper editors. The *demographic* method identifies stakeholders based on particular demographic characteristics that may be relevant; for example, the elderly may have a strong interest in issues related to accessible public transportation. Lastly, the *focal organization* approach identifies those who have a particular relationship with decision makers such as employees, competitors, regulators, and members (Mitroff 1983). These techniques can be used alone or in combination to identify stakeholders.

While stakeholders are often referred to at the level of the organization (e.g., State Fish and Wildlife Agency or the Student Conservation Association), communication occurs with individuals. This means that it is important both to communicate with the appropriate individual stakeholder within the larger stakeholder organization and at the same time to keep in mind that the particular individual may not always accurately represent the larger organization. That individual may have personal interests that intercede or have a particular personality style that is difficult to work with effectively. In some cases it may be in the best interests of the management team to request a different representative from the stakeholder organization, particularly if it is in the best interests of the stakeholder organization to be accurately and effectively represented. Chapter 5 includes a number of practical tools that can be used to identify and recruit stakeholders.

Stakeholder Interests

One of the biggest challenges for decision makers working with multiple stakeholders is managing, integrating, and supporting their competing demands and interests, many of whom may hold widely divergent worldviews. During the early stages of the EPA "Brownfields Economic Redevelopment Initiative" the EPA was criticized for failing to solicit input from residents who could be affected by the cleanup and redevelopment and for focusing solely on the interests of developers and investors. To respond to those concerns, the EPA partnered with the National Environmental Justice Advisory Council (NEJAC) to organize a series of public dialogues to provide a forum for environmental justice advocates and community groups to discuss their policy concerns. The public dialogues were composed of two parts; in the first participants discussed their concerns with the Brownfields Initiative and their visions for healthy and sustainable communities, and in the second government agency representatives, social institutions, and business organizations were brought together to discuss how they could support those visions. In order to maintain the integrity of the process, extensive quotes from participants were used throughout the final report, to ensure that community voices were accurately represented.

Even seemingly like-minded groups may not necessarily have the same goals; conservation groups may differ significantly on the means they view as appropriate for influencing policy, or the scope of government activity. Similarly, falsely lumping "big business" together into one category and making assumptions about their motivations and goals as a stakeholder group ignores industry specific preferences and individual corporate concerns. As such, decision makers must recognize multiple interests, be prepared for the fact that interests may change and evolve over time, and try to see diversity as an advantage and asset to policymaking rather than a liability.

Sources of Interests

Where do stakeholder interests come from? For one, stakeholders may have *economic interests* such as funding or profit motives, which create an underlying interest. For example, stakeholders may try to influence policy to protect their business opportunities or to ensure that they continue to receive government funding for their projects.

Stakeholders, and in particular opportunists, may also be motivated by trying to further the *professional interests* of their organization—for example, using the policymaking process to network and make connections that can be used for professional gain. Stakeholders may also hope to use the experience to raise the profile of their organization, in a sense "resume-building" their organization. Organizations may also be concerned about how a policy change will affect their operations, either positively or negatively—for example, by impacting funding opportunities or changing regulations.

Representatives of stakeholder organizations may also hold *personal interests* that influence their participation, including personal experience, family and friends, political affiliations, or religious values. The pursuit of self-interests, including professional advancement or the search for new experiences, may also help to explain the motivations of stakeholders.

Political interests such as power, advocacy, and campaigning may also be a motivating interest for stakeholders. They may be interested in making a political name for themselves, creating a political alliance with either policymakers or other stakeholders, or becoming known in the political arena. Similarly, some stakeholders may have a *legal interest* in participation, in particular ensuring that legal or ethical requirements are fulfilled. Stakeholders may also have an *academic interest* in the decision-making process, participating for research reasons such as interviewing stakeholders/decision makers or observing the policy process.

Stakeholders may have a *geographic interest* because they are somehow affected by their geographic proximity to an issue—for example, recreation users of a state park or residents living near a wildlife corridor. Some stakeholders may have a *demographic interest* because they are disproportionately affected by a decision. Examples of such disproportionate effects include children and lead poisoning or the elderly and social security. Finally, stakeholders may have a *symbolic/humanistic interest* in which their interest in a policy decision stems from their personal values or emotions. In environmental policy this may be an appreciation of nature, the desire to protect scenic areas, or an attachment to wilderness. Table 2.3 highlights policy stakes and interests.

Conflict and Participation

Conflict is a normal and expected part of policymaking. "The crucial problem in politics is the management of conflict. No regime could endure that did not cope with this problem. All politics, all leadership, all organization involves the management of conflict. All conflict allocates space in the political universe. The consequences of conflict are so important that it is inconceivable that any regime would survive without making an attempt to shape the system" (Schattschneider 1960, p. 71).

Every conflict is made up of issues, positions, and interests.

> Issues are the "what" of a dispute and disputants can argue interminably over an issue without talking about why they are concerned. Positions are specific proposals disputants put forth that suggest a way the conflict can be resolved. Positions are the "how" of a dispute. Interests are the expression of needs. Interests drive a person's behavior and provide the motivation to seek a solution to a problem. In conflict, interest can often be difficult to identify because the disputants are entrenched in their issues and positions. Interests are the "why" of a dispute. (Elias, Jackson, et al. 2004)

Inclusive approaches to stakeholder collaboration may be troubling to some because it means involving those who are opposed to decisions or represent wildly divergent views. For example, fostering a dialogue between both mainstream scientists and holistic healers to manage the overharvesting of herbal remedies such as Echinacea, black cohosh, and wild ginger in the United States is critical from an ecosystem management perspective, although likely to involve very different ways of thinking. However, both groups share an interest in ensuring sustainable

Table 2.3   Policy Stakes and Interests

Policy Stakes	Interests
Economic	• Impact on business practices • Economic gains • Economic losses • Pay the bills
Professional	• Professional benefits by participating • Policymaking will affect organizational operations • Falls within scope of organizational mandate
Personal	• Personal interest in the issue • Personal gain possible through participation (e.g., identify job opportunities) • Social interests • Personal networking
Political	• Make a political name for oneself • Become known by politicians • Power interests • Campaigning/advocacy work
Legal/process	• Ensure that legal or ethical requirements are met
Academic	• Scholarly interest in the issue
Geographic	• Geographic or proximity interest such as live/work/play near affected area
Demographic	• Those disproportionately affected due to particular demographic characteristics (e.g., children and lead poisoning)
Symbolic/ humanistic	• Appreciate nature • Protect beautiful natural areas • Emotional or spiritual attachment to nature • Value protecting nature for nature's sake

growth of these medicinal herbs, which should be the starting point of collaborative decision making. Similarly, different stakeholders have different concerns about old-growth forests in the Pacific Northwest. Wildlife biologists may focus on the spotted owl and minimum habitat requirements. Business investors may be interested in allowable timber volumes and the effects of profits. Local loggers may prioritize pay rates, overtime, and job security. The community may be focused on the tax consequences of policy changes for local municipalities and the potential for job losses.

Conflict is not necessarily a negative state; as long as it is handled and resolved effectively, conflict can lead to innovation and stimulate creative thinking. The discussion that participants engage in through the conflict process can expand people's understanding of the situation and facilitate consideration of alternative perspectives. Conflict can also help stakeholders better understand their own perspectives, priorities, and assumptions as they are forced to articulate their interests and think through their arguments for their positions. Managed conflict as opposed to out-of-control conflict encourages open communication and cooperative problem solving, which at the same time can foster productivity. Key to this is focusing on the real issues at hand and identifying win-win opportunities. It has been argued that being aware of and understanding other people's value systems is an essential preliminary step to consensus-based planning or conflict resolution (Elias, Jackson, et al. 2004). "Very often, the conflicting positions of different stakeholders mask a good deal of commonality in their underlying interests (e.g. improving long term competitiveness of industry)" (Economic and Social Commission for Asia and the Pacific 2001). Once conflict is resolved, a group may actually be stronger if the members develop mutual respect and an appreciation for their ability to work together.

When the conflict is between the agency and stakeholders, issues of conflict resolution and trust are even more important. Establishing trust is very important; however, lack of trust between stakeholders and decision makers should not be an excuse to avoid collaboration. "Even if there is only a low-level of trust among stakeholders, an effective communication and decision-making process can still allow for successful negotiation to take place" (EPA 2001, p. 8).

One of the key challenges for managers collaborating with stakeholders is trying to figure out a balance between competing interests, particularly when there are varying levels of interest and stake. One perspective is that effective managers "do not try either to minimize costs or maximize quality. Nor do they try to meet the demands of all stakeholders. Rather, they minimally satisfy the needs of marginal stakeholders while they attempt to maximize satisfaction of the needs of key stakeholders. Achieving given levels of efficiency and effectiveness are only a means to achieve what policymakers, leaders, and managers really desire: satisfaction of key stakeholders" (Blair, Stanley, et al. 1992, p. 114). Compromise as a group is useful when the cost of conflict and disagreement is higher than the cost of losing ground—for example, when deadlines are approaching or the risk of deadlock could have serious environmental consequences.

Conflict may arise between stakeholders separate from the policy issue at hand. Past history, either professionally or personally, may be a factor, particularly in issue areas in which stakeholders have a high degree of contact and familiarity. Certain issue areas may be especially prone to conflicts between interests. Complex issues like climate change are particularly affected by stakeholder values and perceptions.

Table 2.4   Sources of Conflict in Stakeholder Collaboration

Core personality differences that cause participants in the process to promote conflict regardless of the issue or proposed policy decisions.
Past history of conflicts between participants or with policymakers. Stakeholders may attempt to "punish" policymakers for past grievances or slights, whether real or imagined.
Differing problem definitions and, as such, resistance to accepting the problem definition that has been accepted.
Disagreements about the policy itself, including theory, design, content, timelines, and funding.
Feeling that their voices have not been heard, or that their interests have been misinterpreted.
If stakeholders feel that they are being treated unfairly, either in the decision-making process itself or in the final policy.
Divides between large sophisticated organizations and small grassroots groups, which in some cases may manifest as jealousy.
Interests that evolve and change the character of decision making.

Sometimes policy issues are contentious simply because they affect so many competing interests such as large-scale development projects in the public arena.

Internal conflicts may arise because stakeholders may simultaneously represent multiple interests. For example, in a debate over creation of a wildlife corridor encompassing private land, a stakeholder may on the one hand represent an environmental group supportive of the idea, and at the same time have family members who feel they will be negatively impacted by land use restrictions (Mitroff 1983). Such internal conflicts should not be dismissed as trivial or inconsequential. Other sources of conflict are listed in Table 2.4.

Changing Interests

When decision making stretches over a long time span, stakeholder interests can change and actors may come and go (Elias, Jackson, et al. 2004). It is important to keep in mind that conditions may change, and as a result stakeholder collaboration approaches must have a certain degree of inherent flexibility in order to adjust (Howard 2002). Under what conditions might stakeholder interests change? Institutional factors are certainly important, including personnel changes, budgetary changes that redirect priorities, or changing competition. For example, as the public and government focus more attention on climate change, a market saturation scenario might develop which might force an NGO to change its focus from climate change to a less populated and "competitive" issue area such as endangered species protection. Learning may also be key to changing interests. In fact, a successful stakeholder collaboration process will most likely include evolving interests for that reason. In addition, changing priorities or positions of the community may affect positions for community representatives. Government administration changes, particularly party affiliation, may alter the stakeholder interests and the actor representatives who participate. The broader policy environment may also have an impact such as changes to the agenda or budget constraints.

Stakeholder Participation

Token involvement such as a town hall meeting to announce a decision is not the same as meaningful stakeholder input. Decision making about environmental issues requires not just invitations to participate but also forums that facilitate careful deliberation and a mechanism for incorporating the results into policy or technical analysis. "Many of these efforts to democratize the development of policies—including opinion polls, focus groups, town-hall meetings, open houses, advisory committees, and a variety of economic surveys—have proven useful. However, too often decision makers cast a wide net for hearing citizens' views but then disappear behind closed doors to interpret what they have heard and to work out the tough conflicts that inevitably arise across disparate points of view" (Gregory 2000, p. 1). Stakeholders must be integrated into every stage of the policy process, not just during the early stages of debating ideas.

The goal of this process should not be to mandate the participation of all stakeholders, as that would likely stall decision making entirely. Not all stakeholders should have a decisive power or the right to advise (Verdeyen, Put, et al. 2004). However the reality is that "public participation is growing and transforming environmental decision processes. Many citizens desire to move from providing external reviews of agency plans to direct involvement in identifying and evaluating options" (Burroughs 1999, p. 798). What does stakeholder participation mean? It can mean a number of things. At its most extreme it may be the power to actually make decisions. Less intense participation may include participation in decision processes, nominating representatives, serving in an advisory role, attending meetings, and the right to be informed.

Nonparticipation

While much of the attention of the stakeholder literature has been on the failure of government decision makers to integrate stakeholders into policymaking, stakeholders themselves may also choose not to participate, even when given the opportunity. Nonparticipants include both those who choose not to participate and the would-be participants who would like to but do not know how (e.g., would-be players). Reasons for choosing not to participate include the following:

- Stakeholders lack the resources to participate. For example, traveling to meetings may raise the costs of participation beyond the reach of many small organizations.
- They may not know about the opportunities available.
- They may be waiting to be asked to participate, perhaps unaware of how to navigate access to the process or unsure if they are welcome.
- They may feel that their needs/interests/goals are better met through alternative venues. For example, rather than participating in local decision making, they may be more interested in international treaty negotiations.
- They do not see how they can make a meaningful contribution, whether or not that is actually true.
- They have other or conflicting priorities.
- Stakeholders are disenchanted with the process.
- They may assume decisions have already been made and participation is not worthwhile.
- They prefer to keep a low profile.
- Nonparticipation may also be a way of indicating opposition to either government or the direction the policy is heading.

Levels of Stakeholder Involvement*

In the continuum of stakeholder involvement, *no stakeholder participation* would be the most extreme. The next level of collaboration would be *notification or a good neighbor policy* in which policymakers are not required by law to contact others but choose to inform stakeholders of their planned activities. For example, a decision to set a fire in a local park as part of a prescribed burning policy to reduce the buildup of deadwood may be better received if the neighbors and press are informed in advance about the rationale, scope, and legality of the burn. At this level stakeholder input is not solicited; rather it is simply an opportunity to inform stakeholders about impending actions. In many cases the agency has the legal authority to make decisions without stakeholder input. Decision makers would take the initiative and do all the work of engaging with the stakeholders such as through e-mail or other communication updates about the process. The stakeholders may technically be involved in the process; however, their own level of initiation or engagement is nothing beyond reading the communication. Such passive participation, however, can rapidly change to a more extreme or active level of activity, usually in response to something that comes out of the communication. For these reasons,

---

* Levels of stakeholder involvement are adapted from Meffe, G. K., L. A. Nielsen, et al. (2002). *Ecosystem Management: Adaptive, Community-Based Conservation.* Washington, DC, Island Press.

engagement with these stakeholders is still ultimately worthwhile for decision makers. Techniques discussed in Chapter 5 may include public forums, newsletters, and web postings.

Review and comment is an effort to get stakeholder reactions to a proposed activity, for example, engaging stakeholders in a dialogue to assess preferences among a number of competing options, to develop a preliminary sense of stakeholder reactions to a proposed policy, or to determine preferences from a short list of previously vetted policy options. For example, government environmental impact statements require a period of review and comment in the United States. This may be useful when there are a limited number of options to choose from. Techniques for review and comment participation might include workshops, surveys, focus groups, websites, on-site visits, and public meetings.

Consultation is a request for substantive input from stakeholders at an early stage of the decision-making process. This may include brainstorming policy solutions, identifying issues, or deciding how to allocate a finite resource. Consultation processes can be an effective starting point for building stakeholder support. Consultation techniques may include those listed under review and comment, as well as regular meetings or advisory groups.

Limited partnerships are a formal arrangement with stakeholders based on an agreement to pursue mutual goals with varying degrees of shared assets such as time, money, equipment, or authority. Stakeholders have the authority to make decisions—for example, government agencies and NGOs and citizens sharing responsibility for protecting a watershed. It is limited only in the sense that government retains regulatory authority and assumes liability. Many of the watershed management partnerships fall into the category. The primary advantage of this arrangement is the enduring relationship, which fosters the development of institutional memory and brings some degree of stability to decision making. The disadvantages are the resources required to maintain the partnership, and the fact that a dysfunctional partnership may lead to enduring dysfunctional decision making. An example here might include a partnership grant.

Successful Collaboration

Ineffective stakeholder collaboration techniques have led to widespread dissatisfaction with the quality of stakeholder input (Gregory 2000). What are the characteristics of successful collaboration in environmental policymaking? Chapter 5 provides a series of practical strategies and tactics that decision makers can use to improve stakeholder relations, manage conflicting interests, and facilitate decision making. However, the stakeholder literature suggests a number of guiding principles that policymakers should keep in mind. Most importantly, "a well-designed public involvement process enables all interested stakeholders to hear and understand one another's concerns and needs, review facts, generate and evaluate alternatives and then recommend a course of action" (Meffe, Nielsen, et al. 2002, p. 222).

Successful collaboration should encompass the following elements. First, the willingness to accept the unexpected is critical for effective relationships and activities. A full stakeholder collaboration plan may include changes to human resources, finance, information systems, strategic planning, decision making, production, marketing, organizational structure, and so on (Olden 2003). Good communication strategies are also essential. For example, a stakeholder liaison officer can serve as a point person for stakeholders and facilitate communication. Relationship building often occurs outside of the formal processes that collect official comments such as informal communication. Building on that idea, early and inclusive participation is also important. Along with inclusive participation, ensuring that information is available to all stakeholders and that there are appropriate avenues for participation is important; "open decision making and inclusiveness are the hallmark of many successful collaborative initiatives" (Selin, Schuett, et al. 2000). Consideration of the possible barriers to participation will help to expand participation and make it more inclusive.

Taking the time to understand the motivations or intentions of stakeholders can help to prevent conflict. For example, the person who seems to be stonewalling a decision may be concerned that the proper rules of order are not being followed. Similarly it is important to seek out and acknowledge common goals and express a willingness to compromise/negotiate (Selin, Schuett, et al. 2000). As such, strong agency leadership is also a must. Good leaders will find ways to integrate new members if the situation arises, minimize barriers to participation, make effective use of participants' resources and time, facilitate timely communication, coordinate activities, and provide analytic support such as ongoing evaluations (Selin, Schuett, et al. 2000; Lasker and Weiss 2003).

It is also important to recognize that not all stakeholders are equally important and not every claim is urgent (Mitchell, Agle, et al. 1999; Foote 2002). Effective leadership will take this into account. Stakeholder claims may be diverse and conflicted, representing a challenge to the development of effective and meaningful policy. The policymakers must negotiate a balance between these competing claims.

The case study of Citizen Corps highlights an innovative stakeholder collaboration initiative in the United States. Disaster management is one of the toughest challenges governments around the world face. While many catastrophes cannot be prevented, many types can be avoided, or their effects mitigated. The four essential components of disaster management—prevention, preparation, relief, and recovery—involve not only government decision making but also by necessity the support and involvement of stakeholders from across society. In recognition of the importance of citizen involvement, in January 2002, President George W. Bush announced the creation of USA Freedom Corps to promote volunteerism in the wake of the terrorist attacks of September 11, 2001. Citizen Corps, one of the programs under Freedom Corps, is coordinated by Homeland Security and operates at the national, state, territorial, local, and tribal levels of government. Citizen Corps provides training to citizens to assist in recovery efforts after a disaster or terrorist attack. Each local Citizen Corps Council works with other stakeholders, including organizations (e.g., American Red Cross) and businesses to organize and plan before disaster strikes. Citizen Corps is also an information-sharing mechanism whereby successful local initiatives can be shared and adopted by other groups across the country, creating an environment of innovation and pilot testing of best practices. On the Citizen Corps online portal, "smart practices" and lessons learned are posted to encourage dissemination, and ideas are also shared directly with state coordinators. New ideas can also be shared through the monthly Ready.gov conference call, which is held the first Tuesday of every month. The program is intended in part to alleviate the masses of well-intentioned but untrained volunteers who show up at a disaster and get in the way of disaster relief.

Each council is sponsored or endorsed by an elected local government official or city/county administrator who has responsibility for local government operations. Most of the councils do the following throughout the year: provide educational outreach to households, plan volunteer initiatives with emergency managers, and promote "whole community planning" through discussions, reviews, and planning on topics such as vulnerability, risk assessments, evacuation plans, shelter plans, and mitigation. Citizen Corps does educational outreach to the stakeholders on the councils, as well as citizens. For stakeholders, for example, there are training opportunities and publications on topics such as volunteer liability through the Citizen Volunteer Liability Guide, state liability laws, and how to manage volunteers. Educational outreach programs for citizens include not only the basics of disaster planning but also financial first aid, a Girl Scouts Emergency Preparedness patch, and activity books for kids.

Citizen Corps uses the metaphor of being the "table" to which all stakeholders can come and share ideas and learn about disaster management. One of the interesting things about Citizen Corps is its scope of work. Stakeholders can be involved by participating in training and planning meetings or simply by receiving a pamphlet about household disaster preparedness. Providing a range of commitments helps to bring more stakeholders in, thereby increasing the size of the network. Stakeholders can be an important asset for building capacity when there are shared goals and interests. By harnessing the skills, resources, and strengths of preexisting stakeholder units, governments can greatly increase their outreach and programming. Rather than duplicating what the Red Cross already does, for example, in terms of disaster response, Citizen Corps Councils can strategize with stakeholders to develop efficient and effective disaster response.

Counterarguments to Participation

Despite the previously discussed advantages, why do organizations and government choose not to integrate stakeholders into the decision-making process? The reasons are varied. For one, historical conditions may have limited stakeholder participation. For example, rules to prevent regulatory capture, whereby agencies advance/prioritize the private interests they are supposed to be regulating, as discussed in Chapter 3 may have unwittingly made it difficult for agencies to seek advice from stakeholders. Decision makers may also be concerned about resource constraints, as decision makers envision costly meetings or extensive time commitments. In fact, as illustrated in the previous discussion, stakeholder collaboration can be an effective way to tap into additional resources and need not be an expensive undertaking as highlighted by the wide array of tools in Chapter 5. A general fear of conflict along with more specific concerns about dealing with combative individuals may also discourage decision makers from bringing stakeholders in, assuming that participants will simply want to argue or have an interest in maintaining conflict. Fear that a small vocal minority will co-opt the collaborative process is often a concern (Selin, Schuett, et al. 2000).

There are, of course, challenges and downsides to working with stakeholders and trying to find a compromise, and compromise may be difficult to achieve after years of entrenched conflict. "Some important stakeholders may even refuse to come to the table; others may try to get their way by using pressure tactics. There may be some stakeholders for whom a compromise solution will cause extreme economic hardship. This introduces extra demands for careful negotiation and conflict resolution" (Economic and Social Commission for Asia and the Pacific 2001, p. 42). Fear of conflicts or challenges should not be used as a rationale for not including stakeholders in decision making. Strong leadership, clear priorities, and guidelines can prevent these from happening. Ultimately, policymakers hold the final decision-making power.

Another concern may be that there are simply too many stakeholders, making it impossible to engage any of them effectively, or making it so that any effort would simply take too much time. Even minimal efforts would be better than none at all. As discussed further in Chapter 5, techniques such as snowball sampling, whereby stakeholders themselves help to identify other individuals or groups who would be interested, reduce the burden on decision makers to identify the entire universe of interests. Concern that collaboration is too time consuming is a short-sighted argument. What is really time consuming for decision makers is dealing with lawsuits, appeals, grievances, and the media firestorm in the wake of a poor policy decision.

Decision makers may also falsely assume that stakeholders are not interested in participating. This is common thinking when it comes to getting the general public involved. There may also be an assumption that everyone who shows up will have the same views and therefore will not be very helpful to the process. Conversely, the notion that a camel is a horse made by a committee may also influence thinking on stakeholder collaboration: the idea that nothing effective or meaningful can actually come out of the process, despite persuasive evidence to the contrary (De Lopez 2001; Fletcher 2001; Jonsson 2005; Sabatier, Focht, et al. 2005; Gore, Knuth, et al. 2006; Mangun, Throgmorton, et al. 2007).

Decision makers may assume that stakeholders lack knowledge of the issue or the appropriate expertise and that as a result they will not be able to contribute meaningfully. In some cases, this may be true; however, stakeholders who are given the opportunity to learn may bring a new perspective to an issue. Stakeholders may know more than decision makers think, be willing to learn, or have other kinds of valuable expertise that may be helpful to the process (Moswete, Thapa, et al. 2012).

One of the biggest reasons for the failure to use stakeholder collaboration is that decision makers often do not actually want outside opinions. There may be a fear of losing power and control over the policy process, or they may be worried about exposure of incompetence (Davies and White 2012). If an unpopular decision has to be made, they may want to delay the criticism as long as possible. They may assume that they already know everything or already know what stakeholders want. Similarly, decision makers may feel that they do not want to make changes to their policies or will feel obliged to respond if they know about stakeholder concerns. There may also be a sense that it is easier to apologize for something rather than to ask for input. Decision makers may also feel that there will be fewer people to upset or anger if policy decisions are made in private, perhaps in hopes that either stakeholders will not find out what has been done or in some cases a different administration will deal with the fallout. Opposition to collaborative efforts may stem from apprehension that collaboration will erode agency power and influence (Selin, Schuett, et al. 2000; McDaniel and Miskel 2002).

There may also be an assumption that stakeholder collaboration means everyone has to be pleased with the outcome or that decision makers have to operate from a consensus approach, which is not true. Decision makers ultimately direct the process, and as such, they control the degree to which stakeholders have power and influence over the final decision. As has been argued throughout this chapter, not every stakeholder concern or claim is a priority for policymakers to address. Policymakers must prioritize who should have the most influence over decision making, and such influence may vary over time and across issues (McDaniel and Miskel 2002). Unless there are identified regulations in place mandating consensus or majority or unanimous voting, decision makers retain power over the final decision. Policymaking is, by its very nature, a contentious and complicated process; making decisions in isolation does not ensure less conflict, and in many cases can lead to increased discontent.

Decision makers may also have an interest in fostering stakeholder collaboration but be uncertain of how to do so. While there is extensive recognition of the importance of stakeholder participation, most decision makers lack the experience or knowledge of how to facilitate participation effectively. As such, it is not surprising that there is widespread dissatisfaction with the quality of stakeholder input (Gregory 2000).

Decision makers working in different cultural contexts may also face difficulties in bringing marginalized groups into the policy process. For example, cultural constraints may prevent certain groups such as women or indigenous people from participating effectively. Integrating groups that have difficulty speaking for themselves such as the elderly or immigrants or differently abled populations also poses special challenges. Techniques and applications discussed in the final chapter cover many of those issues from a practical standpoint.

Obviously there may be cases where stakeholder collaboration fails—where stakeholders refuse to collaborate, where their primary interest is policy failure, or where other overwhelming factors supersede success. The possibility of failure, however, is insufficient grounds for ignoring stakeholders. Stakeholder management is important because human elements are often responsible for project success. Identifying key relationships and potential conflicts in advance and working through them are key to successful policymaking.

Conclusion

While the examples and case studies profiled in this book focus largely on environmental policy, the theory and practical applications extend far beyond the environment. Table 2.5 highlights other policy areas, the most prominent stakeholders, and current issues appropriate for inclusive stakeholder participation.

Handled improperly, stakeholder involvement can lead to feelings of disenfranchisement, anger at wasted time, and disappointment with the management team. It is important to recognize that policymaking is not just about science and facts. Whether or not decision makers would choose it to be so, policymaking is also about the process through which decisions are made, the nature of relationships between decision makers and stakeholders, and the way in which decisions are presented.

Over time stakeholders may come and go, and interests may evolve. Particularly, since many environmental issues deal with extraordinarily long time horizons, this can be challenging. Decision makers may spend months nurturing relationships only to have them end abruptly as representatives change jobs or organizational priorities change. Institutional memory is important, and if stakeholders are a revolving door, this may create problems. Facilitators of the process may then have to put effort into ensuring that there is some consistency among the participants to facilitate institutional memory and to create some semblance of stability.

What do different stakeholders need? Stakeholders may be looking for assurance that the process is one that is transparent and abides by rules or particular values. They may also be seeking representation and looking for opportunities to speak in public forums, submit briefs, and receive acknowledgment of their value. Almost all stakeholders want to feel that their participation was meaningful, even if their interests cannot be accommodated.

Stakeholder participation is not in itself an end but rather should be clearly linked to decision making. Too often stakeholders are brought in as token deference to the idea of welcoming diverse viewpoints, but then those ideas and opinions

Table 2.5 Stakeholders in Key Policy Issues

Issue Area	*Key Stakeholders*	*Conflicts*
Health care policy	Hospitals, medical professionals, patients, researchers, health insurance companies, public health departments, American Medical Association	• Funding • Recruitment of medical professionals • Underinsured populations • Medicare/Medicaid eligibility • Access • Consumer costs • Quality control
Agriculture	Farmers, scientists, industry, migrant workers, farm lobby	• Subsidies • Food safety • Immigration • Emergency/disaster management • Nutrient and pest management • Taxation • Agri-food research
Criminal justice	Law enforcement, tribal groups, lawyers, courts, public/private prisons, victims, general public, media, victims	• Crime rates • Incarceration rates • Sentencing • War on drugs • Capital punishment
Education	Teachers, students, parents, academics, school boards, taxpayers, administrators, unions, National Education Association, Federation of Teachers, for-profit education companies	• Standardized testing • School vouchers • Special education funding • Funding formulas • Merit pay for teachers
Humanitarian aid	Those in need, NGOs, donors, military	• Funding • Distribution • Accountability

are never actually integrated into the final decision-making process. Stakeholder collaboration may help decision makers to take advantage of expertise and experience from other organizations, maximize creativity in the identification/development and implementation of policy solutions, build trust between and with other organizations to reduce conflict and promote long-term stable relationships, identify win-win solutions, build openness and accountability in policymaking, and encourage the sharing of responsibility for environmental management.

Chapter 3 explores more specifically the role of stakeholders in environmental policy failure.

References

Banff–Bow Valley Study (1996). "Banff–Bow Valley: At the Crossroads." Technical report of the Banff–Bow Valley Task Force. Ottawa, ON, Ministry of Canadian Heritage.

Baumgartner, F. R. and B. L. Leech (1998). *Basic Interests: The Importance of Groups in Politics and in Political Science.* New Jersey, Princeton University Press.

Berry, J. M. (1989). *The Interest Group Society.* Glenview, IL, Schott, Foresman.

Blair, J. D., J. Stanley, et al. (1992). "A Stakeholder Management Perspective on Military Health Care." *Armed Forces & Society (Transaction Publishers)* 18(4): 548–575.

Bloodgood, E. (2001). "International Non-Governmental Organizations as Interest Groups." *Annual Meeting of the American Political Science Association.* San Francisco, CA.

Bryner, G. (2008). "Failure and Opportunity: Environmental Groups in US Climate Change Policy." *Environmental Politics* 17(2): 319–336.

Bryson, J. M. (2003). "What to Do When Stakeholders Matter: A Guide to Stakeholder Identification and Analysis Techniques." *London School of Economics and Political Science.* London.

Burroughs, R. (1999). "When Stakeholders Choose: Process, Knowledge, and Motivation in Water Quality Decisions." *Society & Natural Resources* 12(8): 797–809.

Cater, D. (1964). *Power in Washington.* New York, Random House.

Cobb, R. W. and C. D. Elder (1981). "Communication and Public Policy." *Handbook of Political Communication.* D. Nimmo and K. Sanders. Beverly Hills, Sage.

Davies, A. and R. White (2012). "Collaboration in Natural Resource Governance: Reconciling Stakeholder Expectations in Deer Management in Scotland." *Journal of Environmental Management* 112(December): 160–169.

De Lopez, T. T. (2001). "Deforestation in Cambodia: A Stakeholder Management Approach." *International Journal for Sustainable Development & World Ecology* 8(4): 380.

Economic and Social Commission for Asia and the Pacific (2001). *Guidelines for Stakeholders Participation in Strategic Environmental Management.* New York, United Nations.

Eden, C. and F. Ackermann (1998). *Making Strategy: The Journey of Strategic Management.* London, Sage.

Elias, A., L. S. Jackson, et al. (2004). "Changing Positions and Interests of Stakeholders in Environmental Conflict: A New Zealand Transport Infrastructure Case." *Asia Pacific Viewpoint* 45(1): 87–104.

EPA (2001). Stakeholder Involvement and Public Participation at the U.S. EPA: Lessons Learned, Barriers and Innovative Approaches.

Eschenbach, R. C. and T. G. Eschenbach (1996). "Understanding Why Stakeholders Matter." *Journal of Management in Engineering* 12(6): 59.

Fletcher, S. (2001). "Using Stakeholder Decision-Making Simulation to Teach Integrated Coastal Management." *Journal of Geography in Higher Education* 25(3): 367–378.

Foote, D. (2002). "Manage Your Stakeholders." *Computerworld* 36(47): 25.

Freeman, R. E. (1984). *Strategic Management: A Stakeholder Approach.* Boston, Pitman.

Gore, M. L., B. A. Knuth, et al. (2006). "Stakeholder Perceptions of Risk Associated with Human-Black Bear Conflicts in New York's Adirondack Park Campgrounds: Implications for Theory and Practice." *Wildlife Society Bulletin* 34(1): 36–43.

Graci, S. (2013). "Collaboration and Partnership Development for Sustainable Tourism." *Tourism Geographies* 15(1): 25–42.

Gregory, R. (2000). "Using Stakeholder Values to Make Smarter Environmental Decisions." *Environment* 42(5): 34.

Hanks, C. D. (2000). "Reexamining the Subsystem Concept." Ph.D. dissertation, Political Science. College Station, Texas A&M University: 185.

Heclo, H. (1978). "Issue Networks and the Executive Establishment." *The New American Political System.* A. King. Washington, DC, American Enterprise Institute for Public Policy Research.

Howard, P. L. (2002). "Beyond the 'Grim Resisters': Towards More Effective Gender Mainstreaming through Stakeholder Participation." *Development in Practice* 12(2): 164–176.

Hula, K. W. (1999). *Lobbying Together: Interest Group Coalitions in Legislative Politics.* Washington, DC, Georgetown University Press.

Jarman, H. (2011). "Collaboration and Consultation: Functional Representation in EU Stakeholder Dialogues." *Journal of European Integration* 33(4): 385–399.

Jonsson, A. (2005). "Public Participation in Water Resources Management: Stakeholder Voices on Degree, Scale, Potential, and Methods in Future Water Management." *AMBIO—A Journal of the Human Environment* 34(7): 495–500.

Kingdon, J. W. (1995). *Agendas, Alternatives, and Public Policies.* New York, HarperCollins.

Kloprogge, P. and J. P. van der Sluijs (2006). "The Inclusion of Stakeholder Knowledge and Perspectives in Integrated Assessment of Climate Change." *Climatic Change* 75(3): 359–389.

Lasker, R. D. and E. S. Weiss (2003). "Creating Partnership Synergy: The Critical Role of Community Stakeholders." *Journal of Health & Human Services Administration* 26(1): 119–139.

Mangun, J. C., K. W. Throgmorton, et al. (2007). "Assessing Stakeholder Perceptions: Listening to Avid Hunters of Western Kentucky." *Human Dimensions of Wildlife* 12(3): 157–168.

McDaniel, J. E. and C. G. Miskel (2002). "Stakeholder Salience: Business and Educational Policy." *Teachers College Record* 104(2): 325.

Meffe, G. K., L. A. Nielsen, et al. (2002). *Ecosystem Management: Adaptive, Community-Based Conservation.* Washington, DC, Island Press.

Mitchell, R. K., B. R. Agle, et al. (1999). "Toward a Theory of Stakeholder Identification and Salience: Defining the Principle of Who and What Really Counts." *Academy of Management Review* 22(4): 853–886.

Mitroff, I. I. (1983). *Stakeholders of the Organizational Mind.* San Francisco, Jossey-Bass Publishers.

Moswete, N. N., B. Thapa, et al. (2012). "Attitudes and Opinions of Local and National Public Sector Stakeholders towards Kgalagadi Transfrontier Park, Botswana." *International Journal of Sustainable Development and World Ecology* 19(1): 67–80.

Olden, P. C. (2003). "Hospital and Community Health: Going from Stakeholder Management to Stakeholder Collaboration." *Journal of Health & Human Services Administration* 26(1): 35–57.

Orr, S. K. (2006). "Policy Subsystems and Regimes: Organized Interests and Climate Change Policy." *Policy Studies Journal* 34(2): 147–169.

Orr, S. K. (2007). "The Evolution of Climate Policy—Business and Environmental Organizations: Between Alliance Building and Entrenchment." *Global Policy Arrangements: Business and the Countervailing Powers of Civil Society.* K. Ronit. London, Routledge.

Sabatier, P. (1999). "The Need for Better Theories." *Theories of the Policy Process.* P. Sabatier. Boulder, Westview.

Sabatier, P. A., W. Focht, et al. (2005). "Collaborative Approaches to Watershed Management." *Swimming Upstream: Collaborative Approaches to Watershed Management.* P. A. Sabatier, W. Focht, M. Lubell, et al. Cambridge, The MIT Press.

Salisbury, R. (1990). *The Paradox of Interest Groups in Washington: More Groups, Less Clout. The New American Political System.* Washington, DC, American Enterprise Institute.

Schattschneider, E. E. (1960). *The Semi-Sovereign People.* New York, Holt, Rinehart and Winston.

Selin, S. W., M. A. Schuett, et al. (2000). "Modeling Stakeholder Perceptions of Collaborative Initiative Effectiveness." *Society & Natural Resources* 13(8): 735–745.

Thurber, J. (1991). "Dynamics of Policy Subsystems in American Politics." *Interest Group Politics.* A. J. Cigler and B. A. Loomis. Washington, DC, CQ Press.

Verdeyen, V., J. Put, et al. (2004). "A Social Stakeholder Model." *International Journal of Social Welfare* 13(4): 325–331.

Wallace, G. (1995). "Managing and Mismanaging Stakeholder Expectations." *Journal for Quality & Participation* 18(3): 76.

Weimer, D. and A. R. Vining (2010). *Policy Analysis: Concepts and Practice.* Englewood Cliffs, Prentice Hall.

West, J. J. and T. W. Clark (2006). "Mapping Stakeholder Capacity in the La Amistad Biosphere Initiative." *Journal of Sustainable Forestry* 22(1/2): 35–48.

Chapter 3

Stakeholders and Decision Making

Introduction

Governments need scientific, technical, and professional advice at every stage of the policymaking process; "decisions that are made without adequate consideration of their technical aspects, or that conflict with strong professional advice, may turn out to be faulty on both technical and political grounds" (Anderson 2006, p. 222). Writing fifteen years ago, Cortner and Moote (1999) identified many of the key challenges to integrating broad participation into environmental decision making, which continue to resonate today. Although the interest, will, and commitment may all be there,

> socially we need to develop the capacity for civic discourse and collective learning. Tools such as community visioning and mapping, collaborative learning, and mediation help develop these social skills and networks. Structurally, we need to break down the barriers to public involvement imposed by excessive bureaucracy, while remaining accountable to all stakeholders, present and potential. Open decision-making processes and all-party monitoring are tools that may address the paradoxes of expert and open decision-making and bureaucracy and accountability. Increasing the governance authority of local communities and drastically reducing the power of large corporations could also foster renewed civic activism and possibly help balance decentralized and centralized governance, but risk undermining national policy and alienating important sectors of society. (Cortner and Moote 1999, p. 105)

This chapter provides an overview of how stakeholders affect, help, and hinder the policy process, as well as an exploration of how agency decision makers can more effectively work with stakeholders to facilitate successful policymaking.

Stakeholders and Public Policymaking

Public policy involves both decisions about how to address societal issues and the legislative or administrative rules to carry out solutions. It begins with the recognition that there is a problem (problem definition), followed by the realization that government is an appropriate venue to deal with it (agenda setting), consideration of solutions (formation), authoritative decision making (legitimation), execution of that policy (implementation), and then assessment of the success or failure (evaluation). While in reality the policymaking process may not flow quite that smoothly, and may take decades during which the process cycles and recycles back on itself, this is a basic starting point from which we can understand policymaking (Birkland 2005; Anderson 2006).

Problem Definition

The problem definition process through which problems become interpreted occurs in a public arena composed of multiple participants and competing problem definitions. The problem definition stage is critical to policymaking because it sets the direction and tone for all future decisions. Stakeholders may be particularly active in the early stages, as they jostle to make their views heard in a variety of arenas such as the media, and with those decision makers empowered to deal with issues once they are on the agenda (Birkland 1997; Anderson 2006).

Different stakeholders may define problems in different ways. Values, information, and experiences will all come into play. Problem definition is an inherently political process, and the outcome will directly affect the solutions that are proposed. The debate over drilling for oil in the Arctic National Wildlife Refuge (ANWR) is a classic example of stakeholders trying to influence the early stages of the policy process. Environmentalists have emphasized the pristine nature of the refuge and pushed energy conservation as an alternative to drilling. Some drilling advocates have framed the issue as a way to reduce foreign dependence on oil, linking drilling to national security concerns. Differing problem definitions, such as those highlighted in the drilling case, are significant because they can destabilize the policy process, delay decision making, and distract policymakers from the most pressing aspects of the problem.

Competing problem definitions can be problematic for policymaking. Presumably stakeholders will select from alternative and competing definitions the one that either best represents or furthers their own interests. This does not necessarily have to be selfishly motivated; such interests may include improving the well-being of the disenfranchised, or some ideal of the common good. What then happens when these definitions conflict? For some there will be a complete dismissal of competing definitions; for others it will be a chance to engage in dialogue about expectations, values, beliefs, and opportunities.

How do stakeholders manipulate the problem definition? Often they will try to stimulate a sense of outrage among the public, galvanizing people, and by extension policymakers, into action as a result (Kraft 2007). Stakeholders in an issue area may also try to manipulate understanding of causation of a problem as a means to further their own interest; for example, the ongoing debate over human versus natural causes of climate change has distracted policymakers in many cases from moving forward on coherent action. Another strategy is to deny that there is a problem; for example, conflicting ideas about the use of forests has led to numerous battles between stakeholders. Conflicts between those who see commercial development of forests as a problem and those who see it as an asset have become a regular feature of forest policy debates.

Agenda Setting

Attention to environmental issues varies in response to changes in the economy, public interest, political economy, and perceptions of problems. The existence of problems, regardless of their severity, does not necessarily mean that the public or government will pay attention. Problems must achieve a certain degree of visibility before they achieve agenda status (Kraft 2007). While policies about nuclear waste disposal affect everyone's quality of life, it is unreasonable to expect that everyone will follow the particulars of nuclear waste disposal policy, which includes issues of safety standards, transportation of hazardous waste, and scientific assessment of possible waste repository sites.

Stakeholders who need decision makers to address their concerns have an interest in influencing the agenda and ensuring that their problems are getting attention. Stakeholders can play a valuable role in bringing problems to the attention of decision makers that might not otherwise attract consideration; however, stakeholders may also try to manipulate the agenda in pursuit of their own self-interests.

How do stakeholders influence agenda setting? They may attempt a number of different strategies, including the following:

- Eliciting public support, for example, through use of media outlets, grassroots organizing campaigns, or protests (Cobb and Elder 1983; Kingdon 1995).
- Appealing directly to decision makers at different levels in order to find a receptive venue that will take up the cause (Schattschneider 1960).
- Collaborating with other groups in order to pool resources. Coalitions can be important for creating and sustaining an issue, which can drain the resources and energies of single individuals or organizations (Ashford, Smith, et al. 2006).

- Taking advantage of electoral changes as newly elected officials may be looking for causes and issues to support. Electoral changes can create openings for new issues to be considered and give space to the voices of previously disadvantaged stakeholders (Cobb and Elder 1983; Kingdon 1995).
- Aligning with changes in social perception; for example, a rise in environmental consciousness in the 1960s and 1970s led to the creation of new environmental groups and greater interest on the part of decision makers to consider environmental policies (Anderson 2006).
- Highlighting changes in indicators, such as statistical evidence that a problem has changed, typically for the worse. For example, changes in pollution levels may drive environmental policy. Indicator changes alone, however, are insufficient to push an issue onto the agenda. Stakeholders, often referred to as "policy entrepreneurs" in this case, will use these numbers to push their own ideas (Kingdon 1995; Birkland 2005).
- Pursuing litigation can also be thought of as another type of venue shopping as stakeholders explore alternative means to get an issue on the agenda (Orr 2006).

Agenda denial is the flip side of agenda setting, whereby stakeholders work to keep issues off the agenda or oppose action on a problem. Stakeholders may also have an interest in prolonging the time it takes for an issue to capture attention. Strategies to oppose agenda status include denying that a problem exists, claiming that it is outside the realm of government action, raising concerns about the consequences of a proposed solution, arguing that nongovernmental entities can deal with the problem, and advocating for further study (Anderson 2006).

Kingdon argues that particular stakeholders, called policy entrepreneurs, are central to agenda setting. Policy entrepreneurs are those members of Congress, agency officials, citizens, and interest group members who work to put issues on the agenda (or keep them there), build support for solutions, and shepherd policies through the formation and implementation processes. According to Kingdon, policy entrepreneurs may be motivated by "their straightforward concern about certain problems, their pursuit of such self serving benefits as protecting or expanding their bureaucracy's budget or claiming credit for accomplishment, their promotion of their policy values, ... their simple pleasure in participating" (Kingdon 1995, p. 24). Policy entrepreneurs serve a number of important roles as they kindle interest in problems, educate, promote new findings, and keep issues simmering until the climate is right to push them forward (Kingdon 1995).

Policy Formulation

Once an issue is on the agenda, stakeholders will then turn their attention to influencing the goals and content of the policies. While there is an extensive body of literature on how groups and individuals attempt to influence policy formulation, two of the most discussed activities are lobbying and monitoring.

Lobbying activities are usually twofold: first, obtaining access to policymakers and, second, influencing decisions. Access may be direct (face-to-face) or indirect (through political aides, mass media, or appeals to public opinion). Access may also depend on the resources available to a group, including physical, organizational, political, and motivational resources, and more specifically money, organizational skills, size, expertise, and the ability to mobilize members (Berry 1989). Nownes and Freeman suggest that groups without money, connections, or access must use outside strategies such as protesting or making use of the media if they want to influence policy formation (Nownes and Freeman 1988).

Stakeholder influence may be particular (a specific vote on a specific bill) or diffuse (general attitudes). Stakeholder groups can serve as an intermediary link between citizens and governments, providing the means through which members can voice their opinions and influence the policy process. The means to do so may include meeting with government representatives, providing policy analysis, protesting, distributing petitions, using the media, and disseminating information on a group's views (Baumgartner and Leech 1998; Orr 2006).

Stakeholders have multiple points of access given the fragmented government arena. Congressional testimony by stakeholders is another way in which groups can promote their interests at any stage of the policy process, but in particular during policy formulation. The large number of congressional committees and subcommittees allows groups to venue shop to find a supportive or at least an open-minded chair who will permit their participation. In addition to the committee system, stakeholders may be able to get access to executive branch officials—for example, the Environmental Protection Agency or the Fish and Wildlife Service—if they cannot get a hearing in the House Resources Committee (Birkland 2005).

Stakeholder groups may propose specific policies to legislators or provide counsel on complex and technical issues that lie outside the scope of legislative expertise. Stakeholders in policy debates have an incentive to selectively present evidence, to discredit other positions, and to distort the positions of their opponents in their efforts to influence the outcome (Sabatier 1999). One of the challenges for stakeholders is to bring new information to policymakers, as they must compete with personal agendas, different ideologies, or entrenched practices that are resistant to change (Ashford, Smith, et al. 2006).

Monitoring as a stakeholder strategy involves keeping track of what policymakers and other groups are doing and then responding appropriately. Heinz, Laumann, et al. (1993) emphasize the fact that most of what lobbyists actually do is not persuade policymakers to change their views but find out what is going on (Heinz, Laumann, et al. 1993). According to Salisbury (1990), the most time-consuming and critical activities that groups engage in "are concerned not so much with persuading government officials to act one way or another as with keeping track of what is happening in the policy process, alerting the client organizations to developments relevant to their interests, and developing appropriate strategies of response and adaptation" (Salisbury 1990, p. 357). As such, monitoring strategies are often used in concert with lobbying. As discussed earlier, monitoring may in fact be the primary interest of stakeholders.

Policy Legitimation

While policy legitimation is largely the purview of government acting alone, such as through a vote in Congress, stakeholders will have had significant influence right up until that moment:

> Policies can…be failures in the sense of never being adopted, or in the sense of being adopted but having unsatisfactory effects….The failure to get a policy adopted is a subject of particular relevance to political science, since adoption failure tends almost always to be due to a lack of interest group support relative to the opposition for the policy being considered. (Nagel 1980, p. 7)

Implementation

Agencies charged with developing and implementing environmental policy face a task that is usually technically and organizationally complex. Environmental policy implementation often requires support beyond simply scientific and technical expertise such as education and communication. Stakeholders who "lost" during the earlier stages may attempt to influence or disrupt policy implementation. "The implementation of environmental policies and plans affects a wide range of stakeholders with differing attitudes and interests. No single outcome is going to be exactly what everybody wants. This means looking for new options that bring different benefits to different people. The aim is to arrive at a 'mutual gain' solution that gives everyone more than if they had not taken part, even if this is less than they might have hoped for in the first place" (Economic and Social Commission for Asia and the Pacific 2001, p. 42).

Agencies charged with implementing policy must often exercise considerable discretion to fill in the details, rules, and directives of policy. Because agencies are able to exercise discretion, stakeholders trying to influence the implementation stage may also target them; thus they are not insulated from politics and the demands of competing interests. Stakeholders may try to work with agency officials as they develop implementation plans, or they may complain about elements of programs that they do not like.

Rulemaking notices are published and available for public review, and stakeholders may monitor these daily publications to determine if there is an issue of interest to them. Stakeholders can exercise significant influence during rulemaking by adding scientific and technical expertise, influencing implementation details, and exploiting or encouraging flexibility.

Evaluation

Stakeholders play a valuable role in the evaluation stage of the policy process. Stakeholders at this stage might include programmatic staff, those personally affected by the program, sponsors, clients, and potential recipients of services, as well as previously involved supporters or detractors. Stakeholders may be able to provide valuable information about the key features of a program including strengths, weaknesses, unanticipated consequences, and areas for improvement.

Stakeholders who asked to participate in an evaluation may be unduly influenced by their own interests and may try to influence the results as such, rather than providing unbiased information. Supporters may be looking for evidence of success, while detractors may be seeking proof of failure, in both cases to validate their previous positions. For this reason broad inclusion of stakeholders is particularly important at the evaluation stage. Decision makers must consider the fact that some stakeholders will wield more influence than others and are in a stronger position to affect evaluation decisions about focus, criteria, methods, and data gathering. Some stakeholders may be difficult to identify or contact, and there may be additional obstacles to incorporating them into the evaluation such as language or cultural barriers. Program beneficiaries such as children, people with disabilities, or the elderly may be particularly difficult to integrate into evaluation.

Stakeholders in the evaluation stage may have very specific information needs. Because information exchange at this stage is often a reciprocal process, it is important for decision makers to have a communication plan in place such as meetings, websites, and reports. Stakeholders can be expected to provide information through surveys, interviews, focus groups, and meetings. One of the issues for the evaluation stage is encouraging use of the results. Stakeholders who disagree with the results are unlikely to facilitate utilization. Conflicts may erupt, particularly in response to perceived criticism. "When stakeholder groups are polarized on an issue, it is likely that evaluation findings will be hard to use. When people hold hardened positions linked to values, evaluation findings may fall on deaf ears or parties may endorse some parts of evaluations while rejecting other parts" (Posavac and Carey 2007, p. 269).

Importance of Stakeholders for Policymaking

The advantages of stakeholder collaboration for policymakers are numerous, including expertise, resource sharing, policy relevance, fostering innovation, anticipating reactions, and trust and legitimacy.

Expertise and Resource Sharing

The inherent complexities of environmental issues, combined with the competing time demands on government, make it increasingly difficult for governments to find sufficient internal resources to address every issue area. Bringing together stakeholders in this way is an easy, budget-conscious, and effective way to use an external pool of expertise for decision making.

Resource sharing is one of the most important assets of collaborative decision making, as stakeholders bring unique experiences, information, goods, services, expertise, and access to target groups which can all be utilized by decision makers (Olden 2003; Treves, Andriamampianina, et al. 2006). Formal collaboration arrangements have been shown to be an effective way to foster the sharing of these resources between stakeholders and decision makers (Davies and White 2012). In addition to material resources such as funding and volunteers, information and expertise are important assets for sharing. Given the highly technical nature of many environmental issues, stakeholders may play an important role in policymaking by providing information to policymakers. Decision makers may not be fully informed about the issue or may lack sufficient technical expertise, and so may rely more heavily on stakeholders for scientific information. Stakeholders as such may in fact provide a valuable service to government if they can provide credible information and analysis (Baumgartner and Leech 1998; Bloodgood 2001; Darnall and Jolley 2004). For example, "because systematic, scientific data on the dynamic and diverse interactions between humans and wildlife are often lacking, conservation planners increasingly make use of stakeholders as sources of expert opinion and to supplement other data collection efforts that may be more time-consuming and expensive as diagnostic measures" (Treves, Andriamampianina, et al. 2006).

Because resource sharing allows participants to exploit their individual strengths and compensate for their weaknesses, diverse participation means a greater variety of knowledge, resources, and skills to tap into compared to arrangements with more homogeneous participants; promoting ongoing discourse among diverse participants enables the group as a whole to overcome individual limitations (Lasker and Weiss 2003).

The FEMA Collaboration Community is an example of one such initiative to tap into stakeholder expertise and resources. The Collaboration Community connects FEMA stakeholders from across the United States in an online forum where users submit their ideas and the community discusses and votes for the best one; the most popular ones then rise up to the top of the list where they can be seen by other stakeholders. Recent topics have included adding disaster preparedness to school curriculums, amateur radio for emergency communication, and developing a mobile app for FEMA employees and the public using GPS data. Participants can also post comments about ideas, fostering a dialogue between stakeholders with vastly different experiences and backgrounds. FEMA leadership also participate in the community, responding to posts, answering questions, and providing updates on implementation on those selected for action.

Policy Relevance

Stakeholder participation ensures that the issues addressed are those most relevant to the key players and those most affected by decisions (Gilliam, Davis, et al. 2002). Stakeholders provide insight into their concerns and illuminate the consequences and the trade-offs that matter most.

Individuals or single organizations such as government agencies often have incomplete information. The failure to see other perspectives, or the reliance on assumptions about what people think, is likely to lead to problems (Lasker and Weiss 2003). Public attitudes on issues such as wildlife are often based more on emotion than fact, which may have an impact on management solutions. For example, understanding how people perceive risks from black bears can be used in turn as a foundation for developing and delivering communication and education programs (Gore, Knuth, et al. 2006). The range of social and political values held by stakeholders can help them to identify problems/issues/solutions from a vantage point that governments and other experts may miss due to incomplete information (Carmin, Darnall, et al. 2003; Darnall and Jolley 2004).

One of the challenges of environmental decision making in a federal system is that federalism combined with insular agency-based decision making may fail to take into account the local contexts of environmental problems. In cases of watershed management, such approaches have often left stakeholders dissatisfied, causing them to turn to the courts for redress (Mostashari and Sussman 2005; Sabatier, Focht, et al. 2005). Stakeholders may have a better understanding of the local context, which includes appreciating the values/politics/history of the local environment, and be in a better position to use this understanding to better develop policy solutions than government decision makers with little local understanding (Mostashari and Sussman 2005). Without stakeholder participation, policies may be overlapping, fragmented, uncoordinated, and insufficient (Olden 2003).

"We the People" is a novel federal government experiment in stakeholder engagement from the office of the President of the United States. It is an online petition system that allows people to directly petition the administration and its policy experts. Petitions that attain a particular threshold of signatures are reviewed by the appropriate staff in the administration and receive an official response. Launched on September 22, 2011, We the People was created as part of a government transparency movement to try to create a new level of openness within the federal government and to engage citizens more directly in government policymaking.

As can be expected with any online, open platform, petition topics have ranged from the serious to the absurd. A 2012 petition urging the government to create a Death Star (from *Star Wars: Episode IV*) as an economic stimulus measure gained sufficient signatures to qualify for a response. The official memo, written by Paul Shawcross, Chief of the White House Office of Management and Budget's science and space branch, stated that "the Administration does not support blowing up planets" and that the cost estimate would be $852 quadrillion, eliminating any economic benefit. The response also questioned the logic of supporting a weapon "with a fundamental flaw that can be exploited by a one-man starship," and so the petition was denied (Shawcross 2013). While the petition was in jest and the response tongue-in-cheek, it received widespread media coverage, driving up traffic and participation on the website. Other more serious recent petition topics have included gun control, humanitarian intervention, immigration, and health policy.

In some ways a literal manifestation of the First Amendment right of U.S. citizens, outlined in the U.S. Constitution, to "petition the Government," as a new avenue for digital civic engagement, the online petition system engages citizens in government in a new way. The initiative has had its critics. For one, many of the petitions are geared toward trying to force the government to take controversial positions, rather than rational and meaningful policy discourse. There are fears that the e-mails used to sign petitions may be used for other purposes, despite reassurances otherwise in the terms of participation. There have also been criticisms of the responses given to petitions as lackluster, disinterested, or even hostile (Scherer 2013).

So what is to be gained by government for this initiative? Such criticism misses one of the fundamental values underlying stakeholder engagement. It can be assumed that the petitions were never intended to result in new policy, although that certainly could happen. The real value of the We the People petition initiative is the opportunity to engage in a dialogue with stakeholders and to share government positions and initiatives with those who have an interest. In an age of social media, where many people get their policy information from Facebook, Twitter, blogs, and other secondary sources, the petitions have afforded the White House a direct link to citizens who may not otherwise listen to the State of the Union address or watch C-SPAN. Web traffic to the site is high, and each individual who signs a petition also agrees that the White House can communicate with them via e-mail about the issue. This is the engagement side of the initiative. Now the government can send out a personal video response to speak directly on the issue to those who care most, whether they are supporters or detractors. A video on gun policy filmed and sent out to petition signers resulted in 400,000 views, and a follow-up study by the president's staff showed that one in four people learned something new, and nearly half said they found President Obama's response helpful (Scherer 2013). Or, the government can send a written response and include links, directing people to government sources for additional information. In response to a petition on green cards for foreign students with advanced U.S. degrees, the administration held a conference call with interested petition signatories and posted a summary on the White House blog. The opportunity to speak directly to people about the issues they care about is a powerful tool for government.

Fostering Innovation

Inviting outsiders into the policy process can be an effective way to create innovative policy solutions (Lasker and Weiss 2003). Stakeholders may be able to provide insight into programmatic ideas in other places, creative thinking about how policies may affect different sectors of society, new ways of looking at issues, and current or novel research on problems and solutions.

Environmental policymakers who are struggling with a broad scope of environmental issues may need stakeholders with more focused expertise on a particular issue area to break down daunting problems into more manageable and solvable parts. Policymakers may also be reluctant to "think outside the box" if they are constrained by elements such as reelection pressures, agency culture, or resource constraints, and so stakeholders may be able to foster the innovation that policymakers cannot do alone.

To build on the idea of stakeholder innovation, the Obama administration has encouraged federal agencies to reach out to the untapped pool of citizen creativity to help solve some of the pressing issues of today. As part of the September 2009 Strategy for American Innovation, President Obama called on federal agencies to stimulate innovation with challenges and prizes to solve public problems. In March 2010 the Office of Management and Budget (OMB) issued a memorandum outlining the policy and legal framework for the initiative. Rather than trying to identify the team most likely to succeed based on a proposal, such as a traditional grant competition, in this case the government pays, in the form of a prize, for the best final submission or product.

The government-wide website Challenge.gov was launched in September 2010 as a one-stop platform for contests sponsored by federal agencies and their partners. Administered by the U.S. General Services Administration, the initiative poses challenges by one party (a seeker) to a third party or parties (a solver) to either identify a solution to a problem or reward contestants for accomplishing a goal. In many cases solvers and winners are not required to transfer exclusive intellectual property rights to the seeker. The solvers instead grant a royalty-free, perpetual, and nonexclusive license to any information that is included in the submission. It is a way to recruit the top talent in the country, whether it is through an individual or a team, to solve public problems in recognition of the fact that the best ideas may come from unexpected places, such as individuals, student groups, or interdisciplinary teams. It is a way to source new ideas, knowledge, and solutions to the challenges faced by government

Challenges have been posed from a wide array of agencies. Table 3.1 highlights a few of those challenges, illustrating the broad range of problems that have been posed.

Anticipate Reactions

One of the most important rationales for stakeholder participation is that it helps managers to anticipate reactions before they become stumbling blocks to project

Table 3.1 Challenge.gov Challenges

Agency	Challenge	Awards
Air Force	Improvements to humanitarian food delivery system	Up to $8,000
Environmental Protection Agency	Contest for K–8 students to design an original poster with sun safety tips	Digital cameras Family trip to Disney World Shade structure
NASA	Development of a mobile app to help the International Space Station Crew track their food intake	$55,000 total in prizes
Federal Partners for Bullying Prevention	Youth ages 13–18 are invited to create a 30- to 60-second video about bullying	$3,000 in prizes
Department of Justice	Development of a methodology to determine if in-service body armor has exceeded its life span	$50,000 total in prizes

success. Compared to the costs of policy failure, stakeholder collaboration can be a minimal investment in time, resources, and energy. When stakeholders are brought in early, policymakers can learn to anticipate their objections and concerns and deal with them up front, rather than waiting until the end when there is much more at stake. Similarly, stakeholder collaboration can help decision makers to understand complexity and anticipate future problems and concerns with the content of the policies under consideration (Elias, Jackson, et al. 2004; Sabatier, Focht, et al. 2005).

In 1983 the EPA piloted "negotiated rulemaking" or "regulatory negotiation" (*reg neg* for short), as an alternative to the highly adversarial traditional rulemaking process. During a reg neg the Agency forms a Federal Advisory Committee of interested and affected stakeholders who are then tasked to negotiate either the outline or actual text of a proposed rule. Although the process is time consuming, most of the committees were able to achieve substantial if not full agreement on the outline or text of a rule, and an EPA evaluation of the process found that the rules developed through reg neg were more practical and easier to implement and were less likely to be challenged in court than those negotiated through traditional means.

Congress passed the Negotiated Rulemaking Action in 1990, and then renewed it indefinitely in 1996, based largely on the EPA experience (EPA 2000).

Trust and Legitimacy

Stakeholder participation helps to integrate democratic values into the decision-making process (Kloprogge and van der Sluijs 2006) and can help to establish credibility for both policymakers and their decisions (Jarman 2011). Public distrust of government can be eased by stakeholder collaboration. Citizens in democratic societies have at minimum a right to speak about the issues and services that affect them (Lasker and Weiss 2003); as such, it is imperative that local communities and other stakeholder groups be involved in environmental decision making, particularly when those decisions affect the social or economic well-being of local people (Redpath, Arroyo, et al. 2004; Treves, Andriamampianina, et al. 2006).

Stakeholders who feel that they had the opportunity to participate meaningfully in the process may be more likely to accept the final result, which may consequently improve the public perception of the decision-making process and increase public trust (Darnall and Jolley 2004). In many ways, then, stakeholder involvement promotes ownership sharing among those who have an interest in the program (Gilliam, Davis, et al. 2002). Collaborators can also have positive trust effects within stakeholder groupings, as working together on decisions may foster trust and common spirit among participants (Selin, Schuett, et al. 2000).

By its very nature, bringing stakeholders into the decision-making process increases the transparency of the process, and as such creates mechanisms for decision makers to be held accountable. Assuming collaboration is orchestrated effectively, stakeholders will gain knowledge about the opportunities and challenges facing decision makers and will be privy to competing viewpoints (Gilliam, Davis, et al. 2002; Kloprogge and van der Sluijs 2006; Jarman 2011).

Another important argument for broad stakeholder involvement is to avoid the appearance of agency favoritism or regulatory capture (Carmin, Darnall, et al. 2003). Regulatory capture occurs when bureaucrats give in to pressure from industry and businesses when developing and enforcing policies. The agency is supposed to work in the public interest but instead gives preferential treatment to commercial or special interests within the sector that it has been charged with regulating. Ultimately a situation may arise whereby regulatory agencies are in fact dominated by the individuals they are charged with regulating (Huntington 1952; Bernstein 1955; Carmin, Darnall, et al. 2003). Broad stakeholder participation can help to avoid both the appearance and occurrence of regulatory capture.

Participatory budgeting is an initiative to engage citizens and stakeholders in allocating part of a public budget. The mission of participatory budgeting is to ensure government accountability and empower citizenship rights by giving citizens an opportunity to identify, debate, and prioritize public funds (Wampler 2007).

The most noted case study of participatory budgeting is the southern Brazilian city of Porto Alegre,* which launched one of the first participatory budgeting initiatives in 1989 led by a coalition of activists and Workers' Party officials. Participatory budgeting was started as part of a wave of reform programs to address inequality in living standards among city residents, in particular those living in isolated slums on the outskirts of the city without access to public services such as water, sanitation, schools, and health care facilities.

The process takes place annually, beginning with a series of neighborhood, regional, and citywide assemblies where city residents and elected budget delegates identify spending priorities and vote on which ones to implement. Not all items are subject to participatory budgeting; debt service and pensions, for example, are not allocated through the participatory process. Delegates are elected to represent specific neighborhoods. The mayor and staff participate in many of the meetings in order to respond to issues and concerns and provide context/expertise when it is requested. At a regional plenary, delegates prioritize the demands of the districts and elect forty-two councilors to represent the districts and cross-cutting thematic areas who will then serve on the Municipal Council of the budget. The Council is tasked with reconciling the requests of each district with the available resources and to then formally propose and approve a municipal budget. The final budget is considered binding, although the mayor technically has the power to veto it or send it back to the Municipal Council.

Although there are ongoing issues, particularly in terms of representation and participation, Porto Alegre has been hailed as a successful example of participatory budgeting. Since the process started, sewer and water connections have increased, the number of schools has quadrupled, and, though the process cannot overcome widespread problems such as unemployment, there have been significant improvements in public welfare amenities.

Participatory budgeting efforts have since spread to more than 1,200 municipalities, particularly in areas such as public housing, schools, and other public services. In Chicago, each municipal district or ward receives $1 million a year to allocate to infrastructure improvements in the ward such as sidewalk repairs, playgrounds streetlights, and the like. Beginning with the 2009–2010 budget cycle, the 49th Ward decided to allocate that money through participatory budgeting, the first political jurisdiction in the United States to do so. Successful projects have included bike lanes, bike racks, a community garden, a convenience shower at a park, a new dog park, sidewalk repairs, underpass murals, and new streetlights. While a few projects have been canceled due to higher than anticipated costs, participatory budgeting has brought citizens into the decision-making process and facilitated more responsive government.

---

* For more information see Bhatnagar, D., A. Rathore, et al. (n.d.). *Participatory Budgeting in Brazil.* Washington, DC, The World Bank.

Participatory budgeting has been shown to promote government transparency and accountability, increase levels of public participation, foster learning about democracy and government, and support more equitable public spending. Public budgeting also brings elected officials closer to their constituents, as together they engage in meaningful discourse about the needs of the community and solutions to address the problems. Bringing citizens into the debate about spending priorities also helps people to understand the larger picture facing government and the challenges inherent in governing modern society.

Stakeholder and Agency Roles

It can be argued that while government has an imperative to collaborate with stakeholders, stakeholders also have responsibilities to government. Particularly in situations where stakeholders are physically brought together, at minimum willingness to hear other positions is key to the entire process. The relationship between stakeholders and policymakers may also be viewed in terms of reciprocity (McDaniel and Miskel 2002). The EPA Common Sense Initiative Council's Stakeholder Involvement Work Group proposed a continuum of stakeholder and agency roles that begins with the degree of influence over the final decision as illustrated in Figure 3.1.

According to the EPA in its review of public participation policies, public and stakeholder participation is a progression. Stakeholder involvement begins when stakeholders seek out information from the agency about an issue that concerns them or when the agency itself contacts a potentially affected party. The next step involves information exchange whereby decision makers, staffers, and stakeholders share ideas, concerns, and solutions. This is followed by collaboration of parties to develop recommendations, followed by a final agreement on action (EPA 2000). The role of agency decision makers in relationship to stakeholders may vary, including seeking assistance with making a decision; working within a cooperative, shared-responsibility relationship with other agencies or stakeholders; or supporting the efforts of a community or region to solve its own environmental problems. The role of the agency in this case can be depicted in a continuum based on degree of final authority held by the agency, as illustrated in Figure 3.2.

As discussed in greater detail in Chapter 5, agencies can reach out to stakeholders through tools such as hotlines, websites, distribution lists, newsletters, Listservs, *Federal Register* notices, documents, electronic bulletin/discussion boards, fact

---

Exchange Information —— Develop Recommendations —— Develop Agreements

---

Figure 3.1   EPA stakeholder involvement continuum.

Decision Maker —— Partner —— Capacity Builder

Figure 3.2 Agency roles.

sheets, exhibits, brochures, formal public meetings, news releases, radio/television public service announcements, briefings, news releases, field offices, partnership grants, and more.

Agency Responsibilities

One of the ongoing controversies in the stakeholder literature is the question of who should plan collaboration activities. Should it be external experts who are skilled in conducting stakeholder collaboration, or should it be an internal planning process run by program staff who are directly responsible for the decision? One of the challenges of working with external organizers is that there is a considerable risk that decision makers will lose the personal investment and ties to the process, and as such be less likely to integrate the outcomes of the process into the final decision making (EPA 1998). Some managers falsely believe that stakeholder management is about stakeholders adapting to the organization (Olden 2003).

While lower-level staffers can run some stakeholder processes, high-ranking decision makers may also need to participate; "it is often essential that EPA senior leadership play a very active role in negotiations. If the EPA does not show high-level support for the process it's advocating, it's clear that other stakeholders may be less than enthusiastic about developing an agreement or product. With high-level participation, EPA can keep other stakeholders at the table and clarify possibilities for agreements" (EPA 2001, p. 8).

Stakeholder Burnout

One problem associated with stakeholder participation is the problem of burnout, when people are tired or drop out of stakeholder arrangements due to too many opportunities or obligations. "There are growing complaints that some stakeholder involvement programs are being conducted just because stakeholder involvement is now considered an *a priori* 'good' without a clear definition of how the program contributes to actual decisions or programs of the agency; there is not always careful analysis or understanding of which type of stakeholder involvement is appropriate in a situation; and, the techniques being used do not always match the audiences the agency is trying to reach, or exclude some segments of the community" (EPA 1998, p. 10).

Stakeholders need to feel that their participation is meaningful in order to continue being involved; "telling people what the EPA did with their comments helps to build a resilient relationship between the EPA and stakeholders. When your responses show that the EPA takes public ideas seriously and that participating really can influence environmental decisions, you help to build trust. This occurs only when people get honest, clear feedback about their comments" (EPA 2003, p. 1). Having realistic expectations and making stakeholders feel valued are critical for successful stakeholder collaboration.

Inclusivity and Working with Marginalized Groups

Theoretical Considerations

McGlashan and Williams (2003) differentiate between two types of stakeholders: institutional and local. Institutional stakeholders tend to be well-organized lobby groups that represent the interests of a large number of people or an industry or other large organization. These organizations tend to have extensive resources at their disposal, including substantive technical expertise. In contrast, local stakeholders are smaller groupings of individuals who lack the technical expertise of the institutional stakeholders and may not participate unless decision makers seek them out or otherwise engage them in the process. One of the challenges is integrating small-scale stakeholders into policymaking; these are stakeholders who may not have the experience or skills to engage with the complexity of the policymaking process, yet could make a valuable contribution (McGlashan and Williams 2003).

Many groups have carved out a deliberate and central niche in government policymaking, in many cases giving them a position of privilege. The advantages for these professionalized interests often include financial resources, organizational assets that can be used for fundraising and political action, and enduring ties with elected and agency officials. In contrast, a local advocacy group will almost always face significant shortcomings due to the absence of these advantages. Although such professional organizations are not always assured of victory over smaller or marginalized groups, they are often able to ensure that their opinions are heard and that processes are monitored, and they are able to mobilize if necessary to protect their interests.

Practical Considerations

Integrating marginalized or underrepresented groups is very important and may require additional efforts to ensure that they feel welcome to participate or are aware of opportunities. Working in an international setting or with a multinational group of stakeholders presents unique challenges for organizers.

It should be noted that one of the challenges for international stakeholder management is applying theory to nondemocratic societies in which notions of community decision making and power may be different; in countries with highly centralized states with governance systems that are less inclusive and transparent, stakeholder participation is particularly challenging (Caffyn and Jobbins 2003). Countries that lack democratic processes, by their very nature, may lack existing forums for stakeholder participation, and the cultural norms to make it effective.

Government should not underestimate how simple choices can have significant consequences on participation. Simple issues such as meeting locations may require special consideration. In the case of a UNAIDS stakeholder process the choice of location proved to be problematic and reinforced the exclusion of marginalized groups. A number of stakeholders were disappointed that the project was based in the corporate offices of Shell Oil (they donated space and ran the scenarios) in London, which helped to reduce costs, rather than in Africa where the majority of stakeholders and those affected by the disease live (Fourie 2004). The seemingly simple choice of location further marginalized African stakeholders. Thinking critically about who needs to participate and the barriers to access helps to prevent such problems.

In some cases, participation by traditionally marginalized groups may be mandated. For example, Executive Order 13175, "Consultation and Coordination with Indian Tribal Governments," requires most federal agencies to facilitate participation/input by tribal governments on regulations, legislative comments, proposed legislation, and policies that have substantial direct impacts on one or more Indian tribes. Similarly Executive Order 12998, "Federal Actions to Address Environmental Justice in Minority Population and Low-Income Populations," requires federal agencies to make environmental justice part of its missions by ensuring meaningful participation by minority and low-income populations, including improving accessibility of public meetings and documents, as well as identifying potential effects and mitigation measures. While broad participation is mandated, it is still up to the agency to ensure that participation is in fact meaningful and effective.

Governments must be proactive in recruiting stakeholders. One way to encourage participation of marginalized groups may be to extend personal invitations. In situations where marginalized groups may not feel comfortable working in tandem with other groups, or fear repercussions from expressing their views, alternative means of participation may be required such as personal interviews rather than group meetings.

Alternative forms of communication may be necessary in order to integrate stakeholders who speak other languages or who cannot read and write. Communication must always be culturally appropriate and relevant. "Current models of stakeholder participation tend to exclude local stakeholders who lack the technical expertise to engage in the process" (McGlashan and Williams 2003, p. 93). The spread of cystic hydatid disease in Kenya was controlled in part by changing local understanding about food and hygiene through discussions and songs about such changes, a communication style that was designed specifically to meet the needs of a population with varying levels of literacy and specific preferences for communication (MacPherson 2004). Communication must always be done in such a way that it facilitates understanding.

Stakeholders themselves can also find ways to participate. They can try to align with another more powerful group that can act as an agent on their behalf. Shared goals may be enough to create an advocacy partnership arrangement. For example, an aboriginal group interested in preserving a section of forest for traditional hunting may be able to align with a conservation group interested in protecting land against development. Despite the different perspectives, the end goals are the same.

When working in unfamiliar communities, whether domestic or abroad, it is important to understand the local context and to be open to the idea that normal operating procedures may not be appropriate. For example, issues of privacy, power structures, and respect may have to be taken into account. Different communities may choose to share information in different ways. By observing how this happens, a facilitator can make the best decision about which tools to use.

Many international initiatives benefit by having those with international expertise join the team. Asking for assistance from those with cultural experience, perhaps a local liaison or someone with knowledge and experience in working with the community, can help ensure that collaboration is culturally appropriate. It is important that the liaison is someone who is acceptable to the local community, as well as to the agency. Translators for both oral and written communication may be necessary. Providing translators at meetings and events may be an important service to ensure that everyone shares a common understanding. If the topic involves scientific terms or specialized lingo, it may be advisable to provide translators with a list of terms and definitions in advance so they are prepared for the translations.

Active listening can be an important tool to check to see if the communication has been accurately understood; this is discussed in greater detail in Chapter 5. Pausing regularly to ask content questions can be one way to ensure that everyone is following the discussion. Intermediaries familiar with the different cultures involved can be helpful in conveying both the substance and the appropriate tone—for example, toning down a strongly worded statement, which may be interpreted as overly aggressive. Rather than focusing on who should be blamed for a communication breakdown, it is key to focus on solutions and identifying how to prevent it from happening in the future. Being aware of possible cultural differences in areas such as conflict, communication styles, sharing of personal information, body language, and postures can be very important for inclusive collaboration (Gudykunst and Kim 1995).

Children present an interesting challenge when it comes to stakeholder engagement. When working with children it is important to develop tools and strategies that are age appropriate. This may be a challenge for facilitators who do not have experience working with children, but the needs and abilities and attention span of a three-year-old are very different from that of a ten-year-old. One of the simplest tools to get children of any age involved as stakeholders is through an art project—for example, drawing their vision of a new park or posters to encourage people to stop littering. Getting children and families involved in a community service project can also be a way to expand conventional notions of stakeholder engagement; examples of community service projects are citizen science activities such as counting birds or cleaning a creek. Children of kindergarten age and higher can participate in surveys, using for example pictures of faces (happy, sad, and neutral) to indicate their preferences. A facilitator trained in working with children could run group activities such as focus groups. Parental permission must be secured before any type of engagement exercise with children, ensuring that parents are given full information about the purpose, activities, and how the information will be used.

In sum, there are a few practical techniques that can be used to encourage inclusivity. First, careful consideration of how to create an atmosphere of equal participation can help to eliminate or reduce power imbalances. For example, a panel conveys authority of a limited few, while a roundtable promotes equality among participants. Where possible, it can be helpful to find ways to recognize and integrate community and indigenous knowledge into discussions and decision making. Identifying key individuals who can speak for those who are unable to speak for themselves can bring marginalized voices into discussions, although it is important to ensure that they actually represent the views of those they claim to represent. Soliciting involvement early in the policy process, and continuing through implementation and evaluation, can be a way both to encourage inclusivity and to learn from mistakes. Establishing a central point of contact within the agency to assist in information exchange and to resolve problems can also help to reduce intimidating bureaucracy. And finally, as has been stated above, it is essential to make information readily accessible and understandable.

Helping Stakeholders Feel Valued

Fostering good relationships between government and stakeholders requires an ongoing effort based on communication and respect. An often forgotten element of inclusivity and stakeholder engagement is the importance of making stakeholders feel valued and appreciated. Such efforts can go a long way to creating a sense of goodwill and encouraging long-term relationships. There are both tangible and intangible tools that can be used to help stakeholders feel valued:

- Making contact early in the decision-making process
- Responding to stakeholder concerns and clearly explaining what actions will be taken in response
- Maintaining a presence in the community or with the stakeholders
- Openly sharing information

- Involving stakeholders in multiple aspects of decision making and data gathering
- Keeping lines of communication open
- Publicly acknowledging participants in stakeholder engagement initiatives on a website, Facebook, or Twitter, in a newspaper ad, or in a newsletter
- Being clear about how stakeholder input will be used
- Sending out copies of reports to those who gave input
- Publicly thanking stakeholders at events
- Ending engagement activities with a discussion about action and implementation. Letting stakeholders know how their input will be used and what the next steps will be can go a long way to making stakeholders feel like they were heard and are valued.

Conflict Management

Conflict may be inevitable when working with stakeholders, particularly when working with those possessing strong passions or dominating personalities. The following is a discussion of sources of conflict and ways to address it if it does arise. Conflict does not mean that the process is a failure or should be abandoned, but it does call for careful thought and consideration.

Sources of Conflict

In a study of black bear management, Lafon, McMullin, et al. (2004) found that while stakeholders actively involved in the policy process gained greater appreciation for other interests, they did not feel that all interests should automatically have input into the decision-making process. For example, they felt that homeowners who experienced property damage from bears should not have much say as they chose to live within the bears' habitat. "Lacking interaction with other stakeholders that committee members experienced, passive participants did not gain greater appreciation or tolerance of other points of view. This suggests that though passive dissemination of information may be somewhat effective in improving knowledge, it is unlikely to reduce conflicts between stakeholder groups. To reduce conflicts, managers must bring conflicting interests together" (Lafon, McMullin, et al. 2004, p. 229).

The "reactive approach" to stakeholder management involves reacting to problems and discontent brought by stakeholders after key decisions have been made. The stakeholder management/collaborative approach would instead support a proactive approach to prevent conflict (Economic and Social Commission for Asia and the Pacific 2001). The key, as described in Eschenbach and Eschenbach's (1996) work, is that stakeholder management too often is delayed beyond the point where stakeholders have any perception of control. For example, when the risks are perceived as high, informing stakeholders about decisions that have already been made will result in backlash because stakeholders have no sense of control. Instead,

Table 3.2 Sources of Stakeholder Conflict

Lack of time or disinterest on the part of participants
Preference for solving problems on one's own rather than relying on a group
Concerns those individuals will not get full recognition for their work
Conflicting goals and interests of participants
Environment conducive to assigning blame
Overbearing or annoying individuals who dominate
Participants who are hesitant to share their opinions
Long-standing feuds or personal conflicts
Impatience to finish quickly rather than listen and work on consensus
Misunderstandings
A need to win rather than an interest in coming to a solution
The wrong people are at the table
Cultural differences and misunderstandings
Poorly run meeting such as unfocused discussions, or a sense that nothing ever gets accomplished
Failure to plan for potential conflict by not setting ground rules or general rapport
Incorrect information or data presented or an overreliance on anecdotal evidence

integrating the stakeholders into the decision-making process earlier at least gives them the perception that they have some control, even if the final decision is ultimately the same.

Conflict has been the downfall of many stakeholder collaboration efforts (Graci 2013). The sources of such conflict are numerous but may include the issues listed in Table 3.2.

Intervention

While the facilitator of a stakeholder engagement initiative typically has responsibility for the success or failure of the initiative, intervention during times of conflict may not always be appropriate or necessary. In some cases the group itself may be able to deal with conflict on its own, or it may be a case where the conflict/issues simply do not interfere with the work of the group. The issue may not be important enough to intervene. It is up to the administrator to use best judgment in this situation and carefully monitor the proceedings to determine if greater intervention is required.

If it becomes apparent that some intervention is necessary, the first step is to try to identify if there is a pattern or particular trigger to the conflict. Is it a conflict between two people? Is there one particular issue that seems to lead to conflict? If the conflict needs to be addressed, there are some low-level interventions that can be used. For example, changing the timing or setting of the meeting may alter existing dynamics. Another option is to focus on creating ample opportunities for participants to discuss their perspectives, ideas, and concerns, without belaboring individual points; allowing people to talk and be heard can be very powerful. Encouraging stakeholders to get to know one another better—for example, a field trip to visit a site, or a social gathering—can help to ease relations as well as help to create a sense of teamwork and unity. Another option is to review general concerns and expectations at the beginning of a meeting, or by e-mail, without singling anyone out to acknowledge existing problems and make others aware of what needs to change; included in this should be a reminder of the purpose of collaboration.

Medium-level interventions require more action on the part of the administrator. If one individual is responsible for the conflict, it may be advisable to discuss the situation with the individual in a private setting. Each stakeholder should be responsible and accountable for the work; in some cases, assigning specific tasks to individuals and minimizing group work may help to ease tensions. Similarly, encouraging those on opposing sides to work together on a separate issue can help each to understand the other and possibly change the relationship dynamic. Another strategy is to emphasize mutual agreement rather than voting. Stakeholders can modify or adjust the options or seek alternatives until everyone agrees the best decision has been reached, or they can encourage stakeholders to think of multiple solutions to satisfy their concerns, rather than focusing on only one solution. The stakeholders may also have to learn to accept that a "good enough" or satisfactory solution may be the best that can be hoped for in some circumstances.

If personal safety is at risk or the initiative itself is at risk of failure, then higher-level interventions may be appropriate, including mediation (whereby a neutral party decides on a solution after hearing multiple sides of the dispute), asking individuals to withdraw, or ending the stakeholder process altogether.

Understanding conflict resolution strategies is important when working with stakeholders. The likelihood of successful collaboration is likely to be poor in the following circumstances: when the conflict is based on core ideological differences, where one stakeholder has the power and ability to take unilateral action, or when the issues are too threatening as a result of historic antagonisms. "Consensus is influenced by politics, personal bias, and persuasion. Consensus building requires informing, facilitating debate, and ensuring that stakeholder concerns are considered. In a democracy, stakeholders typically accept that the process itself represents them, even if they dissent from the prevailing consensus" (MacPherson 2004, p. 290).

Many government programs and offices now use alternative dispute resolution (ADR) techniques to expedite decision making and reduce compliance costs. The EPA defines ADR in the Administrative Dispute Resolution Act of 1996 as "any procedure that is used to resolve issues in controversy, including but not limited to, conciliation, facilitation, mediation, fact finding, mini-trials, arbitration, and use of ombuds, or any combination thereof" (Administrative Dispute Resolution Act of 1996 1996). A neutral third party is brought in to assist others in designing and implementing a process for reaching agreement in a dispute. The neutral third party has no stake in the final outcome. ADR is largely seen as a voluntary process, including participation, the type of process used, and the content of the final agreement. ADR techniques (e.g., facilitation, mediation, fact-finding) can also be used to facilitate participation in decision making (EPA 2000).

In smaller conflicts where full ADR techniques are not necessary, a number of key points can help to improve decision making including making relationships the first priority, keeping people and problems separate, paying attention to the interests that are being presented, listening first and talking second, clarifying facts versus opinions, listening with empathy, seeking what is held in common, and focusing on interests rather than positions.

The last point is critical for working through contentious policy issues. As popularized in the 1981 classic work *Getting to Yes*, navigating conflicting opinions requires a focus on what really matters to participants rather than stating and then defending predetermined positions. If participants focus on positions, then the only options are win, lose, or compromise. For example, if the policy options are no wetland conversion versus full development of all land, some stakeholders will win and others will lose. However, if the interests are maintenance of species that live in wetlands and a chance to secure a comfortable retirement, stakeholders can begin to think about a proposal that protects high-valued wetlands on some land and makes developed land more valuable. The key here is that stakeholders have to appreciate that not all opinions are equally important and not all costs are equally severe. It is the challenge of the administrator to facilitate this realization. All opinions are valid, but they are not all equally important in decision making.

Measuring Effectiveness of Stakeholder Collaboration

One of the challenges from an evaluation standpoint is determining how to measure the success of the stakeholder collaboration. Too often there is a lack of systematic evaluation of collaborative initiatives. As is the case for most programmatic initiatives, human and financial resource constraints often limit the ability of managers to monitor effectiveness. "Collaborative initiatives and supporting agencies are often guilty of using surrogate measures of effectiveness such as whether a final report was submitted to justify the expenditure of scarce resources and ensure agency survival" (Selin, Schuett, et al. 2000, pp. 737–738). What are the measures of partnership effectiveness? Measurable results are crucial both for evaluating the partnership and for learning for the future. Effectiveness measures must reflect the diverse wants and desires of the multiple stakeholders (Weech-Maldonado, Benson, et al. 2003).

A basic measure of effectiveness is whether basic collaborative goals are met— for example, whether participation was inclusive. Another measure is whether or to what extent policy goals are being met. For example, this might include documenting written reports, the amount of resources acquired, or whether a policy was developed. Other measures to consider include outreach, opportunities for equitable participation, cost-effectiveness, efficiency, and likelihood of legal action. "Participant accounts should be an important component of any effectiveness monitoring program. Monitoring programs should be designed to allow continuous feedback to all stakeholders on whether important biological, physical, program, and activity goals are being accomplished" (Selin, Schuett, et al. 2000, p. 737). Surveys to solicit feedback can be used to assess stakeholder opinions of participation and can be used to improve future collaboration—for example, evaluation forms distributed after a public meeting or a web-based survey sent to participants in an advisory group. An often-ignored aspect of assessing stakeholder collaboration is why stakeholders choose not to participate. This information can be valuable, particularly if it reveals trust issues with the agency.

Working with Stakeholders in Policymaking

Initial Assessment

The stakeholder process must begin with the state of conditions as they actually exist, such as knowledge, consciousness, power relations, interests, and players (Howard 2002). Policymakers must use their best judgment to determine when stakeholder participation is appropriate as a starting point for a successful process. Stakeholder input is vital in cases where policymaking is controversial, disproportionately affects certain populations, or encompasses major changes.

For an organization or government manager deciding to explore stakeholder collaboration, it is important to have a very clear vision from the outset about the expectations and limits of the process. Promising more than the organization is able or willing to deliver, for example, creates more problems. Telling stakeholders that participants in the process will determine policies sets up a high expectation on the part of participants; they will only be disappointed and angry if they do not actually have that power and authority.

The EPA advises staff who are planning stakeholder activities to prepare preliminary planning documents outlining their goals, strategies, and tactics. The written document itself is not the most important part; rather it is the thought process that goes into the document that makes a difference. Preparation of such a plan forces dialogue among staffers about what kind of participation is necessary, the institutional requirements and constraints, the stakeholders who should be involved, and the mechanisms through which participation will be carried out. In addition to forcing the agency to think through the process, it also reduces the likelihood of internal disagreements and ensures that agency personnel are all on the same page before participation begins (EPA 1998).

As part of this initial planning, it is imperative to identify and analyze stakeholder interests to ensure adequate representation. Chapter 5 outlines specific tools that can be used to identify and recruit stakeholders, as well as analyze their interests.

Stages of Participation

Once stakeholders have been identified, analyzed, and invited it is time to prepare for participation. One perspective on participation arrangements divides the planning process into four stages (Hoban n.d.). The first stage is the *forming stage* when the collaboration begins to develop. Stakeholders may be cautious, excited, and nervous as they begin to explore the opportunity of working together. Tasks at this stage include defining the collaboration and identifying how to accomplish goals, discussing concepts and issues including what research needs to be done, and identifying potential threats and barriers to accomplish goals. Hoban uses a learning-to-swim analogy throughout this framework and suggests that at this stage participants are like hesitant new swimmers, cautiously exploring but excited about the opportunity.

The second stage is the *storming stage* where stakeholders become impatient and argumentative. Participants may become defensive or competitive, develop unrealistic goals, and seem resistant to change. There may be a sense of increasing tension and jealousy among the group. Using the swimming analogy, this stage is similar to the experiences of new swimmers who have jumped into the water but start to panic that they are going to drown and thrash around in fear.

The third stage is the *normalizing stage* whereby stakeholders accept their position both as and within a team and accept the norms of participating. Stakeholders become more cooperative rather than combative and realize that, like experienced swimmers, they are not going to drown and that as a team they can keep each other afloat. There is a sense of acceptance of the collaboration and relief that progress is being made

The final stage is the *performing stage* by which time the partnership is a well-functioning unit and, like a swimming relay team, the group works well together. This is an opportunity to work through more challenging problems and construct change. The most instructive aspect of this analogy/framework is the recognition that stakeholders may be anxious and hesitant, which, to expand on the idea, may masquerade itself as bravado and defensiveness. As well, it is instructive to keep in mind that some discord/conflict is inevitable in collaborative initiatives and does not necessarily mean that the process is not working or failing. Such discord may disappear as the collaboration experience normalizes.

Information-Sharing Considerations

As has been noted throughout this research, one particular challenge to building consensus is when stakeholders lack information (Dedual, Sague Pla, et al. 2013). For example, in wildlife conservation projects visitors to a national park may be unaware of the extent of their own impact and thus be less likely to accept restrictions on their activities. If the process is changed to empower stakeholders, then information exchanges happen more freely and the knowledge of all participants increases. With empowerment and knowledge also comes motivation to participate, thereby facilitating the development of innovative collaboration (Burroughs 1999).

Promoting Good Communication

Instant communication through e-mail, texting, Twitter, or other online tools is efficient and fast, but it can also lead to misunderstandings and confusion. Communication breakdowns are a common source of stakeholder frustration (Moswete, Thapa, et al. 2012). There are a number of elements to consider when it comes to promoting good communication among stakeholders.

The method of presentation must be appropriate for the information you need to convey and the ways in which your stakeholders learn best. Are there any special needs of individual stakeholders? If so, what do they need? What message is being conveyed? What is common knowledge already? What are the desired actions or responses? Finding ways to share positive messages helps to set the tone for the group, can help to prevent conflict, and can create a shared sense of purpose and accomplishment. If stakeholders express concern, it is affirming to acknowledge those issues; people want to feel like they have been heard.

It may be necessary to reinforce the message by sending an e-mail summary, posting a message on social media, or even placing a personal phone call to ensure that everyone has received and understood the information. People who are absent need to be informed as well. Finding ways to thank participants for a productive meeting, even just through an e-mail, reinforces the importance of the work that everyone is doing and fosters a culture of productivity and appreciation.

One way to facilitate buy-in on the part of stakeholders is if they accept the validity of research and analysis that is being communicated. In 1991 the EPA was criticized for its "Carpet Policy Dialogue," which was a one-year multi-stakeholder policy discussion intended to encourage the carpet industry to reduce volatile organic compound (VOC) emissions. Data for the discussion was provided by the industry without any outside or independent verification, leading to controversy over the adequacy and reliability of the data. In the end, progress on many policy issues was limited because several key stakeholders did not trust the industry's data collection methodology (EPA 2001).

Data must be both transparent and comprehensible to facilitate acceptance. Engaging different organizations in the data collection/analysis may help stakeholders to accept results, recommendations, or new programs. Also, commissioning outside researchers to do research or forming a research panel made up of diverse interests such as industry, research organizations, academics, and NGOs to pool information and formulate recommendations may also bring validity to the research (Economic and Social Commission for Asia and the Pacific 2001).

Dealing with Threats

One of the challenges is figuring out how to encourage/support participation by participants who may be viewed as threats. Understanding power relationships may be instructive here. Those with high power and high interest require careful management; they must be engaged in the work and a reasonable effort needs to be put in to keep them satisfied. Those with high power but low interest require effort on the manager's part to keep them satisfied, but not so much attention that they become bored or irritated. The focus is really on keeping them satisfied. Those with low power and high interest should be kept informed and engaged in a dialogue to ensure that no major issues arise. These stakeholders may be particularly helpful in assisting with the details of the project.

One challenge is dealing with stakeholders who see moral superiority in their view. The ability to engage in rational discourse may be limited by such a position. Establishing trust is very important; however, lack of trust between stakeholders and decision makers should not be an excuse to avoid collaboration. "Even if there is only a low-level of trust among stakeholders, an effective communication and decision-making process can still allow for successful negotiation to take place" (EPA 2001, p. 8).

While it is important to have a clear understanding of how stakeholders can be allies and adversaries, it is important to avoid excessively labeling stakeholders as such, which could alienate groups or limit progress and the potential for adversaries to become allies. While ensuring that important stakeholders are invited to participate should be obvious, decision makers may also have to deal with stakeholders who invite themselves and demand access. For all of the talk about the importance of inclusivity, there are situations in which certain stakeholders may not be welcome to participate—for example, if they lack a minimum requirement of expertise, they are known to cause problems, they have nothing to contribute, the process is too far along or they are joining too late to take part in the process, or their participation would disrupt a preestablished functioning group dynamic.

Ultimately policymakers are also gatekeepers to the policy process, deciding who gets access to the process. Antagonizing or (isolating) the gatekeeper erodes power and influence. Trust between stakeholders and agency staff is critical for effective stakeholder participation efforts. Trust can be fostered through the following: making contact early in the decision-making process; responding to stakeholder concerns and clearly explaining what actions will be taken in response; maintaining a presence in the community or with the stakeholders; openly sharing information; involving stakeholders in multiple aspects of decision making and data gathering; and keeping lines of communication open (EPA 2000; EPA 2001).

Stakeholder relations are difficult because they require the negotiation of the divide between the internal workings of an organization and that of external societal interests. Managing effective relations involves an understanding of human behavior, as stakeholders assume a number of roles related to their work, personal values, and past experiences. Working with stakeholders may be particularly frustrating in highly technical areas where the interests have a different knowledge base. However, it is important for those who work in technical areas to have an understanding of how others think about risk, costs, and benefits in order for policies to ultimately be effective.

Traditionally participation has been based on the exchange of "position statements" presented either orally or in writing to which each side responds. A more proactive approach is instead based on negotiation from a mutual understanding of interests and a willingness to pursue creative options for mutual gain (Economic and Social Commission for Asia and the Pacific 2001). "Without the right kind of leadership and management, it is not possible for people from very different backgrounds, who have rarely worked together and are often skeptical of each other's motivation, to combine their resources and create something new and valuable together" (Lasker and Weiss 2003, p. 130).

Managing Technical Complexity

When stakeholder arrangements include both scientists and nontechnical participants, one of the difficulties is finding a common language (Dedual, Sague Pla, et al. 2013). With scientifically complex decision making, stakeholders are often ill prepared to participate meaningfully. How can we deal with this problem? Involving stakeholders in the policy process early on can help, as can recognizing the issue and taking the steps to create support resources such as accessible reports or holding an information lecture to create a common ground of scientific understanding (Mostashari and Sussman 2005). Simply dismissing stakeholders or downplaying their importance can arouse feelings of animosity and alienation. The challenge is to create a policy that both represents the complexity of the science and at the same time is accessible to key stakeholders (Mostashari and Sussman 2005).

One way to address technical complexity is to consider capacity building, essentially providing support and resources to help stakeholders better understand the issues. The EPA has used Community Advisory Groups as part of the Superfund program to provide local community members with a forum for learning about

Superfund, assessing cleanup options, and giving input to site managers. The EPA has also provided Technical Assistance Grants (TAG) to community nonprofit organizations so that they could hire technical experts to review and explain technical issues associated with the contaminated sites. The TAG support enables the community as a whole to participate more effectively in decision making. Decision makers who are committed to stakeholder participation in policymaking may have to consider the importance of capacity building, particularly in cases where issues are technically complex (EPA 2000).

Decision makers need to consider both the technical competency levels of stakeholders as well as their preferences in developing communication strategies. In cases where problems are complex or ambiguous, a shared context of meaning such as a common set of definitions can make it easier for everyone to participate (EPA 2001).

The amount of time devoted to stakeholder management depends to a large extent on the scope of the project and the likelihood of stakeholder problems, the degree of assistance needed to achieve the results, and the time that the management team has to devote to stakeholder management and communication. If a simple e-mail update once a month is sufficient, then there is no reason to waste time and energy organizing large public forums.

Gregory (2000) studied the use of a structured public involvement process in the Tillamook Bay National Estuary Project (TBNEP), which was tasked to develop a science-based, community-supported management plan for the watershed in northwestern Oregon. The Bay is integral to the local and regional economies that are largely based on natural resources and supports a rich ecological base, although it is degraded due to extensive agricultural and forest development in the area. The TBNEP had held some preliminary open meetings to elicit public concerns; however, the lack of process to examine those concerns and facilitate their incorporation into the final management plan led to feelings of disenfranchisement on the part of many of the stakeholders (Gregory 2000). Decision makers must develop a clear plan that outlines how collaboration activities will be integrated into decision making. For example, videotaping a public forum can create a valuable record of a discussion, but only if someone is actually willing to take the time to transcribe the tape and distribute it to those crafting policy. Too often people rely on these types of records and then never bother using them, which means the information is lost and the effort is wasted.

Efforts to educate stakeholders about highly technical issues such as modeled distributions of water pollutants may ultimately backfire if they become defensive about their lack of expertise. One of the challenges of stakeholder collaboration in scientific areas such as environmental policy is that it exposes the process to pseudoscience, bias, or questionable research (Mostashari and Sussman 2005). Facilitators of collaboration must ensure that there are standards in place to protect the integrity of the process, despite the risks of alienating the participants. For example, a minimum standard of peer-reviewed research may be necessary to help the process from being derailed by speculation and anecdotes. Relying on scientific data to sway the general public or uninformed stakeholders, however, may be problematic. Values, anecdotes, and personal relationships, for example, may have much greater sway for people not technically trained in an area. Decision makers must find a balance between the use of scientific research to make decisions and the types of evidence that may be easier to understand for those lacking science training:

> In stakeholder approaches, experts have knowledge to share, but are only one part of the equation—they have as much to learn from other stakeholders as other stakeholders have to learn from them. Often, the expert's role must be to facilitate the process whereby the diverse stakeholders diagnose their problems and discover and negotiate their own solutions. The expert's role is to provide information, ensure that the enabling resources and environment exist, and to represent their own "stake" in the process. (Howard 2002)

Stakeholder Participation Ideas in Practice

While Chapter 5 outlines different tools for stakeholder collaboration and how to use them, this section will highlight a number of case studies of alternative stakeholder participation in practice.

United Nations Conference on Sustainable Development (Rio+20)

In December 1989 the United Nations passed a resolution that noted that the global environment was under threat and recommended a conference of national leaders to address the problems. The United Nations Conference on Environment and Development (UNCED), popularly referred to as the Earth Summit, was held in Rio de Janeiro June 3–14, 1992. Documents resulting from the meeting included Agenda 21, the Rio Declaration on Environment and Development, the Statement of Forest Principles, the United Nations Framework Convention on Climate Change, and the United Nations Convention on Biological Diversity. The meeting was unprecedented in terms of both its size and scope of issues. On December 24, 2009, the UN General Assembly passed a resolution to hold a twentieth-anniversary meeting in 2012, the United Nations Conference on Sustainable Development (Rio+20) to review previous commitments, the Green Economy in the context of poverty eradication and sustainable development, and an institutional framework for sustainable development. A key component of Rio+20, before, during, and after, has been stakeholder participation on an unprecedented scale.

In addition to the 45,000 people* who participated in the formal negotiations in Rio de Janeiro, collaboration took place online and offline, creating a global community of stakeholders.

The United Nations posed a challenge: how do you engage a planet of stakeholders in a global discussion about sustainable development? In addition to numerous education websites, innovative engagement initiatives were organized around the world. A pocket guide† to sustainable development governance was written and available as a free download in English and Spanish to try to rectify a perceived "knowledge gap" about sustainable development

Social media was an important part of the stakeholder engagement. The social media platforms launched by the secretary-general involved over 50 million participants. On Twitter alone, the English hashtag #RioPlus20 was used over 1 billion times. MyCity+20 was a global youth movement in fourteen cities around the world to get youth engaged in sustainable development through simulations of the Rio+20 negotiations. The organizers of Rio+20 posted a request for people to submit pictures of sustainability. More than one thousand people participated and uploaded their photos, which were displayed in various formats online and at the United Nations meeting. Countless Facebook groups were set up to engage stakeholders in different issue areas. The Twitter hashtags #futurewewant and #Rio+20 were very active in helping stakeholders to share ideas, coordinate activities, and publicize events. One of the most interesting things about Rio+20 was that so many of the stakeholder engagement activities were organized by stakeholders themselves. The environmental group TckTckTck organized a "Date with History" whereby people ages 13–30 were encouraged to upload video speeches telling the world about the "future we want." Videos were shared online, and one winner was selected to travel to Rio to participate in the summit.

A novel stakeholder engagement effort was the development of a Facebook game, "Game Change Rio," created as a joint venture between the Millennium Institute, the Biovision Foundation, and the game company CodeSustainable. Using real-life data, players could explore different policy options to address issues of sustainable development. The game included over 5,000 economic and natural resource indicators and 125 policy options, resulting in over 100 million possible options.

An unprecedented number of nongovernmental organizations participated in Rio+20. The United Nations Commission for Sustainable Development divided accredited NGOs into major groups so that they could work in a coordinated fashion. An organizing partner who helped to coordinate activities and issues

---

* The total number of participants was more than 45,000, which included delegations from 188 countries. Over 100 heads of state and government were there, accompanied by 12,000 government delegates. In addition there were 9,856 NGOs and major groups, 4,075 media representatives, and 5,000 staff. The 1,500 volunteers included 700 young people from vulnerable communities.

† Pocket Guide to Sustainable Development Governance: http://www.stakeholderforum.org/fileadmin/files/PocketGuidetoSDGEdition2webfinal.pdf.

represented each major group and solicited input for a policy paper submitted on behalf of each major group to the UN. Organizing partners were tasked to engage representatives from their major groups for dialogue sessions and input into an official policy document to ensure that stakeholder voices were heard. Prior to the official meeting, the Major Group of Children and Youth organized a Youth Blast in Rio de Janeiro to empower young people to participate meaningfully in Rio+20. For three days youth participated in seminars about sustainable development and how to make the most of the Rio+20 experience. Youth were given an opportunity to share their experiences and solutions on sustainable development and about participation in international decision making.

Across town from the official negotiations, the People's Summit was an official forum for stakeholders to participate in workshops, demonstrations, protests, panels, and networking in a more informal environment. Spread throughout a public park, the People's Summit welcomed local citizens as well as organizations and activists from around the world to engage with the ideas of sustainable development. While geographic distance limited the degree to which there was official interaction with the government delegates at the negotiations across town (which to some was an asset, to others a liability), information flowed between the two venues and many delegates and stakeholders who were formally accredited for the negotiations also at least walked through the sprawling park. Activists at the People's Summit did write a series of fourteen People's Sustainability Treaties, the result of a consultative process with hundreds of civil society organizations.

Much of the negotiations were available for viewing online, and various stakeholder groups posted daily summaries and reports to share with those who could not be there in person. As a follow-up to the conference the United Nations launched the "Sustainable Development Knowledge Platform," an online stakeholder engagement platform that includes downloadable publications, a calendar of events related to sustainable development, United Nations reports and resolutions, and space for stakeholders to continue to register voluntary commitments. After the summit organizations, businesses, governments, and individuals were asked to make formal voluntary commitments that would be shared online. As of February 2013 there were 1,373 commitments representing more than $600 million in projects.

Dialogue on Public Involvement in EPA's Decisions

Opportunities for online participation have changed the way stakeholders can be involved in policymaking. One example of a way to integrate online participation is exemplified by the "Dialogue on Public Involvement in EPA's Decisions"* in July 2001, an online dialogue designed to obtain additional, practical suggestions on how to implement the EPA Public Participation Policy. During the ten-day online event,

---

* An archive of the event is available at http://www.network-democracy.org/epa-pip/.

1,166 people participated, providing input on what the EPA should and should not do to foster effective participation in its decision making. A formal agenda was used as part of the online discussion covering topics such as outreach, best practices for collaborating with tribal governments, and transparency in decision making. Included on the website was a briefing book that included reference materials such as EPA policies and academic papers on stakeholders, and daily summaries of the discussion organized by topic to facilitate education and constructive participation.

The advantages of such an initiative are many. As an inexpensive and relatively simple activity, an online dialogue is a straightforward way to get broad input into decision making. The biggest challenge is publicity and recruitment; spreading the word to interested stakeholders to get enough participation can be difficult for agencies without a well-established network. Chapter 5 includes additional ideas for recruitment.

Citizen Science

Citizen science, sometimes referred to as crowd science, crowd-sourced science, or networked science, is a public participation model of research that brings together interested citizens and research scientists to solve problems that require broad-scale participation. These networks allow scientists to accomplish research tasks that would be too expensive or time consuming through other means. Mobile phones and other consumer electronic devices such as tablets and handheld GPS devices make it easy for citizens to record observations or complete tasks at their own convenience.

Most conventional citizen science projects are focused on data collection. The project Field Exploration: Mongolia is a National Geographic archaeology project in which users assist field researchers in Mongolia by tagging potential archaeological dig sites on satellite images. GLOBE At Night is a global NASA project that invites volunteers to measure the brightness of the night sky and report their observations from a computer or smart phone. The project is both a data collection exercise for future policymaking as well as an educational campaign about light pollution. The American Association of Variable Star Observers has been coordinating and analyzing variable star observations made by amateur astronomers since 1911. They receive nearly one million observations a year, and both amateur and professional astronomers have access to the data for research.

Citizen science projects can also perform important education and engagement functions. This information can in turn be used to help with decision making and policy issues. Citizen science projects can be a valuable tool for government agencies to engage stakeholders in public problems. For example, Neighborland is a crowd-sourced website that allows people to connect with their neighbors, share ideas, and collaborate to make them happen. Citizen science methods could be used in a local community to address a number of public issues such as water quality testing, tracking and counting of feral cats, reporting of potholes using photos uploaded to a community site, tracking of an invasive species such as the emerald ash borer (easily identified by the distinctive marks left in the ash trees), identifying the spread of West Nile disease by posting photos of dead birds, creating a map of green spaces in a community using smart phones and Google Maps, and reporting roadkill to help wildlife offices track incidents.

Online Gaming

Governments have been slow to embrace new technology for stakeholder engagement; however, there are a number of interesting initiatives that have been put into place to bring government to the people in ways that are interesting and engaging. As an interactive medium, online games have the ability to engage users in a way that is active and entertaining. The web-based education project iCivics was started in 2009 by Justice Sandra Day O'Connor to try to improve public civic knowledge and participation. The initiative has grown to include a team of civic leaders including state Supreme Court justices and secretaries of state to expand the scope and reach of the site. The site is made up of 21 games on topics such as elections, civic responsibility, the Constitution and Bill of Rights, budgeting, and the structure of government. Online gaming could also be used to help citizens learn about energy conservation, safe driving, flu prevention, and other public issues.

The United Nations International Strategy for Disaster Reduction (UN ISDR) developed Stop Disasters!, a web-based game intended to educate people about disaster mitigation in one of five common natural disasters: tsunami, hurricane, wildfire, earthquake, and flood. Each scenario takes between 10 to 20 minutes to play. Players are presented with an undeveloped community and a challenge to develop the area within a limited budget to meet specific community needs in terms of housing, schools, hospitals, and landscape. Players must make cost-benefit decisions about building materials (e.g., bamboo, concrete) and landscape (e.g., mangroves, trees) of various costs and resilience. The challenge is to minimize the damage that will occur when the disaster strikes at the end of the game. The game environment is enhanced with fact sheets, pop-up information boxes, and teacher guides to help players make the best decisions. The purpose of the game is to help people around the world think more proactively about natural disasters and risk and what communities can do to mitigate against future threats.

Mobile Apps

With the motto "Only you can prevent wildfires" the United States Forest Service is dependent on its stakeholders to help fulfill one of its core missions of wildfire management. With the Forest Service's Smokey Bear app people can learn how to properly build and extinguish a campfire. The app includes real-time information about wildfires in progress and links to other Smokey Bear social media networks such as a YouTube Channel, Twitter, and Facebook.

A government-created mobile app can be a powerful tool to engage and educate the public. Smartphones are now a reliable way to access the Internet and are cheaper than laptops. The following is a small sample of government mobile apps to highlight the ways in which they are being used for stakeholder engagement and collaboration.

The National Institutes of Health WISER app is designed to support stakeholders in hazmat response. The app includes a searchable database of information on hazardous materials safety, symptoms of exposure to different toxins, as well as access to the Hazardous Substances Databank of the National Library of Medicine.

Rather than develop the technology in house, the city of San Francisco has crowd-sourced transportation information by releasing raw transportation data about train routes, schedules, and real-time locations to the public through web services. In turn, citizen developers have created over ten different apps to help the public navigate the city's transportation systems. By allowing others to use the data to create apps, the city of San Francisco has saved significant money and improved transportation services.

Conclusion

As has been central to this book, the pluralist public policymaking process has both strengths and weaknesses. A primary strength is that multiple voices can be heard, including voices of experts who bring objectivity to a process that can be emotional and politically biased. A weakness is that well-organized, well-heeled groups can prevail over broad national interests. Multiple forces pull government in different directions and make problem solving less coherent than it might be otherwise. Stakeholders, along with agency decision makers, need to develop clear visions, goals, and action items for the process. When goals and objectives are refined into discrete tasks, it is easier to measure results, appreciate the value of the process, and build trust among participants (EPA 2001).

While policy failure may be disappointing, it may provide a learning opportunity. When successful implementation of a policy requires the cooperation of stakeholders, it is only logical that they would be involved from the beginning. The opinions of powerful stakeholders should be used as part of the development process, and their input should be allowed to shape projects at an early stage. This not only increases the likelihood that they will support the work but also can improve the overall quality of the project. Asking people to make changes to their lifestyle, such as reducing energy consumption, is easier when those users have been informed from the beginning. This is about developing trust relations between parties (Kloprogge and van der Sluijs 2006).

Successful leaders need to recruit a broad range of participants, inspire and motivate participants by clearly articulating what can be accomplished and the mutual benefit of collaboration, empower participants, help participants develop relationships with one another, and encourage them to synthesize different ideas and find ways to integrate their complementary assets (Lasker and Weiss 2003).

The following are some proposed summary guidelines based on the theoretical literature and ideas presented above:

- Involve stakeholders before making major decisions.
- Organized opposition should be expected, but decision makers should not be held captive by it.
- The development of trust is a process and is not the automatic outcome of simply sharing information.
- Stakeholders who are asked only for comments will focus on criticism and complaints.
- Stakeholders who are more actively involved can develop a sense of ownership and a more positive and supportive attitude.
- Trained facilitators may be necessary, particularly if consensus seems difficult to achieve.
- Listing stakeholders who participate in decision-making processes as "partners" or some such title helps groups to know that they are being heard and provides them with intangible benefits as well: prestige, publicity, and legitimacy by association. This simple idea can be helpful to creating a team environment and promoting a collaboration ethic rather than one of conflict.

According to Gregory (2000), a structured decision approach to stakeholder participation involves five fundamental tasks. The first task is that decision makers must be clear about the nature of the problem as they see it and the goals of collaboration. The second task is the definition of objectives, including consideration of what values matter most to the stakeholders, and how people think that they will be affected by the proposed solution(s). The third task is to establish alternatives: what are the alternative solutions that might be considered? The fourth task is to identify consequences: what are the possible consequences of the decision and what is the likelihood that they will occur? The final task is to clarify trade-offs by considering the most important conflicts and how can this information be used to design other alternatives.

While the end goal is important, the process by which this happens also deserves attention; decision makers "should avoid being so focused on the *task* of completing an agreement with a stakeholder that they ignore the *process* of completing an agreement. The process by which agreements are reached will be important to nonprofessional and non-executive stakeholders" (Olden 2003, p. 52).

Understanding stakeholders is not just important for those who wish to reach out to multiple interests. Stakeholder participation often occurs against the wishes of managers. Location decisions for hazardous-waste treatment facilities, municipal landfills, prisons, and drug rehabilitation centers are examples of areas where management of stakeholder interests is vital. Often in these cases, self-selection will occur with little effort on the part of the managing agency or organization. Having the skills to manage these interests is important.

Ultimately what should collaboration accomplish? It should improve the policy and management climate by fostering positive relationships between government and stakeholders. It should educate stakeholders, including citizens if appropriate, about the realities of environmental policymaking and management. And of course, most importantly, it should lead to improved policy outcomes.

References

Administrative Dispute Resolution Act of 1996 (1996). Administrative Dispute Resolution Act of 1996. *Pub. Law 104-320.*

Anderson, J. E. (2006). *Public Policymaking.* Boston, Houghton Mifflin.

Ashford, L. S., R. R. Smith, et al. (2006). "Creating Windows of Opportunity for Policy Change: Incorporating Evidence into Decentralized Planning in Kenya." *Bulletin of the World Health Organization* 84(8): 669–672.

Baumgartner, F. R. and B. L. Leech (1998). *Basic Interests: The Importance of Groups in Politics and in Political Science.* New Jersey, Princeton University Press.

Bernstein, M. (1955). *Regulating Business by Independent Commission.* Princeton, Princeton University Press.

Berry, J. M. (1989). *The Interest Group Society.* Glenview, IL, Schott, Foresman.

Bhatnagar, D., A. Rathore, et al. (n.d.). *Participatory Budgeting in Brazil.* Washington, DC, The World Bank.

Birkland, T. A. (1997). *After Disaster: Agenda Setting, Public Policy, and Focusing Events.* Washington, DC, Georgetown University Press.

Birkland, T. A. (2005). *An Introduction to the Policy Process: Theories, Concepts and Models of Public Policy Making.* Armonk, NY, M.E. Sharpe.

Bloodgood, E. (2001). International Non-Governmental Organizations as Interest Groups. *Annual Meeting of the American Political Science Association.* San Francisco, CA.

Burroughs, R. (1999). "When Stakeholders Choose: Process, Knowledge, and Motivation in Water Quality Decisions." *Society & Natural Resources* 12(8): 797–809.

Caffyn, A. and G. Jobbins (2003). "Governance Capacity and Stakeholder Interactions in the Development and Management of Coastal Tourism: Examples from Morocco and Tunisia." *Journal of Sustainable Tourism* 11(2/3): 224.

Carmin, J., N. Darnall, et al. (2003). "Stakeholder Involvement in the Design of U.S. Voluntary Environmental Programs: Does Sponsorship Matter?" *Policy Studies Journal* 31(4): 527.

Clarkson, M. E. (1995) "A Stakeholder Framework for Analysing and Evaluating Corporate Social Performance" *Academy of Management Review,* 20(1): 92117.

Cobb, R. W. and C. D. Elder (1983). *Participation in American Politics: The Dynamics of Agenda Building.* Baltimore, Johns Hopkins University Press.

Cortner, H. J. and M. A. Moote (1999). *The Politics of Ecosystem Management.* Washington, DC, Island Press.

Darnall, N. and G. J. Jolley (2004). "Involving the Public: When Are Surveys and Stakeholder Interviews Effective?" *Review of Policy Research* 21(4): 581–593.

Davies, A. and R. White (2012). "Collaboration in Natural Resource Governance: Reconciling Stakeholder Expectations in Deer Management in Scotland." *Journal of Environmental Management* 112(December): 160–169.

Dedual, M., O. Sague Pla, et al. (2013). "Communication between Scientists, Fishery Managers and Recreational Fishers: Lessons Learned from a Comparative Analysis of International Case Studies." *Fisheries Management & Ecology* 20(2/3): 234–246.

Economic and Social Commission for Asia and the Pacific (2001). *Guidelines for Stakeholders Participation in Strategic Environmental Management.* New York, United Nations.

Elias, A., L. S. Jackson, et al. (2004). "Changing Positions and Interests of Stakeholders in Environmental Conflict: A New Zealand Transport Infrastructure Case." *Asia Pacific Viewpoint* 45(1): 87–104.

EPA (1998). Report of the EPA Common Sense Initiative Council's Stakeholder Involvement Work Group.

EPA (2000). Engaging the American People: A Review of EPA's Public Participation Policy and Regulations with Recommendations for Action. Public Participation Policy Review Workgroup.

EPA (2001). Stakeholder Involvement and Public Participation at the U.S. EPA: Lessons Learned, Barriers and Innovative Approaches.

EPA (2003). How to Review and Use Public Input and Provide Feedback. NSCEP, Environmental Protection Agency.

Eschenbach, R. C. and T. G. Eschenbach (1996). "Understanding Why Stakeholders Matter." *Journal of Management in Engineering* 12(6): 59.

Fisher, R., Ury, W., and Patton, B. (1991). *Getting to Yes: Negotiating Agreement Without Giving In.* New York, Penguin.

Fourie, P. (2004). "Multi-stakeholders with Multiple Perspectives: HIV/AIDS in Africa." *Development* 47(4): 54–59.

Gilliam, A., D. Davis, et al. (2002). "The Value of Engaging Stakeholders in Planning and Implementing Evaluations." *AIDS Education & Prevention* 14: 5.

Gore, M. L., B. A. Knuth, et al. (2006). "Stakeholder Perceptions of Risk Associated with Human-Black Bear Conflicts in New York's Adirondack Park Campgrounds: Implications for Theory and Practice." *Wildlife Society Bulletin* 34(1): 36–43.

Graci, S. (2013). "Collaboration and Partnership Development for Sustainable Tourism." *Tourism Geographies* 15(1): 25–42.

Gregory, R. (2000). "Using Stakeholder Values to Make Smarter Environmental Decisions." *Environment* 42(5): 34.

Gudykunst, W. and Y. Y. Kim (1995). Communicating with Strangers: An Approach to Intercultural Communication. *Bridges Not Walls.* J. Stewart. New York, McGraw-Hill.

Heinz, J. P., E. O. Laumann, et al. (1993). *The Hollow Core: Private Interests in National Policymaking.* Cambridge, Harvard University Press.

Hoban, T. J. (n.d.). "Building Local Partnerships." Retrieved January 29, 2009, from http://www.ctic.purdue.edu/media/files/Building%20Local%20Partnerships.pdf.

Howard, P. L. (2002). "Beyond the 'Grim Resisters': Towards More Effective Gender Mainstreaming through Stakeholder Participation." *Development in Practice* 12(2): 164–176.

Huntington, S. (1952). "The Marasmus of the ICC: The Commission, the Railroads, and the Public Interest." *Yale Law Journal* 614: 467–509.

Jarman, H. (2011). "Collaboration and Consultation: Functional Representation in EU Stakeholder Dialogues." *Journal of European Integration* 33(4): 385–399.

Kingdon, J. W. (1995). *Agendas, Alternatives, and Public Policies*. New York, HarperCollins.

Kloprogge, P. and J. P. van der Sluijs (2006). "The Inclusion of Stakeholder Knowledge and Perspectives in Integrated Assessment of Climate Change." *Climatic Change* 75(3): 359–389.

Kraft, M. E. (2007). *Environmental Policy and Politics*. New York, Pearson.

Lafon, N. W., S. L. McMullin, et al. (2004). "Improving Stakeholder Knowledge and Agency Image through Collaborative Planning." *Wildlife Society Bulletin* 32(1): 220–231.

Lasker, R. D. and E. S. Weiss (2003). "Creating Partnership Synergy: The Critical Role of Community Stakeholders." *Journal of Health & Human Services Administration* 26(1): 119–139.

MacPherson, C. C. (2004). "To Strengthen Consensus, Consult the Stakeholders." *Bioethics* 18(3): 283–292.

McDaniel, J. E. and C. G. Miskel (2002). "Stakeholder Salience: Business and Educational Policy." *Teachers College Record* 104(2): 325.

McGlashan, D. J. and E. Williams (2003). "Stakeholder Involvement in Coastal Decision-Making Processes." *Local Environment* 8(1): 85.

Mostashari, A. and J. Sussman (2005). "Stakeholder-Assisted Modeling and Policy Design Process for Environmental Decision-Making." *Journal of Environmental Assessment Policy and Management* 7(3): 355–386.

Moswete, N. N., B. Thapa, et al. (2012). "Attitudes and Opinions of Local and National Public Sector Stakeholders towards Kgalagadi Transfrontier Park, Botswana." *International Journal of Sustainable Development and World Ecology* 19(1): 67–80.

Nagel, S. S. (1980). Series Editor's Introduction. *Why Policies Succeed or Fail*. H. M. Ingram and D. E. Mann. Beverly Hills, CA, Sage.

Nownes, A. J. and P. Freeman (1988). "Interest Group Activity in the States." *Journal of Politics* 60(1).

Olden, P. C. (2003). "Hospital and Community Health: Going from Stakeholder Management to Stakeholder Collaboration." *Journal of Health & Human Services Administration* 26(1): 35–57.

Orr, S. K. (2006). "Policy Subsystems and Regimes: Organized Interests and Climate Change Policy." *Policy Studies Journal* 34(2): 147–169.

Posavac, E. J. and R. G. Carey (2007). *Program Evaluation: Methods and Case Studies*. Upper Saddle River, NJ, Pearson Education.

Redpath, S. M., B. E. Arroyo, et al. (2004). "Conservation in Practice Using Decision Modeling with Stakeholders to Reduce Human-Wildlife Conflict: A Raptor Grouse Case Study." *Conservation Biology* 18(2): 350–359.

Sabatier, P. (1999). The Need for Better Theories. *Theories of the Policy Process*. P. Sabatier. Boulder, Westview Press.

Sabatier, P. A., W. Focht, et al. (2005). Collaborative Approaches to Watershed Management. *Swimming Upstream: Collaborative Approaches to Watershed Management*. P. A. Sabatier, W. Focht, M. Lubell, et al. Cambridge, The MIT Press.

Salisbury, R. (1990). *The Paradox of Interest Groups in Washington: More Groups, Less Clout*. *The New American Political System*. Washington, DC, American Enterprise Institute.

Schattschneider, E. E. (1960). *The Semi-Sovereign People*. New York, Holt, Rinehart and Winston.

Scherer, M. (2013). "Why the White House Loves Your Death Star Petition." *Time* http://swampland.time.com/2013/01/31/we-the-people/ (January 31, 2013).

Selin, S. W., M. A. Schuett, et al. (2000). "Modeling Stakeholder Perceptions of Collaborative Initiative Effectiveness." *Society & Natural Resources* 13(8): 735–745.

Shawcross, P. (2013). "Official White House Response to Secure Resources and Funding, and Begin Construction of a Death Star by 2016." Washington, DC, White House Office of Management and Budget.

Treves, A., L. Andriamampianina, et al. (2006). "A Simple, Cost-Effective Method for Involving Stakeholders in Spatial Assessments of Threats to Biodiversity." *Human Dimensions of Wildlife* 11(1): 43–54.

Wampler, B. (2007). *Participatory Budgeting in Brazil.* University Park, PA, Penn State University Press.

Weech-Maldonado, R., K. J. Benson, et al. (2003). "Evaluating the Effectiveness of Community Health Partnerships: A Stakeholder Accountability Approach." *Journal of Health & Human Services Administration* 26(1): 58–92.

Chapter 4

Case Study: Yellowstone National Park

Introduction

National parks in the United States have a challenging mission, to serve as both protected wilderness and tourist attraction for the general public. The first involves isolating parks from human impacts, the second encouraging and supporting access and use. When President Ulysses S. Grant signed a law in 1872 declaring that Yellowstone National Park would forever be "dedicated and set apart as a public park or pleasuring ground for the benefit and enjoyment of the people," he likely had no idea that national parks could become battlegrounds for competing visions about the purpose and mission of these lands (Orr and Humphreys 2012). Supporters of untamed wilderness are often at odds with those who favor year-round commercial tourism, particularly as such areas become increasingly rare in a country consumed by urban sprawl. For some, the meaning of a national park is found in its isolation from society; for others, the accoutrements of society including fast-food restaurants and retail shops only serve to enhance the national park experience:

> The happy convergence of many disparate interests permitted Congress and the public to sustain contradictory, but compatible beliefs that permitted a park system to flourish: On one side the repugnance of the seemingly boundless materialism that infused American life, a spiritual attachment to untrammeled nature, and a self-congratulatory attitude toward the preservation of nature's bounty; and on the other

a commitment to economic progress wherever it could be exacted, nationalistic pride, and the practical uses of nature as a commodity supportive of tourism and commercial recreation. (Sax 1981)

Management of national parks in the United States falls under the auspices of the Department of the Interior and the National Park Service (NPS), which was created in 1916 to administer national parks and monuments. The stated purpose of the 1916 National Parks Service Organic Act is to "conserve the scenery and the natural and historic objects and the wildlife therein and to provide for the enjoyment of the same in such manner and by such means as will leave them unimpaired for the enjoyment of future generations." Congress expanded this policy in 1978 by directing that "the protection, management, and administration of these areas... shall not be exercised in derogation of the values and purposes for which these various areas have been established." These seemingly contradictory values have created extensive management challenges for the NPS as they struggle to develop policy that serves both public and environmental interests.

This chapter reviews five key policy challenges within Yellowstone National Park—winter use, wolf reintroduction, bioprospecting, bear management, and wildfire policy—and explores how stakeholders have both improved and complicated agency decision making within Yellowstone National Park. Each case study is used to highlight a different aspect of policymaking and stakeholder collaboration.*

Yellowstone National Park

Established in 1872, Yellowstone National Park, spanning an area of 3,468 square miles, was the first national park in the United States. The park reaches across three state borders: Wyoming, Montana, and Idaho, although most of the park is in Wyoming. Early administration of the park was under the authority of the U.S. Army; however, in 1917 such responsibility was transferred to the newly created NPS. The natural features of the park are extensive including lakes, canyons, mountain ranges, and rivers. The many geothermal features, including Old Faithful geyser, are some of the most popular features for visitors. Hundreds of species of wildlife have been documented within the park including grizzly bears, wolves, free-ranging herds of bison, and elk.

After Yellowstone was established as a national park, visitation grew quickly from 300 visitors in 1872 to more than 5,000 in 1883. Today more than two million tourists visit Yellowstone each year. The park now has more than one thousand historic structures and features and has been designated an International Biosphere

---

* Background information for these case studies came from the NPS website (www.nps.gov) unless otherwise noted.

Reserve (October 26, 1976) and a United Nations World Heritage Site (September 8, 1978).

In addition to the controversies highlighted throughout this chapter, Yellowstone National Park faces a number of policy and management challenges: funding shortfalls, extensive exotic non-native species within the park that threaten native species, outbreaks of disease/pests/fungus that threaten the flora and fauna, and climate change. While the causes of these problems are numerous, policy is particularly complicated in Yellowstone National Park due to the expansive range of stakeholders who are passionate about park problems and solutions. Visitors, local residents, recreationists, elected officials, government appointees, scientists, ranchers, environmental organizations, concessionaires, and the concerned public often have very divergent views about the role and future of national parks in the United States. In some of the policy issues discussed in the following sections these differences have been reconciled, sometimes quickly (bioprospecting), sometimes reluctantly (wildfire), and at other times with great unease (wolf reintroduction). Other issues are an ongoing process of incremental changes (bear management) or show little hope of resolution (winter use).

Bear Management

Policy Background

Some of the most challenging issues for the NPS at Yellowstone National Park are related to the management of bears within the park, in particular human-bear interactions. Early visitors to the park were enchanted by the sight of the park's abundant wildlife, in particular the bears. Park garbage dumps became a popular tourist attraction as people gathered at night to watch the bears feed on garbage. Although hand-feeding bears was technically banned in 1902, visitors continued to try to interact with the bears, giving them food handouts, posing for pictures, and causing regular "bear jams"—traffic jams due to visitors stopping their cars to view wildlife, and all too often feed the bears as they graze or rest by the roadside. In wilderness areas such as Yellowstone National Park, when bears and people come into regular, benign contact, bears will habituate to people, exhibiting a reduction in their normal behavioral response. The term *habituate* is often used to describe what happens to wildlife when they lose their natural fear of humans and become a public safety hazard as a result. Habituated wildlife, for example, are more likely to enter campgrounds and other public areas. Wildlife that become habituated are usually relocated to other parts of the park or killed to reduce the threat to human visitors.

In 1931, park managers began to realize that rapidly growing numbers of visitors were also leading to increased bear-human conflicts. Official record keeping of incidents began in that year to track human injuries, property damage, and bear control actions. On average it was found that between 1931 and 1969 bears caused

48 human injuries and 100 property damage incidents per year within the park. In 1960 a black bear management program was developed to try to reduce injuries and damages. The program included visitor education addressing garbage removal and proper food storage, the development and use of bear-proof garbage cans, removal of potentially problematic or habituated bears, and stricter enforcement of regulations that prohibited the feeding of bears. After 10 years, bear-human conflicts were reduced only slightly, and so in 1970 a more intensive program was developed that included such elements as the closure of open-pit garbage dumps inside and adjacent to the park, and weaning bears off of garbage back to a natural and native diet. The program was considered a relative success, with reported declines in the numbers of bear-caused human injuries, human-bear conflicts, and necessary control actions.

In 1983 a companion grizzly bear program was developed to improve management of grizzly bears within the park. The program focused on habitat protection in the backcountry areas of the park including restricted recreational use in areas with seasonal concentrations of bears. The goals of the program were to minimize bear-human interaction that might lead to habituation of bears, prevent the need to displace bears from prime food sources due to human presence, and decrease the risks of injury to humans from bear encounters. The program is still in use today.

In 1975 the grizzly bear was listed as threatened under the Endangered Species Act. It was believed that outside of Alaska, grizzlies in the United States had been reduced to 2 percent of their former range, and that only five or six small populations remained, totaling 800–1,000 bears. Listing of the grizzly led to an end of grizzly bear hunting in the Greater Yellowstone Ecosystem and numerous management plans to expand protection efforts. A Yellowstone grizzly bear recovery area was established that encompassed approximately 9,500 square miles, including surrounding areas outside the park, to focus research on the primary area of habitat and to ensure that key land use issues outside the park were also taken into account in future management plans.

Since the initial listing of grizzlies as threatened, policy planning for grizzly bear management has been filtered through a number of different specialized stakeholder collaboration groups. In 1975 research and management of grizzlies intensified after the establishment of the Interagency Grizzly Bear Study Team (IGBST). Still in place today, the team works with state wildlife officials in Idaho, Montana, and Wyoming to improve understanding of grizzly bears and to facilitate science-based decision making. In 1983 the Interagency Grizzly Bear Committee (IGBC) was created to improve communication and cooperation throughout the recovery area and across multiple federal lands and state lines.

In 1993 the Grizzly Bear Recovery Plan was developed to try to bring the grizzly bears to a viable and sustainable population level. In 2000 a team of biologists and agency managers from the USFS, NPS, USFWS, and the states of Idaho, Wyoming, and Montana developed a *Draft Conservation Strategy for the Grizzly Bear in the Greater Yellowstone Ecosystem*. This was followed by a two-year public comment period that included a series of public meetings resulting in 16,794 public comments. In 2002 the Conservation Strategy was approved. In 2007 the grizzly bear population in the Greater Yellowstone Ecosystem was removed from the federal threatened species list. In 2009 that ruling was overturned and the bears were returned to the list. The grizzly conservation strategy is based on the following:

■ Develop a long-term guide for managing the population and ensuring sufficient habitat to maintain recovery.
■ Develop cooperative relationships between stakeholders.
■ Delegate management of bears outside the parks to state wildlife agencies.
■ Sustain population at or above 500 bears.
■ Implement improved monitoring.
■ Remove/relocate aggressive bears.

Despite extensive bear management policies, threats to bears in Yellowstone continue to be problematic. Bear habitat has been narrowed by rural development, oil and gas drilling, logging, road building, and off-road vehicle use. Because the bear habitat extends beyond the park borders, there are limits to how much the park service can control; reports of grizzly bears preying on nearby ranches are an ongoing concern. Grizzly bear mortality is highest on private land, which is outside of NPS control. As well, threats to grizzly food sources such as the white pine blister rust fungus and mountain pine beetle outbreaks have resulted in growing concern that the population will not be able to be sustained at the present level. Scientists and the NPS have warned that careful policy planning must continue to ensure that grizzly bears maintain a sustainable population.

Policy and Stakeholder Analysis

Over the years, Yellowstone bear issues have been defined in a number of different ways. These definitions seem to stretch along a continuum ranging from the best interest of the bear, which would be living in the wild with minimal human intrusion, to the other extreme in which bears are reduced to mere spectacle and tourist attraction. Today, many visitors feel that a visit to Yellowstone is not complete without seeing a bear, and so agency personnel continue to struggle with meeting the needs of both the fee-paying/voting public and the wildlife they are charged to protect.

Bear policy is an ongoing struggle for Yellowstone because the makeup of one of the key stakeholder groups, the visiting public, changes daily. The revolving door of visitors means that policy education is an unrelenting duty to ensure that every day visitors are aware of their responsibilities within the park. Education programs within the park are extensive, including lectures, signs, pamphlets, staff training, website information, bear reporting forms, food poles at backcountry campsites, and ranger intervention at bear jams. Bear policy in Yellowstone highlights the importance of educating those most affected by a policy about the underlying rationale of a policy, as well as providing clear guidelines and expectations. To ensure compliance with bear policy, visitors, particularly those unfamiliar with wilderness, must be educated about proper bear management and must understand why it is so vitally important to protect the bears.

Wolf Reintroduction

Policy Background

At the time of the establishment of Yellowstone National Park in 1872, the gray wolf population thrived within the park boundaries; however, park-sanctioned predator elimination programs of the late 1800s and early 1900s led to a rapid decline of the species. The last wolf in Yellowstone National Park was killed in 1926.

Wolf reintroduction was initially proposed by biologists in 1966 due to concerns about the critically high elk population in the park. After the eradication of the wolf, the top of the food pyramid within the park ecosystem, elk and other large prey populations soared, and new growth vegetation suffered as a result. Deciduous woody species such as upland aspen and riparian cottonwood crashed due to overgrazing. Coyote populations also increased in response to the absence of wolves and had a noticeably negative effect on other species such as the red fox. Biologists argued that reintroduction of the native gray wolf was necessary to stabilize the park ecosystem. The local community, and in particular ranchers in the region, however, were concerned that wolves would be a threat outside the park and prey on cattle.

As this early disagreement indicates, restoration/reintroduction of native species is often a challenging proposition in terms of conflicting stakeholder interests. According to NPS policy native species can be restored under the following conditions:

1. Sufficient habitat exists to support the species.
2. Reintroduction poses limited threat to other species.
3. The same species that was lost can be restored.
4. The species that was lost was affected by human activity.

The NPS struggled to develop a policy that would serve both the interests of the local community and the environmental needs of the park. Draft recovery plans were released in 1982, 1985, and 1987; however, each was met with significant disagreement. In 1993 a Draft Environmental Impact Statement (DEIS) was released for public comment, receiving more than 150,000 comments from stakeholders and the general public. The policy was finalized in May 1994 with plans to reintroduce wolves as an "experimental non-essential" population as listed in article 10(j) in the Endangered Species Act in two recovery zones: Idaho and the Greater

Yellowstone Area. To encourage ranchers to support wolf reintroduction, the environmental organization Defenders of Wildlife created a "wolf compensation fund" that would use donations to compensate ranchers for the market value of any livestock lost due to the wolves.

In response to the reintroduction policy, two lawsuits were filed in late 1994. The first was filed by the Wyoming Farm Bureau to halt the program out of concern for local livestock populations. The second suit, filed by a coalition of environmental groups, argued that recent unofficial sightings of wolves in the park meant that wolves should be given full protection under the Endangered Species Act, rather than the limited protection afforded by the "experimental" classification. Both cases were thrown out of court.

Implementation of the wolf reintroduction program began in 1995, with the transfer of adolescent wolves from Alberta, Canada. Since then, the wolves have adapted well to the park and are now considered to be fully recovered, having surpassed the target goal of 30 breeding pairs. In addition, as a result of the wolf reintroduction, biodiversity has increased within the park, most notably new-growth vegetation such as aspen and willow trees. The beaver and red fox have also recovered, most likely due to wolves controlling the coyote population. In 2009, with the demonstrated recovery of the wolf population, hunting was allowed to resume outside the park boundaries despite a court challenge filed by the Defenders of Wildlife. The status of hunting continues to be a subject of court and legislative battles.

Policy and Stakeholder Analysis

A number of challenges have faced the wolf reintroduction program. From a policy perspective, authority and control of large carnivores such as wolves is highly fragmented in the region, making it difficult to develop and implement an overall system for management. Conflicts between different agencies at the federal and state levels are ongoing, particularly over management policies when wolves leave the protected confines of the park. As the U.S. Fish and Wildlife Service, in concert with the NPS, had managed the wolf population since reintroduction, state officials have regularly complained about the overstepping of jurisdictions. The federal government ultimately agreed to allow state management of the wolves, as long as state plans were approved by the U.S. Fish and Wildlife Service. Officials in Wyoming had resisted assuming management without government funding, saying they did not ask for wolves to be reintroduced and should not be burdened with the expense. Changes in habitat and wildlife such as fragmentation of private lands and escalating recreational use of public lands are also a problem.

For nongovernmental stakeholders, the wolf reintroduction program has been extremely controversial, pitting scientists and environmentalists against local ranchers and hunting outfitters. Opponents of the wolf restoration argue that the Yellowstone reintroductions were unnecessary, as American wolves were never in danger of biological extinction and that wolves are of little commercial benefit due to the high cost of reintroduction. Hunters have also cited concerns about the possibility of large ungulate population declines within the park due to wolf predation. The Wyoming Farm Bureau Federation representing local livestock producers opposed the policy, arguing that the wolves posed a real threat to the livestock and that the very presence of wolves would disturb the natural grazing patterns.

While the primary policy goal has been achieved, there have been hundreds of confirmed incidents of wolves killing local livestock, largely due to a few isolated wolves or wolf packs. Between 1987 and 2010, the Defenders of Wildlife spent more than $1.4 million compensating private owners for proven and probable livestock depredation. Although the Defenders program did have government support and was transitioned into a federal program in 2010 based on its successes, it raised important questions about the role of stakeholders in policymaking. Essentially, the organization interjected itself into the policy process, taking on a decision-making role entirely separate from that of the government. From one perspective the Defenders of Wildlife usurped authority from government; from another the organization stepped in and saved the day in a way that the government would never be able to, given the circumstances and prevailing public opinion of the time. The line between stakeholder and government decision making becomes blurred. While in this case the stakeholder was able to facilitate reconciliation between opposing interests, it raises the question of what happens when stakeholders intervene without government support. "Vigilante policymaking" could backfire and in fact destabilize policymaking. Or, as in the case of wolf reintroduction, it can also be used to support decision making, facilitate actions that are beyond the capabilities of government, support resource sharing, and be a way to reach out to multiple stakeholder interests to resolve differences.

Snowmobiles

Policy Background

In 1955 the first multi-passenger snowcoaches were brought into Yellowstone for winter tourists, followed by modern snowmobiles in 1963. In 1968 the park opened up the asphalt roads in winter to snowmobiles and encouraged snowmobile use as a way for recreationists to experience the winter beauty of the park and to increase winter use of the Old Faithful Lodge. In 1971 the NPS began grooming roads to improve snowmobile access. Snowmobile use expanded through the 1970s and 1980s, along with concerns and visitor complaints about noise and air pollution and allegations of wildlife harassment. In 1990 a Winter Use Plan Environmental Assessment was completed with a commitment to examine the issue of whether winter visitation exceeded sustainability thresholds. In 1994 the Greater Yellowstone Coordinating Committee began work on an interagency assessment of winter activities in the park, culminating in the 1999 report *The Winter Visitor*

Use Management Assessment. In 1997, the Fund for Animals filed a lawsuit against Yellowstone opposing snow grooming of roads in the park. The lawsuit was settled and the court ordered the NPS to do an Environmental Impact Study (EIS) on winter use. The EIS found adverse impacts from emissions, persistent noise from engines, and stress to wildlife, particularly bison. The Park Service and EPA both independently concluded that the use of Best Available Technology (BAT) and guided trips would not prevent adverse impacts from continued snowmobile use within the park. As a result of the EIS findings, the Assistant Secretary for the Department of the Interior issued a Record of Decision (ROD)* on November 22, 2000, announcing his decision to eliminate snowmobiling in the park entirely and allow only multi-passenger snowcoaches.

On December 6, 2000, the International Snowmobile Manufacturers Association (ISMA), the national recreational organization The Blue Ribbon Coalition, and the Wyoming State Snowmobile Association filed a joint lawsuit requesting that the ROD be set aside and to permit snowmobile access within the park. The lawsuit argued that (1) the National Environmental Policy Act (NEPA) process was not duly followed when the EIS was conducted, (2) the Department of the Interior and the NPS had been unduly pressured by environmental organizations to eliminate snowmobiles from the park, and (3) the NPS and EIS authors had preconceived plans to close the park to snowmobiling regardless of the EIS findings. The Department of the Interior and the NPS agreed to conduct a Supplemental Environmental Impact Statement (SEIS) to consider new snowmobile technology as part of the condition of settlement from the ISMA court case, which required the Park Service to consider "any significant new or additional information or data submitted with respect to a winter use plan."†

The 2001 supplemental EIS again concluded that even with the new technology, limited daily entries, and guided tour requirements, snowmobile usage would have unacceptable adverse impacts on the environment and wildlife. The EIS concluded that snowcoaches would best allow visitors to enjoy the park and at the same time cause the least amount of damage to the environment. Despite these findings, in 2003 the Park Service published a ROD and a final rule authorizing 950 daily snowmobile entries and requiring the use of BAT snowmobiles. In addition snowmobiles would be restricted to snow-covered roads and would only be permitted in designated areas representing 1 percent of the park.

In December 2003 the U.S. District Court for the District of Columbia invalidated the 2003 ROD/final rule/Supplemental EIS and sided with environmental plaintiffs that the NPS had violated the Administrative Procedure Act in failing to explain its decision to allow continued snowmobile use "[i]n light of

---

* A Record of Decision is a document that is prepared to substantiate a decision based on an environmental impact statement. It includes a statement of the decision, a detailed rationale, and a justification for not adopting all mitigation measures if appropriate.
† 72 Fed. Reg. 70781.

its clear conservation mandate, and the previous conclusion that snowmobile use amounted to unlawful impairment."[*] The court ordered the NPS to re-implement the 2001 final rule, which would replace snowmobiles with snowcoaches. Until then, up to 493 snowmobiles would be permitted per day in Yellowstone. In June 2004 the District of Columbia court ordered the Park Service to craft a new rule consistent with that decision at least thirty days prior to the start of the winter season.

In March 2007 the NPS released a draft copy of the new EIS that evaluated six alternatives for winter use in the park. As part of an extensive stakeholder collaboration process, 122,000 people filed comments about the EIS and planners organized more than 60 public meetings with stakeholders. The final EIS, released in September 2007 and subsequently adopted in the November 2007 ROD, approved up to 540 snowmobiles daily in groups of eleven with commercial guides, along with the entry of 78 to 83 snowcoaches operated under concession contracts with the Park Service. The rule authorized the NPS to use principles of adaptive management to change the number of snowmobiles allowed and to open/close areas of the park to traffic as necessary. As well, the NPS would conduct a five-year study to assess the impact of winter vehicle use on bison. According to the Park Service, the rule

> strikes a balance between the use of snowmobiles and snowcoaches in the Parks and is designed to protect against the adverse impacts that occurred from the historical types and numbers of snowmobiles used. Experience over the past several winters, during which a temporary plan has guided winter use management of the Parks, has shown that the combination of strict limits on the number of snowmobiles allowed to enter the Parks, the use of snowmobiles that meet NPS requirements for air and sound emissions…, the requirement that visitors touring Yellowstone on snowmobiles be accompanied by a commercial guide, and the availability of snowcoaches, allows for an appropriate range of visitor experiences while ensuring that the integrity of park resources and values is not harmed.[†]

A coalition of environmental organizations represented by the environmental law firm Earthjustice challenged the 2007 ROD in the District Court for the District of Columbia before the final rule was actually issued, arguing that (1) the permitted level of recreational snowmobiling would have adverse impacts on the park, (2) the NPS violated NEPA through inadequate analysis of effects on air/soundscape/wildlife, and (3) once again the NPS had failed to adequately explain its rationale for departing from the original 2001 findings. The National

---

[*] The Fund for Animals v. Norton, 294 F. Supp. 2d 92, 108 (D.DC 2003).
[†] 72 Fed. Reg. 70782 (Dec.13, 2007).

Park Conservation Association filed a petition for review of the Record of Decision based on similar arguments.

On September 15, 2008, the U.S. District Court for the District of Columbia issued an opinion that vacated and remanded to the NPS the 2007 Final Environmental Impact Statement (FEIS), 2007 ROD, and 2007 Final Rule. The NPS issued the Winter Use Plans Environmental Assessment on November 3, 2008, as a result, which would allow up to 318 snowmobiles and 78 snow-coaches per day into Yellowstone for three years. On November 7, 2008, the U.S. District Court for the District of Wyoming issued an order to the NPS to reinstate the 2004 rule for snowmobile and snowcoach use. In January 2010 a new public input period began. In May 2011 a DEIS was published for public review and comment. In November 2011 the NPS issued an FEIS including a one-year ruling for 2011–2012 winter use. A Supplemental Environmental Impact Statement (SEIS) is being developed that will include a long-term regulation for winter use. Table 4.1 summarizes the policy history of the snowmobile issue.

Policy and Stakeholder Analysis

Winter use policy in Yellowstone highlights the challenges and frustrations of stakeholder collaboration. Stakeholders have successfully used the court system to interject themselves into the policymaking process, to overturn policies, and to prolong decision making. In some ways this highlights how would-be stakeholders with sufficient resources can transform themselves into players. In many ways, the NPS has lost control of the policy process, as every policy decision they make is scrutinized, questioned, and often overruled. Every formulated policy leads directly back to the problem definition and agenda-setting stages.

Bioprospecting and Benefits Sharing[*]

Policy Background

Budget cutbacks for national parks have made funding an ongoing concern. Options for raising revenue are limited, and recent attempts to develop corporate sponsorships for national parks and monuments were met with public outrage and ridicule. Although controversial, bioprospecting has been heralded as a new way to increase park revenue.

---

[*] For more detailed information on the Diversa case presented here see Kate, K. T. (1998). "Yellowstone National Park and Diversa Corporation," from http://www.cbd.int/doc/case-studies//abs/cs-abs-yellowstone.pdf.

Table 4.1 Winter Use Policy History

1949: First snowplanes carry visitors into Yellowstone.
1955: Snowcoaches enter the park.
1963: First snowmobiles (six, total) enter the park.
1967: Congressional hearing held on winter access to the park.
1968: Yellowstone managers decide to formalize over-snow use.
1971: Managers begin grooming roads and Old Faithful Snowlodge opens.
1990: NPS issues first winter environmental assessment for Yellowstone.
1997: NPS is sued by groups who believe bison used groomed roads to leave the park, which led to their slaughter. NPS must develop a new winter use plan and Environmental Impact Statement (EIS).
1999: Draft EIS released; more than 48,000 public comments are received.
2000: The final EIS released; record of decision (ROD) signed; would ban snowmobiles from Yellowstone and Grand Teton in the winter of 2003–04.
2000: December: Snowmobile group files suit against the ban.
2001: NPS settles with snowmobilers group and agrees to prepare a Supplemental Environmental Impact Statement (SEIS).
2002: Draft SEIS released—more than 300,000 comments received.
2003: December 11: Final rule published in *Federal Register*; allowed 950 Best Available Technology (BAT) guided snowmobiles daily.
2003: December 16: Judge Sullivan directs NPS to phase out snowmobile use.
2004: February 10: Judge Brimmer issues preliminary injunction against banning snowmobiles.
2004: NPS completes another EA for Yellowstone; 95,000 comments received.
2004–2007: Under a temporary plan, limited numbers of snowmobiles with professional guides are allowed in the park.
2007: *Winter Use Plans EIS* completed; 122,000 comments received; final rule published in December.
2008: Federal Court (DC) rejects the 2007 plan. Park prepares new temporary plan allowing 318 snowmobiles and 78 snowcoaches per day.

(Continued)

Table 4.1   Winter Use Policy History (Continued)

2009: NPS completes temporary plan.
2010: New public input period begins.
2011: NPS issues Draft and Final Environmental Impact Statements following extensive public input period.

Bioprospecting is research that searches for useful products, applications, or processes in nature. Discoveries may include, for example, enzymes or biological molecules that serve as catalysts for chemical reactions. Within national parks in the United States, most of the bioprospecting is focused on the study of microorganisms. According to national park regulations, in order to study microorganisms within national parks, researchers must obtain a research permit conditional on assurance that there will be no adverse impacts from their research. Permits are not issued for those who wish to harvest natural products such as herbs, as federal regulations prohibit harvesting natural products from national parks. Small research samples may be removed from the park for research; however, those samples cannot be sold or commercialized. Knowledge derived from research on those samples, however, can be commercialized.

In 1969 Dr. Thomas Brock, a bacteriologist from Indiana University researching the hot springs of Yellowstone, discovered a new microorganism, *Thermus aquaticus*. His discovery proved that bacterial life could survive at temperatures above 55°C, a major milestone in the history of microbiology. Subsequent research with the bacteria eventually led to a Nobel Prize and patent right sales of more than $300 million. The commercial use of enzymes derived from *Thermus aquaticus* was highly controversial. After Dr. Brock's initial research, the samples were deposited in the American Type Culture Collection, a public repository. Other scientists obtained the samples from the public repository and were able to derive significant profits from their work. Despite its initial and critical role in the process, Yellowstone received no financial benefits. As a result the NPS began to explore opportunities for benefits sharing from research conducted within the park.

The "Old Faithful Symposium" was a stakeholder discussion organized in September 1995 during which NPS managers discussed their intention to seek a share of commercial profits that are generated by products developed from Yellowstone samples. Stakeholders at the symposium included academics, seventeen biotechnology companies, members of the press, and selected environmental organizations supportive of bioprospecting profit sharing. The sense of the symposium was that the park should enter into benefit-sharing agreements; however, there was no clear consensus on the kinds of arrangement that would be appropriate for the park.

Diversa Corporation (originally known as Recombinant Biocatalysis Inc.) was formed in 1994 and specializes in the discovery, modification, and manufacturing of novel enzymes and bioactive compounds that result from research on biological samples. Under a Cooperative Research and Development Agreement (CRADA) signed on August 19, 1997, between Yellowstone and Diversa, Yellowstone granted Diversa access to samples of genetic resources within the park. Diversa would collect samples in collaboration with the park and conduct research and development of the samples. The Federal Technology Transfer Act requires each CRADA negotiated and signed between a federal laboratory and a company be subject to a statutory 30-day review of its terms by the head of the relevant federal agency. Diversa volunteered to add an additional 60-day period to the review, given the novelty of the agreement. As part of the review the park held public comment meetings and the White House also reviewed the agreement.

The CRADA was met with controversy even before it was finalized. The Edmonds Institute (EI) and the International Center for Technology Assessment (ICTA) opposed the Yellowstone/Diversa partnership, and on July 1, 1997, they filed Freedom of Information Act requests with the Secretary of the Interior and the NPS to see the terms of the CRADA. The NPS responded that negotiations were ongoing and the terms that might be subject to public review had not yet been finalized. On August 15, 1997, they filed a petition requesting that the proposed CRADA be dropped and that information related to the agreement be made public.

On February 6, 1998, the Department of the Interior settled the Freedom of Information Act lawsuit out of court, paying the Edmonds Institute $8,000 in legal fees and making most of the requested information available, except for the financial details of the agreement, which included confidential commercial and pricing information for products generated from the biological samples.

On February 25, 1998, the Edmonds Institute filed another Freedom of Information Act lawsuit against the NPS for withholding from public disclosure the financial arrangements. On March 5, 1998, the Edmonds Institute and a coalition of other concerned stakeholders filed a suit against the Department of the Interior and the NPS to stop implementation of the Yellowstone-Diversa CRADA due to alleged violations of the Federal Technology Transfer Act of 1986. The complaint was based on three allegations:

1. The agreement violates the Federal Technology Transfer Act as it only allows federal laboratories to enter into CRADAs with private organizations to exchange resources.
2. The CRADA violates implementation of the NPS Organic Act of 1916, which mandates conservation of the environment. Commercial and consumptive uses of natural resources are generally considered to be contrary to the intention of the act.
3. The CRADA was not subjected to public scrutiny to analyze its environmental impact.

The court ruled in favor of Yellowstone, stating that the CRADA contributed funds and knowledge that would be used in support of the conservation mission of the park.

The final agreement gives Diversa nonexclusive access to the genetic resources in Yellowstone such as microorganisms in the thermal features and the alpine tundra. As part of the financial agreement, the company gave the park an up-front payment of US$100,000, payable in five yearly installments of US$20,000, to be offset against any future royalty payments received by the park under the agreement. In addition to monetary benefits, the park has received equipment donations such as DNA extraction kits and staff training in current molecular biology techniques. As a result of these services, and continued interest in bioprospecting, the park has been able to support its own research projects such as detection of brucellosis, an infectious disease, in Yellowstone bison. The technology transfer has been valued at $75,000 per year for the park.

Policy and Stakeholder Analysis

Bioprospecting provides an excellent example of the policy cycle in action. Commercialization of *Thermus aquaticus* and demonstrable profit potential of natural resources, in concert with budget concerns, led to the awareness and definition of a problem. The problem was defined not as one of unlawful exploitation of protected resources but rather as a question of how Yellowstone could share in the profits derived from park resources. The realization of what could be at stake pushed the issue onto the agenda. Policy formulation occurred through internal debates as well as through the stakeholder gathering at the "Old Faithful Symposium." Stakeholders tried to change the direction of policy through Freedom of Information Act requests and ultimately through an unsuccessful court challenge. Policy implementation has been on a small scale thus far, with the Diversa CRADA serving in many ways as a pilot project to work out the details of bioprospecting policy. As a highly technical policy issue that has a limited impact on most traditional Yellowstone stakeholders such as local residents and visitors, the likelihood of conflict is low. Unless there are dramatic changes, it is likely that bioprospecting policy will continue to be refined, implemented, and evaluated with very little controversy.

Wildfires

Policy Background

Throughout early history, the landscape of Yellowstone was shaped by fire as periodic lightning strikes burned grass and surface vegetation and cleared out underbrush. Fire can help to restore depleted stands of aspen and increase populations of insects, birds, and mammals that prefer new growth. Native Americans also used fire regularly to facilitate hunting and gathering (Carle 2002). Fire suppression can have devastating consequences for natural areas such as Yellowstone, in particular by allowing ground fuel to build up and thereby creating fuel for fires to burn hotter and higher and consume more area (Busenberg 2004).

Despite the history of fire and demonstrated benefits of fire for the Yellowstone ecosystem, wildfire policy is a contentious issue (Fifer and Orr 2013). The summer of 1988 was a keen reminder of the challenges of managing stakeholders in issue areas that are both scientifically complex and emotionally powerful.

The summer of 1988 was one of the hottest and driest seasons in Yellowstone National Park, leading to an unprecedented 248 individual wildfires affecting 1 million acres or 45 percent of the park. Wildfire management policy at the time was based on a philosophy of natural management, so administrators allowed wildfires contained within the boundaries of the park to burn as long as they posed no threat to lives, property, or specific natural/cultural sites of unusual value (Schullery and Despain 1989). By the end of the summer, however, continued high winds and limited rain caused the fires to spread and the park dramatically increased its firefighting effort, spending up to $3 million a day until rain and snow in mid-September helped the suppression effort and the wildfires were all out. In all, more than 25,000 firefighters were involved in the firefighting effort, with a total cost of $120 million (Pyne 1989; Franke 2000).

Media coverage of the fires was extensive, and the public response was predictably outraged at the idea that the country's crown jewel could be in jeopardy and allowed to burn. The NPS was vilified for being inept and unprofessional. Politicians declared Yellowstone wildfire policy to be a resounding failure and demanded policy change.

In 1972 the NPS adopted a let-it-burn policy to allow spontaneous fires to burn. Until the summer of 1988 both the agency and conservation groups considered that policy a success. An extensive education plan was developed to educate visitors about the value of fire. After the fires, however, critics argued that the fires should have been suppressed and fought much earlier and that only a limited number of fires should have been allowed to burn at all, given the scope of the fires and the unusually hot, dry conditions. "The fire fighting effort was largely driven by public outcry from who saw a policy failure" (Lichtman 1998, p. 3). Wyoming Senators Malcolm Wallop and Alan Simpson publicly demanded Park Service Director William Mott to resign from his post because the NPS had "destroyed Yellowstone by tolerating wildfire" (Williams 2002).

Policy and Stakeholder Analysis

The real policy failure in the wildfire case was not the decision to let the fires burn, but rather the failure of stakeholders such as citizens and elected officials to understand the ecological benefit of wildfire, and the idea that such extensive burning was in fact a correction of the unfortunate historical policy to suppress fires. The failure in Yellowstone is due in large part to the disconnect between stakeholders and policymakers. One of the key problems underlying this case is the failure of decision makers to adequately collaborate with stakeholders in such a way to bridge support across the scientific divide. Labels of policy failure stem not from the policy itself but from the failure of the general public, the media, and elected officials to understand how fire could be an ecologically beneficial condition. For a society raised on Smokey Bear and Bambi, such a thought conflicts with childhood notions that "only you [and maybe the government] can prevent forest fires." Policymakers, in this case the NPS, failed to work collaboratively with stakeholders in the wake of the fires to help them understand the policy decision. The consequences of this failure included public ridicule and distrust and increased political oversight of future NPS decisions. "We must start by restoring public confidence in federal land management agencies, and then we need to develop processes that will allow for genuine public dialogue about the issues…an honest appraisal of how much control humans have over wildfires must be communicated to the public. And the ecological objectives of a natural fire policy should be persuasively presented to resource constituencies and policymakers" (Lichtman 1998, p. 8).

Conclusion

National parks represent different things to different people. They stimulate tourism and economic development, they inspire poetry and art, they are research laboratories, and they serve recreational and educational purposes. National parks cannot be looked at from a single perspective; the very heart of the national parks idea is to find a balance between competing values. As demonstrated in Table 4.2 stakeholders play a number of important and complicated roles in national parks policy. Like so many other case studies in public policy, stakeholders are both a great strength and a liability for policymaking. From those who are simply curious about what is happening to those who take policy matters into their own hands by filing lawsuits or developing complementary programming, stakeholders are a key component to the policy process.

Table 4.2 Stakeholders and National Parks Policy in Yellowstone

	Players	Would-Be Players	Curious	Monitors	Opportunists
Bear Management	• Grizzly Bear Study Team • Environmental organizations • State governments	• Tourists	• Tourists	• Other areas dealing with bear issues	
Wolf Reintroduction	• Defenders of Wildlife • Wyoming Farm Bureau		• Tourists	• Others interested in reintroduction programs	• Ranchers who receive compensation from Defenders of Wildlife
Winter Use	• Snowmobile groups • Concessionaires • GYC • Fund for Animals	• Snowmobilers	• Snowmobilers • Winter tourists	• Tourists	• Snowcoach operators

Bioprospecting	• Diversa • Edmunds Institute • International Center for Technical Assistance			• Other biotech companies	• Agency staff who receive specialized training to support Diversa
Wildfires	• NPS	• Public	• Public	• Public • Other park agencies interested in fire policy	• Politicians seeking media attention • Media

References

Busenberg, G. (2004). "Wildfire Management in the United States: The Evolution of a Policy Failure." *Review of Policy Research* 21(2): 145–156.

Carle, D. (2002). *Burning Questions: America's Fight with Nature's Fire.* Westport, CT, Praeger Publishers.

Fifer, N. and S. K. Orr (2013). "The Influence of Problem Definitions on Environmental Policy Change: A Comparative Study of the Yellowstone Wildfires." *Policy Studies Journal* 41(4).

Franke, M. A. (2000). "Yellowstone in the Afterglow." Yellowstone National Park, Yellowstone Center for Resources.

Kate, K. T. (1998). "Yellowstone National Park and Diversa Corporation." From http://www.cbd.int/doc/case-studies//abs/cs-abs-yellowstone.pdf.

Lichtman, P. (1998). "The Politics of Wildfire: Lessons from Yellowstone." *Journal of Forestry* 96(5).

Orr, S. K. and R. L. Humphreys (2012). "Mission Rivalry: Use and Preservation Conflicts in National Parks Policy." *Public Organization Review* 12(1): 85–98.

Pyne, S. (1989). "The Summer We Let Wildfire Loose." *Natural History* 98(8).

Sax, J. (1981). *Mountains without Handrails.* Ann Arbor, University of Michigan Press.

Schullery, P. and D. G. Despain (1989). "Prescribed Burning in Yellowstone National Park: A Doubtful Proposition." *Western Wildlands* 15(2).

Williams, T. (2002). "Only You Can Postpone Wildfires." *Sierra Club Magazine* July/August.

Chapter 5

Stakeholder Collaboration Tools

Introduction

As argued throughout this book, "involving a wide range of groups...helps win support, raise awareness and build capacity within key organizations and communities. The investment up-front is substantive, but the results will be rewarding" (Economic and Social Commission for Asia and the Pacific 2001, p. 4). While the previous chapters have explored stakeholder collaboration from more theoretical and case-based perspectives, this chapter explores the practical techniques necessary to encourage and support effective collaboration within a multi-stakeholder environment. The tools presented here have a wide array of applications, but not all tools will be appropriate for all stakeholder audiences. Table 5.1 provides an overview of each of the tools presented in this chapter.

Planning

Every stakeholder engagement effort must include a thoughtful preplanning process in order to be successful. While the specifics of stakeholder activities will vary, there are some general requirements that apply universally to all stakeholder collaborations from advisory councils to public forums. Figure 5.1 is a general outline of the steps necessary to organize stakeholder initiatives.

Step 1 is to identify the *purpose* of the stakeholder collaboration process, specifically the mission and goals. What is the agency hoping to achieve through this

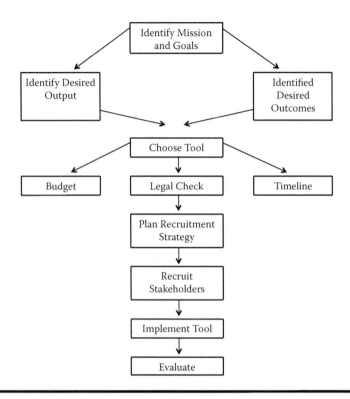

Figure 5.1   Steps to organize stakeholder initiatives.

initiative? This statement should serve as a guide for decision making and measuring progress. The mission is the long-term desired end-result (e.g., protect the watershed) and the goals define the accomplishments necessary to achieve that mission (e.g., identify ways to protect the economic resources of the local watershed and ensure that future generations can do the same). Collaborative arrangements may have both short- and long-term goals. In some cases a purpose statement may need to be revised with input from stakeholders during the initial stages of stakeholder activities.

Step 2 is to determine the *output and outcomes*. Outputs typically refer to the accomplishments or products, while outcomes refer to the impact. For example, the desired output may be a compendium of comments from the public or a set of policy recommendations. The outcomes may be managed use of the watershed and greater awareness of the watershed by the general public.

Using the statements of purpose, outputs, and outcomes will help to *choose the stakeholder collaboration tool* to use, which is step 3. Questions to consider are listed in Table 5.2.

The fourth step is to develop a *budget and timeline*. The budget should include details about all anticipated expenses with exact dollar amounts specified such as staffing, facilities, printing/publication costs, and reimbursements for stakeholders (e.g., transportation, food), and publicity. The timeline should include all tasks to be completed and the names of those responsible. It should be anticipated that some degree of flexibility will be necessary as the planning takes place; ideally all project personnel should be aware that their responsibilities may have to change as necessary.

The fifth step, unique to government agencies, is to determine if there are *statutory or regulatory requirements* that must be followed, for example through the Office of Management and Budget or Federal Advisory Committee Act.

The sixth step is to identify stakeholders and develop a *recruitment plan*. Additional ideas for recruitment are discussed in the Recruitment Tools section. During the *implementation of the recruitment plan*, it is essential to communicate expectations to stakeholders including the purpose, participation requirements, and expectations.

The next step is to *implement* the collaboration, using the guidelines discussed with each of the tools.

The final step is *evaluation*. Although listed as the final step, in fact ongoing evaluation of stakeholder participation is important. By keeping evaluation in mind from the beginning, there is a greater likelihood of being able to make improvements as time goes on, as well as preventing problems from arising in the first place. Having a sense of evaluation indicators prior to beginning the collaboration process will help to keep the process on track and allow for monitoring throughout, rather than simply a final evaluation when it is too late to make changes.

The following evaluation tools can be combined in different ways to create an appropriate evaluation of participation. At minimum, there must be an assessment of whether or not the mission, goals, output, and outcomes were achieved. If not, what went wrong? Were they misidentified in the beginning or was there a failure of implementation? The issue of utility should also be considered: Was it useful? Will the findings be used in a meaningful way as part of the policy process?

Another possibility is to look at quantitative data; for example, the number of stakeholders participating and the scope of that participation. The evaluation could include counting the number of people who participate in town hall meetings, who stop and engage with a road show display, or who leave comments on a Facebook page. A more refined evaluation would include more detail about those numbers: for example, what is the breakdown of demographics at the town halls, and if there were multiple meetings in different areas of the city, which geographic zones were most successful and why? For the road show, how long did people spend interacting with the display? Which parts were most engaging? Careful planning beforehand is vital to ensure that such records are being kept.

Another evaluation tool is to survey stakeholders and government staff involved in stakeholder activities (e.g., speakers, facilitators, event organizers) to solicit their opinion. What worked, what did not work, and what are the areas for improvement are all questions that can be asked here as part of an evaluation.

- Did stakeholders feel their views were heard?
- Did they learn anything during this process?

- Were they satisfied with their own level of participation?
- Did they achieve what they hoped to achieve?
  - What were the strengths and weaknesses of the process?
- What could have been improved?

Qualitative assessments are also important to capture some of the intangibles of the stakeholder participation experience. Description and interpretation are important elements of the qualitative assessment.

Table 5.1 is a summary of all the tools presented in this chapter, along with their purpose, target audience, suggestions for evaluation and degree of effort involved. The table can be used as a quick reference for identifying and comparing stakeholder tools.

Recruitment Tools

Recruiting numbers of stakeholders can be a challenge, but it is one of the cornerstones of a successful stakeholder collaboration project. A quick search of the Internet for engagement examples will result in countless message boards with no posts, Facebook pages with few likes, and Twitter feeds with limited followers. Recruitment must be a part of the planning and implementation of any engagement strategy. There are a number of strategies that can be used to publicize and recruit stakeholders to participate as discussed below.

Networking

One option to recruit stakeholders is to map out the networks of stakeholders—for example, people in a geographic region, or those with an interest in the outdoors—and then try to identify and reach out to leaders of those networks or organizations. This is an opportunity both to test the recruitment message that will be used and to ask leaders to help with recruitment. Once one stakeholder is identified he or she can be asked to identify others who may be interested, a technique commonly referred to as snowball sampling. Similarly, asking other government or organization employees for stakeholder suggestions can be highly effective. An ongoing stakeholder file should be maintained and updated on a regular basis to simplify future recruitment initiatives.

The Federal Register

Many organizations and individuals active in policy issues subscribe to the *Federal Register* as a way to follow policy debates and changes. Posting notices of public meetings in the online *Federal Register* can be one way for federal government agencies to recruit stakeholders, although this is limited to those who are actively engaged in such matters and have a high degree of policy sophistication.

Table 5.1   Stakeholder Tools Summary

	Purpose	Target Audience	Evaluation	Effort
Recruitment Tools				
Networking	Identify stakeholders	Professionals Special interests	Count of numbers of stakeholders	Low
Federal Register	Identify stakeholders	Special interests Government employees	Number of responses	Low
Sampling	Identify stakeholders	All stakeholders	Count of number of stakeholders	Low
Public notices	Recruit stakeholders	General public	Count of number of stakeholders	Low
Stakeholder analysis	Analyze stakeholder interests and needs	For internal use	Follow-up comparison to determine accuracy	Low
Proximity and power	Visualize relationships between stakeholders and government	For internal use	Assessment of utility— did it help the stakeholder collaboration process?	Low
Fishbowl	Share views and be heard	Special interests	Survey of participants and facilitator	Medium
Electoral process	Vote on policy options	General public	Election results Voter turnout	High

(Continued)

Table 5.1   Stakeholder Tools Summary (Continued)

	Purpose	*Target Audience*	*Evaluation*	*Effort*
Imbizo	Dialogue with community	Community Government	Survey or interviews with participants	High
Focus group	Identify interests Share opinions	Special interests	Survey or interviews with participants	Medium
Dot poster	Identify interests Vote on choices	General public	Count of participants	Low
Mobility map	Identify mobility patterns and use	General public Users of a resource Community members	Survey or interview of participants or users of the map	Low
Village walk	Informal sense of a community	Government	Survey or interview of government participants	Low
Seasonal calendar	Document stakeholder activities	General public	Survey or interview of participants or users of the calendars	Low
Participatory cost/benefit analysis	Identify stakeholder preferences	Special interests General public	Survey or interview of participants	Low
Surveys	Identify stakeholder preferences and behavior Solicit ideas	General public Special interests Professionals	Response rate	Medium

(Continued)

Table 5.1 Stakeholder Tools Summary (Continued)

	Purpose	Target Audience	Evaluation	Effort
Public comments	Identify stakeholder preferences Solicit ideas Educate	General public Special interests	Count of responses Assessment of utility— were comments used in a meaningful way?	Low
Experimental auction	Identify how stakeholders value nonmarket goods	General public Special interests	Survey or interviews of participants	Medium
Engagement Tools				
Road show	Engage with stakeholders Educate	General public	Count of visitors Survey or interviews of visitors	High
Community-directed visual images	Capturing stakeholder emotions and perspectives	General public Special interests	Count of images and participants Survey or interviews of participants	Low-high
Listserv	Discussion Education Announcements Updates	Special interests	Count of users Frequency of posts by unique users Survey or interview of users	Low

(Continued)

Table 5.1 Stakeholder Tools Summary (Continued)

	Purpose	*Target Audience*	*Evaluation*	*Effort*
Retreat	Strategic planning Discussion Education	Special interests	Survey or interview of participants	Medium
Town hall meeting	Discussion	General public Community	Attendance Survey or interview of participants	Medium
Historical mapping	Documenting history and change	Community Special interests	Count of participants Survey or interview of participants	Low
Kitchen table discussion	Engage with stakeholders Educate Listen	Community	Count of discussions and number of participants Survey or interview of participants	Medium
Mobile apps	Engagement Education Entertainment	General public Special interests	Count of downloads Ratings and reviews	High
Field trip	Education Team building	Special interests	Survey or interview of participants	Medium
Citizen jury	Engagement Identify opinions and beliefs Education	Randomly selected citizens	Survey or interview of participants	High

(Continued)

Table 5.1 Stakeholder Tools Summary (Continued)

	Purpose	*Target Audience*	*Evaluation*	*Effort*
Partnership grants	Pilot projects	Special interests	Survey or interview of participants	Medium
Public forum	Answer questions Education	General public	Attendance Count of questions Survey or interview of participants	Medium
Social media	Engagement Education Identify perspectives Networking Recruiting stakeholders Announcements and updates Solicit ideas Publicity	General public Special interests Government	Count of users Count of active participants Survey of users	Low-high
Impact/effort matrix	Prioritize ideas	Special interests Government	Assessment of utility	Low
Charrette	Develop and refine ideas	Special interests	Survey or interview of participants	Medium
Force Field Analysis	Identify and assess factors working for and against a decision	Special interests Government	Survey or interview of participants	Low

(Continued)

Table 5.1 Stakeholder Tools Summary (Continued)

	Purpose	Target Audience	Evaluation	Effort
Ranking and sorting	Understand preferences Decide among choices	General public Special interests	Survey or interview of participants	Low
Problem tree	Visualize causes and consequences	General public Special interests	Survey or interview of participants	Low
Consensus workshop	Identify policy solutions Strategic thinking	Special interests	Survey or interview of participants	Medium
Social audit	Evaluate performance	Special interests General public Government	Survey or interview of participants Assessment of utility	High
Citizen Report Card/ Community Scorecard	Increase accountability and responsiveness	Government Special interests General public	Survey or interview of participants Assessment of utility	High
Delphi study	Generate ideas	Special interests	Survey or interview of participants	Medium
Concentric circles	Prioritize ideas	Special interests General public	Survey or interview of participants Assessment of utility	Low
Risk chart	Strategic thinking about risk	Special interests	Survey or interview of participants	Low

(Continued)

Table 5.1   Stakeholder Tools Summary (Continued)

	Purpose	*Target Audience*	*Evaluation*	*Effort*
Open-ended stories	Strategic thinking Icebreaker Reduce conflict	Special interests Children	Survey or interview of participants	Low
Advisory committee	Strategic thinking Consultation	Special interests	Survey or interview of participants Assessment of utility	Medium
Resident's panel	Public input in decision making	General public	Survey or interview of participants	Medium
SWOT analysis	Strategic thinking	Special interests	Survey or interview of participants	Medium
Brain-storming	Generating ideas	Special interests	Survey or interview of participants	Medium
Education Tools				
Public exhibition	Education Publicity	General public	Count of visitors Survey or interview of visitors	Low
Speakers' bureau	Education Engagement Publicity	General public	Count of speeches Survey or interview of speakers and audience members	Medium

(Continued)

Table 5.1 Stakeholder Tools Summary (Continued)

	Purpose	*Target Audience*	*Evaluation*	*Effort*
Website	Education Limited engagement	General public Special interests	Count of visits Survey of visitors	Medium
Storefront	Education Engagement	General public	Count of visits Survey or interview of visitors	High
Deliberative polling	Education Track opinion changes	Random sample of citizens	Survey or interview of participants	Medium
Workshop	Education	General public Special interests	Survey or interview of participants	Medium
Conference	Education Share information	Special interests Government	Survey or interview of participants	Medium-high
Technical report	Share research or policy findings	Special interests Government	Count of readers (e.g., downloads) Review and critique by other experts	Medium-high
Press conference	Share information Publicity	Media General public	Count of media that attend and amount of coverage	Medium

(Continued)

Table 5.1   Stakeholder Tools Summary (Continued)

	Purpose	*Target Audience*	*Evaluation*	*Effort*
Telephone hotline	Education Answer questions	General public	Count of calls Survey of callers	Low-high
Brochure	Education Refer to other sources of information	General public	Count of number of brochures distributed	Low-medium
Agency open house	Education Engagement Networking Identifying and recruiting stakeholders	General public Special interests Government	Count of visitors Exit survey	Low-medium
Mailouts	Education Publicity	General public Special interests	Counts of mailouts Survey of recipients	Low-medium
Public speaking	Education Publicity	General public Community organiza-tions	Count of speeches Survey of participants	Low-medium
Featured media stories	Share information Publicity Education	Media General public	Count of number of feature stories Review of online comments for stories on the Internet	Medium

(Continued)

Table 5.1 Stakeholder Tools Summary (Continued)

	Purpose	*Target Audience*	*Evaluation*	*Effort*
Inserts and advertisements In newspapers	Share information Publicity	Media General public	Count of distribution	Medium
Newsletters	Share information Education Publicity News and updates	Special interests	Count of distribution Survey of readers	Medium
Project Management Tools				
Meeting planning tools	Run effective meetings and events	For internal use	Assessment of utility	Low
Project scope chart	Project organization	For internal use	Assessment of utility	Low
Gantt chart	Project time management	For internal use	Assessment of utility	Low
Logical framework	Strategic planning	For internal use	Assessment of utility	Low
Communication and Teamwork Tools				
Communication needs assessment	Identify communication needs of stakeholders	For internal use	Assessment of utility	Low
Active listening	Promote communication	For internal use	Assessment of utility	Low-medium
Stakeholder introductions	Improve group dynamics	Participants at events	Assessment of utility Feedback from participants	Low

(Continued)

Table 5.1   Stakeholder Tools Summary (Continued)

	Purpose	*Target Audience*	*Evaluation*	*Effort*
Team-building exercises	Improve group dynamics Improve communication skills	Participants at events	Assessment of utility Feedback from participants	Low

Sampling

Sampling techniques can be useful when large numbers of participants are required, especially from the general population. *Systematic sampling* can be used when there is a list of members of the population (e.g., households or individuals) of interest. In this case every member is assigned a number, and then every nth number (e.g., every second or fifth or tenth) is chosen for the sample until the desired sample size is reached. In a *simple random sample* a list of households, people, or some other unit is created and each is assigned a number. Using a random number generator (easily found online), each unit that matches the random numbers is selected as a participant. A more low-tech option is to put each number (or name) into a basket and draw one by one from the basket until the desired sample size is chosen. In a *stratified random sample* groups (or strata) of the population are separated into categories (e.g., tent campers, RV campers, lodge visitors, day-use visitors at a park), and then a random sample is chosen from each group. This method ensures that a sufficient number of participants are selected from each group.

To create a *cluster sample* groups or clusters are identified and randomly sampled. From each sampled cluster, the individual subjects are selected by random sampling. For example, to survey university student attitudes toward energy conservation in Ohio, the investigator would make a list of all of the universities in Ohio and take a random sample of those universities. Then a random sample of students would be selected from each of those universities.

Public Notices

The distribution of public notices can be another way to recruit stakeholders. Examples here include advertisements in local media, billboards, featured stories in newspapers, announcements in local utility bills, inserts in newspapers, signs on public vehicles such as garbage trucks, and posters in public places.

Table 5.2   Questions to Consider When Choosing a Collaboration Tool

Questions	Options and Considerations
What kinds of collaboration are feasible?	• Online • Short-term or long-term • One in-person meeting • A series of in-person meetings
Who will run the meetings/events?	• A substantive chairperson has expertise in the policy issue • A process chairperson has meeting management and/or conflict resolution skills • Some issue areas will need one or both depending on the circumstances
How many voices should be included?	• Are there people who should participate but face barriers? • How can participation be facilitated to reach those who should be involved?
How will decisions be made?	• Individual opinion—each stakeholder gives his or her opinion with no attempt to reconcile the opinions of others (e.g., comment cards at a public meeting). • Convergence of opinions—identify one or more general themes within the group. • General concurrence—facilitator announces general sense of the group and unless someone disagrees strongly, that is the decision. • Weighing the dissent—determine if dissent is strongly felt (e.g., ask dissenter to obtain a second, show of hands to identify who agrees with dissenter). • Voting—a majority or supermajority (usually 2/3 or 3/4). A majority and minority report can be included with the vote record. • Consensus—there are many variations here, but essentially the group affirmatively concurs with a decision. • Government makes the decision.

(Continued)

Table 5.2   Questions to Consider When Choosing a Collaboration Tool (Continued)

Questions	Options and Considerations
What type of records will be kept?	• Note taking • Videotaping • Photos • Archive
What are the limitations?	• Funding • Staffing • Confidentiality concerns • Regulatory requirements

Social Media

The use of social media, discussed in greater detail in the Engagement Tools section of this chapter, can be an excellent tool for recruitment. For example, posting information on Facebook and Twitter can be a cost-effective way to identify and recruit stakeholders.

Identifying Stakeholder Interests

Stakeholder Analysis

As part of the collaboration process, it may be useful to formally identify and map out stakeholder interests, including both overt and hidden interests. This level of analysis will help to sort out threats and potential conflicts, as well as assist in identifying potential allies and assets. Decision makers must make two critical assessments: namely, how could each stakeholder pose a threat, and what is their contribution to the process, and what, if any, threats do they pose? A number of authors have developed ways to analyze stakeholder interests (Bryson 2003; Smith and Love 2004; Kirby 2006; West and Clark 2006). Table 5.3 is a synthesis of these different approaches into one straightforward analytical tool. Creating a table for each potential stakeholder (within reason, of course) can help to track interests and think about the different roles individual stakeholders or groups may play in the process.

Proximity and Power Diagram

Another tool to help understand stakeholders is a proximity and power diagram to visually illustrate the relationships between stakeholders and the organization

Table 5.3   Stakeholder Analysis

Stakeholder	Group name/representative(s)
Interest	List specific interests
Level of interest	Estimate level of interest (e.g., low to high)
Resources available	What can the stakeholder bring to the process (e.g., legitimacy, financial support, volunteers)?
Who does the stakeholder represent?	For example, citizens, business interests
What does the stakeholder want?	Protect interests, gather information, and so on, as discussed in Chapter 2
Type of stakeholder	Player, would-be player, curious, defensive monitor, opportunist (see Chapter 2)
Issue position	Supportive, mixed, antagonistic, unclear, etc.
Preferred form of communication	For example, e-mail, social networking, postal, telephone

(Figure 5.2). The first step is to draw a rectangle in the middle of a page and write the name of the organization inside. The next step is to write out a list of stakeholders and rate them on their importance to the organization and the closeness of the relationship with the organization. Next, stakeholders are drawn in circles around the main center circle, with each stakeholder in one circle. Large circles indicate high importance and small circles indicate low importance. The closeness of the stakeholder to the organization is represented by the closeness of the circle to the organization in the center.

The following questions should be asked after the mapping is completed: Is there anything unexpected or unusual? Are there any patterns that can be observed, particularly in terms of closeness to the organization (e.g., is one set of stakeholders consistently farther away?)? Is there anyone who should have a stronger relationship? Is there anyone who is missing? Are there any problems or opportunities apparent from the diagram?

In the figure, Stakeholder A is of high importance and has a close relationship with the agency; however, Stakeholder B is of low importance and also has a close relationship with the agency. This suggests that the agency may be spending unnecessary time and energy on the relationship with Stakeholder B. Stakeholder C, who is identified as being of high importance, does not have a close relationship with the agency, which may be a liability.

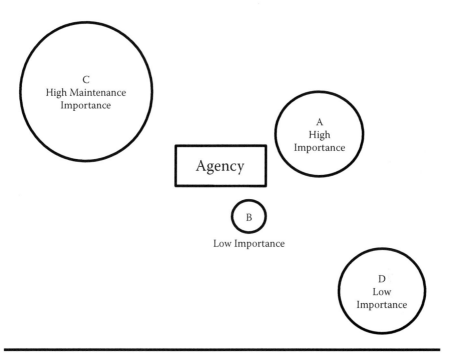

Figure 5.2   Proximity and power diagram for stakeholder analysis.

Fishbowl

A fishbowl exercise is a safe discussion space where participants in a small- to medium-size group can voice their opinions without direct challenges from others, which can help to reduce tensions and also create opportunities for other opinions and ideas to be heard. Fishbowl exercises traditionally involve two concentric rings of participants. The inside circle discusses the issue while the outside ring observes.

The role of the observers is to learn and listen to the discussion so they can later contribute feedback. The participants in the inner circle are led by a designated facilitator who ensures that the discussion flows properly and that everyone in the group is given an opportunity to speak. After the discussion, small groups made up of representatives from both the inner and outer circles can discuss what transpired. This allows individuals to gain perspectives from each other. Alternatively, the circles can switch, and the observers become the discussants and vice versa. The final discussion is conducted with the entire group to process the events of the fishbowl exercise. This discussion is important to gain general reactions of the individuals to the fishbowl. The final question of the exercise should be posed at the end of the discussion asking individuals what they learned from the exercise.

Fishbowl exercises may be particularly useful when there are two different "sides" to an issue, as this can force each side to hear the other without arguing or thinking about a response. For example, if an issue divides property owners and environmentalists, this may be an opportunity for them to understand the underlying interests of their different positions.

Electoral Process

A ballot initiative, proposition, plebiscite, referendum, or vote on a ballot question is another way to engage citizen stakeholders and identify interests. The ballot is a direct vote on a policy proposal or piece of legislation. Depending on electoral law, the referendum may originate from a petition by citizens (often called an initiative) or from the legislature (often called a referendum). Depending on the circumstances, these efforts may be binding or nonbinding. A nonbinding ballot question means that the results will be used under advisement by the government. A measure may be approved through different means—for example, a simple majority of votes, a supermajority, or a majority of districts voting in favor. These measures are a form of direct democracy, engaging citizen stakeholders directly in the electoral process. Ballot measures can be an expensive process, as those representing both sides of the issue become involved in campaigns to sway voters and increase turnout of their supporters.

Imbizo*

Imbizo is the Zulu word for *gathering*. A popular stakeholder engagement tool in South Africa, the Imbizo can be applied to other contexts as well. During the Imbizo, the president and other government officials travel to remote communities to meet with local people to exchange views and engage in a dialogue about community issues. In its traditional form, as an important part of the indigenous African political system for centuries, the Imbizo is more than just a communication tool; it is intended to also be a sharing of information that will be used for future decision making, and in particular to improve the implementation of policy and service delivery.

The Imbizo may combine site and project visits (e.g., schools, factories, parks, rivers), formal stakeholder meetings, community gatherings, and informal discussions. Although the government may have issues for an agenda, the community should also be allowed to raise new agenda items.

In many ways, the Imbizo is a tool of evaluation, whereby decision makers and those with political authority go out and see or experience the effects of the policies that have been passed. The Imbizo is intended to increase transparency and accountability and promote inclusivity and participation in decision making. The Imbizo implicitly recognizes the value of lay and indigenous

---

* For more information on Imbizo see Hartslief, O. (2005). "The South African Presidential Participation Programme (Presidential Imbizo): Engaging Communities for a Better Life." International Conference on Engaging Communities. Queensland, Australia.

knowledge. The Imbizo works when those with the power to make changes and decisions participate and when the citizens are able to speak and share honestly. The Imbizo does not work if government officials are not willing to make changes based on what they have learned or if the citizens are not forthcoming about their experiences, thoughts, and ideas, for instance, because of fear of retribution of some kind, loss of funding, or an unwillingness to discuss failures or embarrass the government.

Focus Group

Focus groups facilitate two-way communication and learning between stakeholders and government. In decision making, a focus group can be an important way to discuss and evaluate decisions and identify stakeholder interests. The goal of the discussion is to tap into feelings and beliefs of the participants on a particular topic to understand how and why opinions are formed.

A good focus group begins with planning. The purpose of the focus group should be identified and clarified. The quality of the output from a focus group first and foremost depends on the participants. Thinking carefully about which stakeholders to invite so that the organization can effectively achieve their purpose can make a significant difference in the final result. Typically focus groups are made up of five to ten (or up to twenty-five) individuals who represent a particular interest directly related to the decisions that need to be made.

Krueger (1994) developed an outline to guide a focus group that is useful for stakeholder engagement. The first step is to begin with group introductions and a quick overview of the purpose of the focus group. Nametags can be helpful for encouraging participants to build on each other's ideas and become more comfortable in the setting. The first question should be an easy, noncontroversial introduction to help everyone feel comfortable with the process. Introductory questions can help the group to warm up by discussing their own experiences within the general topic of the focus group. Transition topics take the discussion to a broader scope and highlight how opinions may be diverse. The key questions (five or six) are the heart of the discussion and are derived from the purpose of the focus group. Ending questions deal with encouraging participants to summarize their positions and to give feedback on the facilitator's interpretation of the group results/discussion. One thing to keep in mind is that a focus group is not a forum to change minds and opinions. While that may be an unintentional consequence of the discussion, it is in no way the purpose of the focus group. There are no "winners" or arguments here; it is the open sharing of thoughts of all the participants.

There are a number of options for capturing the information from a focus group. The most common technique is to use a combination of note taking and audiotape. Some participants may not feel comfortable being videotaped, and it may hinder the discussion. Participants must be told if they are being taped. While audio taping can be helpful, it does not capture the nonverbal expression of individuals and it may be difficult to identify who is speaking. If audio taping is going to be used, and the facilitator limits his or her note taking accordingly, it is very important then that the audio recording is in fact analyzed/transcribed afterward. If the facilitator is not willing to put in the time and energy to use the audiotape afterward, then valuable information will be lost unless the notes were comprehensive.

The role of the facilitator is to run the discussion without either dominating or unduly influencing responses. When facilitating a focus group it is important to ensure that all participants have the opportunity to speak and that a select few do not dominate the discussion. If necessary, quieter participants may be called on to answer questions to ensure that their opinions are heard. The facilitator should bring objectivity and expertise to the process. The facilitator should be someone who is good at drawing people out, controlling a group, listening, and summarizing quickly. At no point should the facilitator be involved in the discussion such as by agreeing or disagreeing with something that has been said. The facilitator guides the discussion, keeps it on track, ensures that a respectful discussion takes place, and ensures that everyone gets an opportunity to speak. The facilitator should be careful not to dominate the group but needs to be assertive enough to keep the group on task. Before the session the facilitator should plan out the questions and topics to be discussed. These should be relatively detailed as a focus group is typically a structured discussion, more like a group interview than a free-flowing conversation. A good facilitator will be able to provide objective conclusions based on the interpretation of the discussion.

Focus groups should not go longer than 90 minutes, although participants should be told it is a two-hour exercise to give some flexibility. In that time period no more than five main questions, each with subquestions and/or probes for more information, should be asked. Running more than one focus group on the same topic will ensure that the results of one focus group were not due to unusual group dynamics, such as the persuasive skills or aggressive communication style of one participant.

Focus groups are not without their challenges. They can be a time-intensive operation involving planning, recruitment, meeting, analysis of results, and evaluation. Combative participants or a weak facilitator can derail focus groups. Focus groups are a good choice when the participants will all be able to speak openly and comfortably and if the organization needs more in-depth information than can be obtained through other means such as a survey. Focus groups do not always work well when the topics are sensitive and personal, as participants may be uncomfortable sharing that information in a group setting. Focus groups can also be used when it is important for stakeholders to have a sense of being listened to, or even to feel empowered. The opportunity to be listened to can have powerfully positive unintended consequences for participants of focus groups. Lastly, focus groups may also be appropriate when it is necessary to determine if there is a true consensus among stakeholders on an issue, a nuance that may not be obvious from a survey.

Dot Poster

Dot posters can be a useful tool to visually display individual preferences within a group. Decision choices, generated either by the agency or by stakeholders, are listed on large pieces of paper posted on a wall. Each person is given a sticker, usually a color circle, to put on the paper to mark his or her preference. This can be customized depending on the situation; for example, it can be used to rank preferences, where blue indicates first choice, red indicates second, and so on. Or different groups/regions/interests can each have a different color to see how choices vary. It may also be worthwhile to note demographic information about the respondents to ensure that the participants are representative of the population of interest. A dot poster could be used for example at a farmer's market to identify where people live (which provides information about awareness of the market and how far people are willing to travel) or how much they value organic food.

A dot poster can help to get a sense of a group's preferences and how different options are ranked. Everyone can see how others feel and how their opinions compare with the rest. Dot posters also allow everyone a voice, not just those who speak the loudest. Dot posters can be used in combination with many of the other tools here, such as public forums, conferences, and road shows. A record of the posters can be kept by simply taking a picture of each poster. Dot posters are inexpensive and easy to use, can be set up almost anywhere, and are faster than administering a survey. The major downside is "social desirability bias" whereby some individuals may feel uncomfortable deviating from the majority. It is up to the decision makers to decide if this is an issue.

*Mobility Map**

A mobility map illustrates patterns of spatial mobility for a neighborhood or community. A mobility map can be drawn on top of an actual map of the area, or a blank piece of paper can be used with a central point identified for reference. Stakeholders are asked to indicate important places, the locations they visit, or routes along which they travel by marking them on the map/paper and labeling them for reference. Although the map can be developed with the aid of cartographers, a mobility map can also be simply sketched on a piece of paper or chalkboard. Distances and scale are not important; rather the goal is to identify centers and patterns of activity. If transportation and access are important, different colors and symbols can be used to highlight how people get to these places (e.g., walking, drive, bus, carpool). Thick lines can indicate activities that are undertaken most frequently or by the most people. Depending on the audience and purpose there are

---

* For more information see Beck, C. (1997). *Introduction of a Participatory and Integrated Development Process (PIDEP) in Kalomo District, Zambia, Volume 1.* Weikersheim, Margraf Verlag.

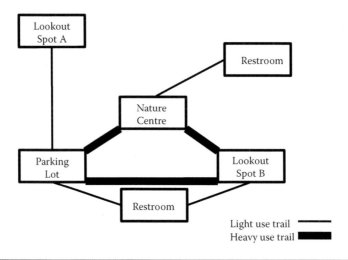

Figure 5.3 Mobility map of city nature preserve.

additional ways to customize the map such as by season, time spent, necessity, aesthetics, or amenities. A mobility map can be used to identify future walking trails, bus routes, issues of accessibility, and the like. The mobility map in Figure 5.3 can be used to make decisions about trail maintenance and facility upgrades. Lookout Spot A is underutilized, suggesting that additional research is necessary to determine why; perhaps new signage is necessary or there are barriers to access that need to be addressed.

Village Walk*

For government workers doing fieldwork in a new community, the opportunity to get an informal sense of the community and stakeholders can be invaluable. A guided walk through the community can help to develop an understanding of the problems and potential of the area, as well as familiarity with the terrain, amenities, population, and surroundings. This can also be a time for a more casual conversation with a few stakeholder "tour guides" about the history, the people, resources, facilities, outsider groups, and special concerns.

Typically a village walk involves a small group led by one or two local people. Larger groups may need to be broken into smaller groups to facilitate informal conversation during the tour. This is an opportunity to talk, observe, and contextualize. Afterward, the groups should have a debriefing session without their guides to discuss their observations and experiences.

---

* For more information see Case, D. A. D. (1990). *The Community's Toolbox: The Idea, Methods and Tools for Participatory Assessment, Monitoring and Evaluation in Community Forestry.* Rome, Food and Agriculture Organization of the United Nations.

Seasonal Calendar*

For policy issues that have a seasonal component—for example, use of natural areas—a seasonal calendar can be one way for stakeholders to document their activities over the calendar year. Seasonal calendars can be used to identify workloads, resource use, income patterns, gender differences, or variation in productivity over time.

A group of stakeholders can create the calendar by discussing each month in turn and discussing what should be filled in, or individuals can each complete their own. Afterward, a discussion can examine patterns, strengths, weaknesses, opportunities, and challenges that are apparent from looking at the calendar. Table 5.4 is a sample seasonal calendar highlighting threats to local agriculture throughout the year, which can be used for planning.

Table 5.5 includes categories of visitation at a local nature preserve, which can be used to make decisions about hours of operation and staffing needs.

Table 5.4   Threats to Local Agriculture

	Predators	Flooding	Parasites	Drought
Jan			High	
Feb			High	
Mar	High		Low	
Apr	High	High	Low	
May	High	High	Low	High
Jun	High		High	High
Jul	High		High	High
Aug	High		High	
Sept	High		Low	
Oct			Low	
Nov			Low	
Dec			High	

---

* For more information see Guijt, I. and J. Woodhill (2002). *Managing for Impact in Rural Development: A Guide for Project M & E.* Rome, Italy: International Fund for Agricultural Development.

Table 5.5 Seasonal Calendar for Local Nature Preserve Activities

	Day Trip Visits	Overnight Activity	School Groups
Jan	Snow shoeing	Lodge	Low
Feb			Low
Mar			High
Apr	Hiking		High
May		Camping and Lodge	High
Jun			High
Jul			No group visits
Aug			
Sept		Lodge	
Oct	Few visitors		
Nov			Low
Dec			Low

Participatory Cost/Benefit Analysis[*]

Participatory cost/benefit analysis is a tool to both identify stakeholders' preferences and educate people about the implications (costs and benefits) of different policy options.

Participants may be selected from stakeholder lists or through a general call to the public. The facilitator begins by providing an overview of the issue and the policy options to ensure that there is a common basis of understanding. The presentation of the options should be done in a carefully neutral manner. Participants are presented with a number of policy options and asked to identify the costs associated with each, including for example materials, supplies, and labor. Dollar values are assigned to each cost and a total cost is calculated. The same exercise is repeated with the benefits of each option. The total cost is compared with the total benefit as a ratio of cost/benefit. The ratio for each policy is calculated and the stakeholders then discuss the results. This exercise can help stakeholders think strategically and comparatively about different policy options, but it is limited by the fact that arithmetic skills and a certain degree of expertise are required to identify and value the costs and benefits. Although this is an exercise that may be better suited to

---

[*] For more information see Bamberger, M., J. Rugh, et al. (2012). *Real-World Evaluation: Working under Budget, Time, Data, and Political Constraints.* Thousand Oaks, CA, Sage.

stakeholders with some expertise in the issue area, it is a valuable experience for helping participants to better understand the challenges of policymaking and an opportunity to get different perspectives on the costs and benefits of policy.

Surveys

Surveys can be a useful tool for identifying stakeholder perspectives and concerns, as well as to generate ideas. The advantages are numerous: it is easy to reach large numbers of people, they can produce quantitative or qualitative results, and they can be offered online or in hard copy. Surveys can be used to obtain a variety of information including facts, behavior, opinion, attitudes/beliefs, motives, and knowledge. The disadvantages of surveys as collaborative tools are that they do not really facilitate in-depth responses, response rates may be low, and it can be a challenge to present sufficient background on the issue without losing the attention of the respondent.

A well-designed survey should in a sense tell a story, with a clear introduction, plot development (in the form of sections made up of questions that flow together), and a conclusion. Surveys should begin with a few easy warm-up questions to help people get comfortable; personal questions should be saved for later in the survey. Questions about demographics (e.g., age, gender) should be included only if they are actually relevant and should go at the end as they can turn people off from completing the survey. It is important to have sensitivity about what people feel comfortable sharing in a survey. People may be unwilling to answer because they are not comfortable sharing information with a stranger, fear their opinions are wrong or they will be ridiculed, or are uncertain about the appropriateness of their answer or how the information will be used. The introduction of the survey should address these concerns.

In terms of developing questions, there are a few guidelines to keep in mind. All instructions should be clearly worded—for example, "check all that apply" or "check the most important issue to you." Questions must be written at the level of the audience who will be taking it; for example, the use of acronyms or lingo should be avoided unless the administrator is certain that the target audience will understand it. Items must be clear and precise. For example, asking the question "Do you work every day of the week?" may create confusion over whether a week is Monday–Friday or Monday–Sunday in this context.

Wherever possible, questions should avoid the use of negative items as people will often read over those words; for example, "The boat ramp should not be closed on Sunday" may be misinterpreted by respondents. A better question would be "Should the boat ramp be closed on Sunday?" Questions should not include biased terms and items that lead the respondent in a particular direction.

Open-ended questions require the respondent to write out a response: for example, "Why do you think some people do not recycle at home?" These questions can help to identify the range of possible responses and avoid bias that a list of options can introduce, and they can be a way to get rich, detailed comments from people, giving them a chance to elaborate if they so choose. However, the survey administrators must then read and interpret the answers, a time-consuming endeavor, and may introduce bias due to misinterpretation. Closed-ended questions require respondents to select an answer from the options provided by the administrator. Response options in this case must be exhaustive (or include an "other" option) and mutually exclusive, meaning they do not overlap.

A survey should go through a pilot testing process whereby a small group of people takes the survey to identifying potentially confusing or problematic questions. Those in the pilot test should have the same reading level and expertise as those who will be taking the actual survey.

Online surveys are cost effective (and can be free using Google Forms) and straightforward to administer, but it may be difficult to get respondents unless there is a comprehensive list available of their e-mail addresses. Surveys distributed through social media such as Facebook and Twitter and posted on a website tend to have very low response rates. Mail-back surveys, which are distributed through the mail, in newspapers, or in municipal bills, are more expensive to distribute due to printing and mailing costs; however, they typically have a wider reach in terms of audience and are likely to get more responses.

Ensuring a good response rate is always a challenge. Providing return postage will help to encourage people to return surveys, as will sending out reminders and providing incentives to respond such as a token gift (e.g., a bookmark), or entering respondents into a raffle drawing. Giving recipients a compelling reason to take the survey—for example, details on how this will affect decision making—will also encourage more people to take the survey.

Public Comments

Public comments may be solicited online, at public events, or by mail. The purpose is usually to obtain a broad sense of public opinion, give people the opportunity to speak, or generate new and innovative solutions to public problems (although this is rarely successful). Before a public comment period is begun, it is important to think about what the purpose and goals are for such an activity; will the comments actually be integrated into decision making, and what will be done with the information that is learned?

Because public comment opportunities can often be abused, it is often advisable to include some sort of accountability measures for public comments. If comments are to be solicited online and published as they are posted, then it may be important to moderate the postings to remove posts that are offensive or spam. The guidelines for moderating and for appropriate posts should be clearly indicated. For example, while anonymous posts may be appropriate in some cases, most organizations require at least an e-mail address, a zip code, or a region, if not full name and contact information, to limit problems. The downside is that such control may discourage honest critique; the advantage, however, is that it promotes account-ability and validity in the comments. It can also be an excellent way to generate a contact list of concerned citizens for future projects.

Participants should be informed of ways to follow the rest of the proceedings, for example, via a website or Facebook page or by signing up for news and reports.

*Experimental Auction**

An experimental auction is a tool to determine the monetary value that people place on nonmarket goods. For example, how much are people willing to pay for clean air or for an endangered species? These are critical questions, especially for a government trying to determine if the benefits of policy outweigh the costs to provide them. Traditional methods to try to answer these questions often involve asking people directly how much they would spend for something or figuring out some sort of proxy dollar value; for example, calculating how much people spend to visit the Grand Canyon gives an approximation of how much they believe it is worth. Experimental auctions can be used to identify the preferences and values held by stakeholders.

There is an alternative, however. Rather than using hypothetical questions about how people might behave, or making inferences based on quasi-related behavior, experimental auctions involve people using real money for real goods in an active market. In the experimental auction, people bid to buy real goods and products. There are many variations on the experimental auction. One strat-egy is to have people bid to upgrade from a typical good (e.g., a bag of apples) to a new good (e.g., a bag of organic apples); the difference between the two prices is how much people value the "organic" label in real money terms. A second design is where people bid simultaneously on two (or more) items, such as organic and nonorganic bags of apples, and then a random drawing is done to determine which auction is binding. A third option is a sealed-bid auction where participants simultaneously submit sealed bids and the participant with the highest bid wins. Another variation of the sealed bid auction is a "second price auction" (also called a Vickrey auction) in which the winner (who sub-mitted the highest bid) buys the good at the price listed in the second-highest bid (Lusk 2007, p. 310). The advantage of this type of stakeholder engagement is that it helps them to think about the value of goods and services in a more meaningful way, while also providing government with valuable information about monetary value.

---

* For more information see Lusk, J. L. and J. Shogren (2007). *Experimental Auctions: Methods and Applications in Economic and Marketing Research.* Cambridge, Cambridge University Press.

Engagement Tools

Road Show

A road show approach to stakeholder engagement is a way to bring the stakeholder engagement process directly to the stakeholders, rather than waiting for them to volunteer. The road show is a self-contained mobile unit that goes to where stakeholders or the general public gather such as conferences, malls, schools, and local fairs and may include displays, interactive activities, speakers, performances, models, and the like. A road show can function as a mobile workshop as well, hosting on-site small group educational discussions. Technology can be a way to make a road show more engaging and interactive—for example, having a poll or survey available on a tablet device, trivia games, contests, or videos. Technology is not the only option. Many of the other tools presented in this section such as historical mapping and dot posters are appropriate for a road show. While it is easy to target a large number of people with a road show, the quality of the interaction may be low due to the short amount of time spent with each individual. This should be taken into account during the design of the road show.

Community-Directed Visual Images[*]

Community-directed visual images involve creating drawings, photographs, or videos that are directed by the stakeholders in order to convey a message or capture the emotions of a policy issue. Stakeholders can either create the images themselves, or they can direct a professional artist or photographer to help create them. Images can be uploaded to an online forum, sent in via post, or created on-site during a stakeholder event. During the Rio+20 negotiations discussed earlier, stakeholders around the world posted photos of "sustainability," creating a provocative montage of the global environment.

One advantage of this tool is that it can be a way to engage stakeholders who may be hesitant to speak up vocally. Making drawing tools available at a stakeholder event and asking people to draw (e.g., their vision for a new public park) may help people to feel more comfortable sharing their ideas. It may be necessary to have stakeholders add a short narrative of explanation, as amateur drawings may not always be clear.

These community-directed visual images could be used to help outsiders understand a particular context through the eyes of the people or can be used as part of an information-gathering process whereby stakeholders visually document a problem. They can help to share information such as group dynamics that may be difficult to explain using other means such as a focus group. This is also a way to engage those

---

[*] For more information see Case, D. A. D. (1990). *The Community's Toolbox: The Idea, Methods and Tools for Participatory Assessment, Monitoring and Evaluation in Community Forestry.* Rome, Food and Agriculture Organization of the United Nations.

who may be illiterate or speak a different language. Using a smartphone, capturing photos or video is now an easy process that can be widely shared. At its most simple, stakeholders could be sent out for an hour to create a video with a smartphone. At the other extreme the stakeholders would sketch out a narrative they want to share, meet with a videographer, shoot the necessary footage, edit, and reshoot as necessary to create a more polished and professional production. The decision of where to fall along that continuum depends on the purpose of the exercise and the time and resources available.

Listserv

A Listserv can be another option to engage a large number of stakeholders in an ongoing discussion, as well as to disseminate news and reminders. A Listserv is a means to distribute information to an entire group at once by sending a message to one e-mail address; everyone who receives the e-mail is considered to be a subscriber to that list. Listservs are typically used to deliver information about events, to share news, and to serve as limited discussion forums. They can also be a way to connect stakeholders with complementary interests; for example, farmers can post the food they have available to sell that day, and chefs can post what they are looking for, as a way to promote the development of a local food movement. Stakeholders can engage in a discussion about issues that are of interest to them at their own convenience over e-mail.

There are a few guidelines for developing a good Listserv. A Google search for *Listserv or e-mail list management software* will show many options for free or paid Listserv services, and many Internet providers/website hosts also include Listserv services in their packages. Most Listservs are moderated, meaning a moderator approves each message that gets posted. This is intended not to screen out critical messages but rather to limit spam and off-topic messages, which are irritating to Listserv members. Members should receive a periodic reminder of how to remove themselves from the list, which means they will no longer receive messages or be able to post messages to the list. To control the number of messages, if members are posting questions asking for ideas (e.g., references on human-wildlife interactions), it is a good idea to encourage other members to respond personally ("off list") to the person asking the question; this person can then send one e-mail summarizing all the responses.

Retreat

A stakeholder retreat is an opportunity for stakeholders to get away as a group to focus on issues, strategic planning, or decision making. A retreat may be as simple as a few hours at an off-site, neutral location or a more elaborate multiple-day trip. The intention is to create a focused, distraction-free environment where stakeholders can fully engage with the topics at hand. The location should be accessible and quiet with all of the necessary amenities available such as washrooms, food preparation areas if necessary, computer/technology needs (including Wi-Fi), and space for meeting or working. The hosts should provide all the food necessary, although if a lack of funds makes this difficult, participants should be made aware in advance to bring their own food.

Like all stakeholder activities, planning is essential for a successful retreat. The facilitator(s) and participants should have a clear idea of the purpose and goals of the retreat, and there should be an agenda of activities to ensure those are accomplished. Many of the tools listed in this chapter can be applied to a retreat such as focus groups, brainstorming, and fishbowls.

Town Hall Meeting*

A town hall meeting is an opportunity for citizen stakeholders to engage in discussion, work through issues, and discuss pros, cons, strengths, and weaknesses of different ideas. The town hall meeting is typically open to everyone in the community and participants are given the opportunity to voice their opinion, as well as ask questions directly of public figures.

Advertising is an important part of a town hall meeting. Publicity may include advertisements on city vehicles (such as garbage trucks), ads in the local newspaper, social media, and flyers sent out via mail or in utility bills. A moderator who is skilled at keeping a meeting running smoothly and handling conflict is essential. In many cases the moderator is a neutral person chosen for his or her moderating skills, and the public officials are available to answer questions. The meeting should have an agenda with ample time for public feedback and questions.

Historical Mapping†

Historical mapping is a very simple tool to help stakeholders focus on documenting the history of a problem or change in a community. A timeline is displayed—for example, poster boards with years posted chronologically around a room. Participants then work either individually or as a group to post relevant events under each of the dates. By encouraging stakeholders to post their events even if they are duplicates, facilitators can get a sense of the importance of each event. Individuals could also be given a sheet of star stickers to indicate their support for events that have been posted as another way to measure relevance and importance.

---

* For more information see Bryan, F. (2003). *Real Democracy: The New England Town Meeting and How It Works*. Chicago, University of Chicago Press.
† For more information see Case, D. A. D. (1990). *The Community's Toolbox: The Idea, Methods and Tools for Participatory Assessment, Monitoring and Evaluation in Community Forestry.* Rome, Food and Agriculture Organization of the United Nations.

This tool can be an effective way to understand the roots of a problem and to understand how past events connect to present problems. Afterward, a group discussion can be held to work through each time period and ensure that nothing was missed. If sensitive issues are raised (e.g., a crime), the facilitator must not allow the discussion to get stuck on that event; instead, the facilitator should give it sufficient attention and then move the discussion on to the next event or time period.

While this could be a meaningful exercise for a small group of stakeholders, a timeline and an explanatory poster could also be developed in a public venue, such as a community center or public library, to engage the general public in the historical mapping process as well.

Kitchen Table Discussion

A common tool during election campaigns, kitchen table discussions are small group meetings in comfortable, neutral spaces such as a local coffee shop or someone's home. This setting creates a relaxed and informal atmosphere that encourages discussion and two-way communication. The host (or facilitator) plays an important role in opening the discussion, sharing information, reminding everyone that there are no right or wrong answers, encouraging people to both talk and listen, and easing tension if necessary. Participants benefit by learning new things (such as information about new programs) and by having an opportunity to share ideas in a nonthreatening environment. In addition, it can be a way for people to meet others in their community. For example, a series of kitchen table discussions could be held in a farming community to discuss an ongoing drought; a government official could talk about government support programs, and farmers could discuss the impact the drought is having on their crops and their lives. Going out directly into the community this way creates a more supportive sense of engagement and empowers local people through a sense of "home court advantage." Kitchen table discussions also reduce the travel burden on stakeholders and are ideal for those who may be intimidated by walking into government buildings or participating in larger forums.

The facilitators of the kitchen table discussions should be people who are comfortable leading discussions and listening to others. The locations should be neutral with limited distractions. The groups should be around eight to ten people to ensure that everyone has the opportunity to speak and that there are a variety of perspectives represented.

Mobile Apps

Smartphones and mobile applications (or apps) have created new opportunities for stakeholder engagement; in particular, they can be a way to disseminate information, educate the public, and facilitate two-way communication. There are some important considerations. To ensure broad scope, the app should be available for as many devices as possible, namely iPhones, iPads, Androids, and BlackBerrys. For agencies that do not have the internal resources to build the app, that work may have to be contracted out to an app developer, of which there are plentiful options.

Although the technical specifications for app development extend beyond the intentions of this book, a stakeholder collaboration app should meet the same expectations of all of the other tools presented here: it should be purposeful, efficient, and engaging for the user. The app should be accessible to the target audience and should assist the users in engaging with the policy process in a more meaningful way.

Field Trip

A field trip allows for personal interaction and team building and can help participants get a better understanding of an issue. Field trips can be a way for stakeholders to deepen their understanding of a physical location, how processes work, or the people who live there. By their very nature, field trips also provide participants with a chance to get to know one another and to interact in a more informal manner. Field trips are not decision-making forums, but rather information-sharing and information-gathering activities. The purpose of a field trip is to visit a specific site, such as a watershed, in order to gain firsthand experience with a location to better inform the stakeholder collaboration process. While field trips may be expensive and time consuming, they provide an active learning experience that is difficult to replicate in other ways.

Citizen Jury*

A citizen jury can be used to solicit the opinions and beliefs of the public to assist in decision making. As developed by the Jefferson Center, the process brings together eighteen to twenty-four randomly selected citizens for five days of hearings, including opportunities to question witnesses, followed by a report of the findings. A citizen jury allows the individuals involved to learn more about an issue or topic and helps decision makers to gather information on what people are thinking once they have all the facts. Recommendations and opinions of the jury are revealed after everyone has had the opportunity to listen to a variety of witnesses and have discussed the issue as a group. At the conclusion, the jury presents their thoughts on the issue and makes recommendations or renders a decision.

The citizen jury model can be modified in different ways; for example, rather than a random sample of citizens, a representative from each stakeholder interest could serve on a panel and question agency decision makers about a policy, with the option to also call on witnesses as needed. This process forces transparency onto an

---

* For more information see the Jefferson Center, http://jefferson-center.org.

agency and may lead to the resolution of problems, as well as a greater understanding on the part of stakeholders about the complexity of the policy process. Such tools can also encourage decision makers to grapple with the concerns of stakeholders, or at the very least hear and acknowledge them.

Partnership Grants

Partnership grants are competitive monetary awards to facilitate stakeholder participation in decision making, program development, or policy implementation. For example, agencies can provide monetary grants to stakeholder groups to offset the costs of participating in policymaking, such as travel to meetings; they may be used by stakeholders to hire outside consultants, such as scientists to explain the scientific complexity of a project as unbiased nongovernmental experts; and different stakeholders could use grants to run a number of pilot projects to test different proposals.

Partnership grants require oversight and accountability, the agency should be clear about how the money is to be used by the stakeholder group, and monitoring or evaluation of the funds should be mandated. Ultimately these grants can be an effective way to give power to stakeholders to help agencies make policy decisions.

Public Forum

Public meetings allow for government officials to make a formal presentation to the public, followed by audience questions and comments. Public meetings can be effective ways to introduce a problem or proposed project, explain constraints and options, or report a final decision. Public debate is at the same time an opportunity to resolve issues/controversies, facilitate education, and disseminate information. As divergent views are presented participants may come to appreciate the complexity of environmental policy and begin to appreciate the range of perspectives and the varying degree of importance of these opinions.

Events such as public forums targeted to the general public can be excellent engagement tools, but they do require special consideration to be successful. Planning, as outlined in the first section of this chapter, is critically important when working with large groups of public stakeholders both to ensure an effective event and to make certain that participation is meaningful.

Planners must ensure that the event is accessible for those who need to attend, taking into account issues such as public transportation, travel times, child care, disability services/access, parking costs, and signage. The time of day and year should accommodate the needs of those attending; for example, evening and weekend meetings may be more convenient for most working people, while summer meetings may be difficult for farmers to attend.

Advertising a public event can take many forms including print/radio/television ads, social media, press releases, handouts and posters at public sites (e.g., parks,

Table 5.6   Floor Plan Options for a Public Event

Floor Plan	Best for	Advantages	Disadvantages
Head table	Panel discussions	Conveys authority Clear who has authority	Not very inviting
Round tables	Discussion	Encourages participation	Some people will have their backs to the front of the room
Chairs in rows	Listening to a presentation	Orderly	Limits participation
No chairs	Mingling and moving around	Encourages conversation	Difficult to hold the attention of the entire group
Floor seating	Children's activities or creating a casual environment	Creates an open atmosphere for participation	Limited accessibility
Large circle	Encouraging participation in a medium-sized group	Easy to identify who is speaking, promotes interaction	May be difficult to convey authority

recycling facilities, city hall), inserts in local bills (e.g., water, utility), notices sent home to schoolchildren, and posters on city garbage trucks.

The choice of the facility itself is important, as it will set the tone for the proceedings. A room that is too large suggests a lack of turnout, regardless of actual attendance. A small crowded room may create the sense of high turnout but may also make the participants uncomfortable. The choice of floor plan layouts will also impact the nature of the event, as illustrated in Table 5.6.

The event should begin with an explanation of the purpose and ground rules. Agency staff members should be adequately prepared to talk about the issues clearly and have a preliminary sense of the public's interest and potential questions. Developing a written agenda beforehand and confirming who will speak when will help the event run more smoothly.

Another consideration is how to manage public comments. A microphone on a stand in a center aisle will encourage those who wish to speak to form a line, creating order but discouraging those who are physically unable to stand in line. Another option is for those interested in speaking to sign a form with their name, address, the name of the organization they represent, and the issue they wish to address. This creates a public record of the speakers and enables the moderator to call on attendees in an orderly fashion, although it limits spontaneous responses and rebuttals. Speakers should be informed of the time limit (two to three minutes is usually sufficient), and this should be strictly enforced. A signal at the halfway mark and again indicating thirty seconds remaining can help to keep speakers on track. The moderator should decide in advance how partisan political statements or inflammatory statements would be handled. It is the role of the moderator to go over the guidelines of what is acceptable at the beginning of the meeting, and periodically throughout the comments as necessary. The public can also be given the option of submitting written comments, by dropping comments into a box for further review or using an online portal.

Although public forums are often used in government, there are some concerns. Oftentimes these forums masquerade as two-way communication even when government decision makers have no intention of making changes to their policy. These forums can actually generate more conflict, as a vocal minority may dominate and distort proceedings so that they seem to represent the majority. Ultimately, these forums are usually best used to convey information or answer questions about policy rather than solicit new ideas.

While required by many environmental laws and regulations, public consultation is a challenge. For one, participation often extends the decision-making process timeline particularly when divergent opinions create controversies that require additional time to address or require stakeholders to obtain new knowledge. Public hearings as a stakeholder process can be problematic because they can be inaccessible to key stakeholders, are easily dominated by a few narrow interests, and are often token or superficial proceedings. The public forum setting makes it difficult to convey detailed or technical information, it can be difficult to obtain consensus given the size, large events need a strong chairperson/moderator to ensure that particular individuals/groups do not dominate the discussion, and it can be difficult to predict attendance in advance.

A public meeting has a number of advantages, however: it can be an effective way to disseminate information to a medium-size crowd and is a way to obtain immediate feedback.

Social Media

Online collaborative communication tools, or *social networking*, can connect disparate stakeholders in interactive and inexpensive forums, giving them opportunities to exchange ideas, highlight projects, network, track events, monitor deadlines, leave notes for others, and stay in touch. While an informative website is important for every organization and agency, people now rely on social media for up-to-date information and interaction. Social media is a chance to share messages, craft an image, respond to current events, develop personal connections, solicit input, and mobilize stakeholders.

With any type of social media it is important to think about the "brand" or image that is crafted, as well as the goal. What are you trying to achieve, and how will you know if you've achieved it? Social media requires attention to ensure that the brand is consistently portrayed and controlled. Postings should be frequent and someone should be in charge of daily monitoring of the sites to remove offensive comments and/or ban problematic users if necessary.

What are the advantages of using online social networking tools? For one it is convenient; stakeholders can go online at their convenience to read, write, or participate in discussions, and updates can be made by government quickly and easily. It is a way to bring government directly to the people. Social media also serves an archiving function by keeping everything in one place and online. Social media is also a way to keep people informed. The primary disadvantage of these tools is that they require reliable Internet access and use in order to be effective. Stakeholders who prefer more traditional tools may be left out of the policy process if everyone else is using social networking tools. Careful thought must go into the decision to use these tools, and staff must make sure that everyone is familiar with their use.

Every organization and government agency should have a Facebook page, and engaging, informative status updates should be posted on a regular basis. Facebook can be useful for promoting stakeholder events, asking questions, generating ideas, soliciting public comments, sharing information, identifying stakeholders, showing appreciation to stakeholders for their participation, and staying abreast of what stakeholders are doing. Tracking responses to status updates—for example, the number of likes or page shares—can help to identify the most successful types of posts in terms of engagement.

Twitter is another tool that can be used by stakeholders for communication. Twitter is a micro-blogging service through which users send and read updates (or *tweets*) of up to 140 characters in length. Twitter can be a quick way to ask questions, get feedback, or post a reminder about meetings or deadlines. Twitter can be used as a communication tool to get feedback from stakeholders, to brainstorm among diverse interests, and to respond to stakeholder concerns. Twitter also has uses beyond simply social networking. The Red Cross, for example, is using Twitter to exchange minute-to-minute updates and critical information such as directions during local disasters.

One way to build exposure on Twitter is by following popular Twitter users, retweeting other people's tweets if they are relevant, and tagging people and organizations in messages. Using trending hashtags (if they are appropriate to the mission) can also help to expand the reach of the Twitter feed. To use Twitter successfully for stakeholder engagement it is key to write tweets that are interesting, relevant, and clear. Tweets should be personal but professional and, if at all possible, should be useful to followers.

YouTube can be an effective tool for giving stakeholders access to speeches and presentations. These videos can be easily uploaded to YouTube, a video-sharing site that is very user-friendly. The link to the videos can also be posted on the agency website, Facebook, or Twitter or sent by e-mail to a contact list. YouTube can also be an excellent tool for stakeholder education.

A *wiki*, a Hawaiian word meaning *fast* or *quick*, is an online tool for stakeholder collaboration. A wiki is a website that allows visitors to add, modify, or delete content using a web browser. Wikis can be powerful tools for note taking, project communication, group learning, knowledge sharing, and, most importantly, collaboration. Wiki tools, such as Google Docs, are intended to be simple and straightforward, without requiring any background knowledge in software programming. A wiki document may be made publicly available, whereby anyone can edit the document, or can be limited to specific users. Typically edits to a wiki page are unrestricted without any sort of moderation or approval, which can sometimes lead to abuse through deletions or unwanted edits; however, most wiki websites save archived versions to ensure that all is not lost under such a scenario.

Flickr is an online photo and video hosting website that can be used by government to foster collaboration through the sharing and collecting of visual images. By creating groups and unique tags, stakeholders and the general public can upload photos or videos to create collaborative stories, identify problem areas in a community, keep others apprised of progress on a project, or celebrate successes. For example, Flickr could be used to share photos of a watershed restoration project, to share the environmental history of the community, to track the spread of an invasive species, or to highlight regrowth of a forest affected by wildfire.

LinkedIn is a professional social networking website that can be useful for identifying, recruiting, and engaging with stakeholders. Agencies can use LinkedIn to connect directly with individuals and to create groups to bring together people and organizations with shared interests. LinkedIn can be particularly useful for recruiting stakeholders and identifying their interests.

Blogs are discussion or informational websites that are updated on a regular basis, rather than being static, and often encourage comments, feedback, and discussion with readers. As another form of social networking, blogs can be a way to reach out to stakeholders and to identify/recruit individuals who are passionate about particular issues. Blogs may be used for advertising, as an online journal, or to provide commentary.

Creating an *online collaboration community* for stakeholders can be a long-term way to engage stakeholders in a dialogue about issues and ideas. Most appropriate for an issue area with a broad range of stakeholders, it can also serve as an online resource for others. An online collaboration community is ideal for longer-term engagement. A group of stakeholders can work together over the Internet on documents, brainstorm, or share best practices.

An online collaboration community must be set up with a sense of purpose and a sufficient audience to make it work. The online community can help to foster communication, transparency, and participation. The community should bring together diverse stakeholders such as government, science, NGOs, corporations, and citizens in order to nurture a dialogue on the issues. It should be easy to use and also needs to be secure, such as by requiring a password or login as well as encryption. The features of the online collaboration community should match the needs— for example, a whiteboard for brainstorming sessions, a calendar if it is important to track dates, project management tools, a message board for starting discussions, messaging between members to facilitate communication, or file sharing. Websites such as huddle.net provide online workspaces with project and collaboration tools such as discussion boards, forums for sharing documents online, and whiteboards for brainstorming, which can facilitate collaboration from a distance.

What are the benefits of an online stakeholder forum? For one, it can be focused on sharing information and ideas. Stakeholders can visit the community and engage at their leisure, ideal for those with busy schedules or who are geographically disparate. Active online communities can also foster relationships and networking between stakeholders; as people get to know one another from their posts, relationships can form. Forums can also be a way to consolidate knowledge, information, and ideas in one place.

If an agency is fearful of what stakeholders will say or is not interested in what stakeholders have to say, simple one-way communication tools such as a website would be better. If the community of stakeholders is small and unlikely to visit the forum, then other forms of online media, such as Facebook, might be better. Private and sensitive information should not be shared over a public forum. Private forums that require authorization of participants can be created, and that might be a better option for some issue areas, although it could reduce participation.

Strategic Thinking Tools

Impact/Effort Matrix*

When efforts such as brainstorming have generated too many ideas, it may be useful to think in terms of impact and effort in order to prioritize. The process begins with a numbered list of all the potential ideas. Participants are asked to rate each idea based on its impact (high or low) and effort (easy or hard). Ideas are then slotted into the matrix shown in Figure 5.4. "A" priority ideas are easy with a high impact and should be implemented first. "B" priority ideas are worthwhile but will take more effort. "C" priority ideas would be a lower concern as the impact is low. "D" priority ideas are not worth the effort, as they will have a low impact for a high degree of effort. This tool is a useful way to sort through a large amount of information and see how time and effort can be prioritized.

---

* For more information see Office of Quality Improvement (2007). *Facilitator Tool Kit.* Madison, University of Wisconsin–Madison.

		A	B
Impact	High	Priority	Priority
	Low	C Priority	D Priority
		Easy	Hard

Effort

Figure 5.4 Impact/effort matrix.

Charrette*

The Charrette procedure (sometimes spelled *Charette*) is a collaborative technique to develop and refine ideas. Originally derived from the French word for *little cart*, Charrette has a history rooted in nineteenth-century Paris when professors at the École de Beaux Arts would use little carts to go around and collect the final drawings from their architecture students. Students would jump on the Charrette to put finishing touches on their designs in the final minutes before the deadline. Typically applied to building design, a Charrette can also be a powerful tool for stakeholder engagement. While there are many different ways to structure a Charrette, a basic design is outlined here that is easy to customize.

To begin, a larger group of people is broken into several small working groups. A group of seven or less plus a recorder is ideal for an interactive discussion; diverse groups tend to be more creative than more homogeneous groups. Each group is assigned an issue; depending on the number of issues some issues may be given to more than one group.

Each group is tasked with brainstorming ideas or solutions following traditional brainstorming guidelines (discussed in this chapter). When the time is up, each recorder moves to the next group and reviews their issue and the results of the previous brainstorming session. Brainstorming begins again, with each group now discussing the issue brought by the new recorder. The task of the group is to build on the existing ideas as well as generate new ones. This is repeated until each group has discussed each issue. In the final group session the results can be presented, prioritized, or voted upon.

The advantage of a Charrette is that participants develop a vested interest in the final decisions or vision. With an emphasis on collaboration and iterative design, a Charrette can facilitate consensus and overcome creative stumbling blocks. A

---

* Lindsey, G., J. A. Todd, et al. (2009). *A Handbook for Planning and Conducting Charrettes for High Performance Projects*. Washington, DC, National Renewable Energy Laboratory.

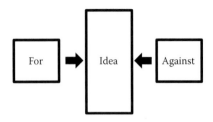

Figure 5.5   Force Field Analysis.

successful Charrette encourages group ownership of the ideas and results and can help to defuse conflict between different interests.

Force Field Analysis

The Force Field Analysis was created by Lewin (1943) as a way to identify and assess the factors (or forces) working for and against a decision or idea. Each factor is then scored based on its influence, and the scores are totaled to determine which side wins. The analysis can help stakeholders or managers to identify what forces need to be strengthened to support change and what forces working against the idea need to be managed strategically.

As illustrated in Figure 5.5, to begin the Force Field Analysis a narrow box is drawn down the middle of a large piece of paper or on a whiteboard, with the plan, proposal, or idea in the middle. The forces for change go in a column on the left-hand side and the forces against change are listed on the right. Each force is given a score, for example 1 (weak) to 5 (strong), and then the scores for each column are added up. An idea that has a higher score in the for column has a greater likelihood of success than one with a higher score in the against column.

Ranking and Sorting*

Ranking and sorting can be used to understand how stakeholders make choices and why: for example, why some farmers choose to plant certain crops, or why a particular energy efficiency strategy is preferred. It can also be used to compare differences between groups, such as organic versus conventional farmers, and give insight into group decision making.

In a *ranking exercise*, participants are given picture cards (or text cards) and asked to rank the cards from first to last choice. Paired comparisons could also be used, where participants must choose between pairs of options. For example,

---

* For more information see Case, D. A. D. (1990). *The Community's Toolbox: The Idea, Methods and Tools for Participatory Assessment, Monitoring and Evaluation in Community Forestry.* Rome, Food and Agriculture Organization of the United Nations.

participants could be given cards that include different visions of a new public park such as playground, naturalized area, basketball courts, skateboard ramps, and picnic tables and asked to rank the options. Typically six options or fewer work best for this exercise. Participants can be asked to comment on their decision-making process. One example of how this was used was a development project in Ethiopia where six tree species were being promoted as part of a community forestry project. Adoption of some of the trees was quite low, so interviewers used a paired ranking exercise to ask farmers which ones they preferred and why. The exercise revealed differences between the preferences of the extensionists running the project (who preferred trees with rapid growth) and the farmers (who preferred tress with greater uses).

In a *sorting exercise* participants are given a stack of cards (150 or less) and asked to sort them according to predetermined categories into baskets. For example, the cards could list problems previously identified as being issues in the community. The participant would sort them into "not a problem," "somewhat of a problem," and "a significant problem." This is similar to the ranking but is a way to deal with a larger number of issues. The total for each basket can be recorded and then the sorting exercise repeated with other participants.

Problem Tree

A problem tree is a visualization technique to help stakeholders think about the causes and consequences of a particular problem. A diagram of a tree (or a box) is sketched out and the problem is written in the middle of the trunk. Causes of the problem are drawn as roots of the tree, and consequences of the problem are added as leaves. Figure 5.6 illustrates the basic format of the problem tree. This is a useful tool for clarifying complex problems as it encourages consideration of multiple and complex causes, as well as broad consequences. Participants should be encouraged to think about both intended and unintended consequences, which can be highlighted in different colors. Figure 5.7 is a sample problem tree for a community dealing with clean water issues.

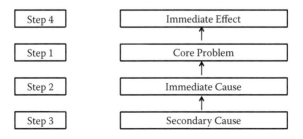

Figure 5.6   Problem tree construction.

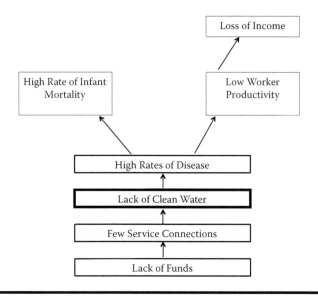

Figure 5.7 Sample problem tree—lack of clean water.

Consensus Workshop[*]

The Consensus Workshop method was developed by the Institute of Cultural Affairs based on experience with hundreds of people in community development initiatives from the 1950s to the 1990s. The purpose is to facilitate large group learning and strategic thinking through a discussion of a complex issue. In this case, a diversity of perspectives and ideas is an asset.

There are five basic steps:

1. Set a context—A single, open-ended question is posed to help participants begin to think about the topic (e.g., "What can be done to reduce wildlife-human interactions?" or "What could we do with this green space in the middle of town?").
2. Brainstorm in layers—Individuals are asked to silently brainstorm ideas individually and then share their favorite ideas in a small group. The small group then writes individual ideas onto large cards, one idea per card, which are then read aloud and posted on the wall.
3. Cluster ideas—The large group sorts the cards in clusters of similar ideas.
4. Name the clusters—Each cluster is then given a three- to five-word title that answers the initial question posed for the exercise.

---

[*] The Consensus Workshop is a method of The Technology of Participation[®], a registered trademark of the Institute of Cultural Affairs (ICA).

5. Confirm the resolve—The titles are reviewed with the group and confirm that they represent the consensus of the group. This is then used as a foundation for strategic action.

Social Audit*

A social audit can take many different forms and can be initiated by government, by stakeholders, or as a collaborative venture between the two. The purpose is to examine the social performance as perceived by stakeholders (or the general public) with respect to the core values of an agency or a specific program.

The steps to designing and implementing a social audit are as follows:

1. Background preparation
   - Define scope of audit and identify key stakeholders.
   - Outline and assign responsibilities.
   - Develop performance indicators in consultation with stakeholders.
   - Develop and implement a public awareness campaign about the goals of the social audit by using mailouts, social media, traditional media, and door-to-door visits if necessary to ensure that all stakeholders are reached.
2. Information gathering
   - Using tools such as surveys, focus groups, and public forums, collect data from stakeholders about their perceptions and experiences of the agency or service/program under study. Examples might include the following: Do you believe agency X is interested in the views of stakeholders? Does agency X promote the well-being of people in your community? Is agency X a leader in your community?
   - Review public documents as appropriate, such as managerial records and budgets. The purpose of the records review is to assess gaps between needs and resources and ensure fairness and transparency.
3. Analyze collected data
4. Share findings
   - Develop a dissemination strategy to share findings with stakeholders such as a public forum or sending out a media release.
   - Share information with stakeholders and others who should be informed of the results.
   - Organize a public forum to allow all stakeholders to give feedback and discuss ideas for change.

---

* For more information see *FAO Training Module on Social Audit*, http://www.fao.org/docrep/006/ad346e/ad346e09.htm; Centre for Good Governance, *Social Audit: A Toolkit*, http://unpan1.un.org/intradoc/groups/public/documents/cgg/unpan023752.pdf.

A social audit is a way to engage stakeholders by focusing on social and ethical performance. Social auditing improves governance by strengthening accountability and transparency and by strengthening relationships with stakeholders. A social audit also provides valuable evaluation information that can be used to improve governance. By bringing together policymakers and stakeholders for a common purpose, there is an opportunity to facilitate understanding of concerns. Such an exercise can also help to improve trust between stakeholders and government. Falling under the realm of participatory evaluation, social audits can also be used as an empowerment tool by training stakeholders, particularly those who are traditionally disenfranchised, in social audit methodology and analysis.

The social audit in some ways makes government vulnerable to criticism and to expectations that issues that are raised will be effectively addressed. Policymakers may end up feeling threatened by the process, rather than engaged and supported. In order to be successful, decision makers and stakeholders must be committed to the process, there must be a plan for implementation of changes based on the results of the study, and there must be broad involvement of stakeholders. In order to be effective, the principles for identifying stakeholders for participation should be inclusive, representative, relevant, and balanced.

Citizen Report Card and Community Scorecard*

The Citizen Report Card and Community Scorecard are similar in many ways; both are intended to increase social and public accountability and responsiveness from government. These tools may be useful for publicizing policies and programs. These tools may be initiated by governments or by stakeholders seeking accountability and can also be used in concert.

The Citizen Report Card is a survey that is distributed to the public to assess user perceptions about the quality, efficiency, and adequacy of public services. The survey results are compiled and a report issued, with summary findings distributed to the public and media. The advantage of the Report Card is that it is relatively simple to reach a large number of citizens; for example, a local government could include the survey with another government mailing such as a tax bill, or trash collectors can tape them onto a random sample of trash containers in areas that have public trash pickup and a high proportion of single-family homes.

The Community Scorecard is a qualitative tool that is used for monitoring and evaluation to determine how well an agency is meetings its goals. The main source of information collection is through focus group discussions, which are concerned less with actual data and more with feedback and accountability. The dialogue between government and citizens allows citizens to articulate their views and demand change

---

* For more information see The World Bank. (2009). "Participation at Project, Program & Policy Level." Retrieved April 1, 2013, from http://go.worldbank.org/1S57LH08E0.

and allows governments to respond to those demands directly. This information can also be used as a way to identify the questions that community members may have, which can be addressed through a website or a direct mail newsletter.

Delphi Study*

A Delphi study is similar to a focus group; however, the participants do not actually have to physically meet, making it easier to involve stakeholders with limited time or from geographically disparate locations. The purpose is to engage selected stakeholders in a process of generating ideas in a series of online questionnaires and arriving at a consensus through a systematic, iterative process. The participants who are selected to participate should reflect a diversity of interests and experience and should have special knowledge to share. The outcome should be an agreed-upon set of guidelines or recommendations that include the input of everyone in the group. While traditionally used for forecasting, the technique has much broader potential such as policy analysis, idea generation, and program decision making.

The advantage of a Delphi study is that it allows for the sharing of ideas from stakeholder experts through a transparent and democratic process. It prioritizes expediency for the participants, as they can work from home or the office at a time that is convenient for them, and is also cost-effective for agencies to use. The online Delphi study also eliminates some of the negative experiences of group meetings such as conflict, personal differences, and domineering by one participant. As well, unlike in a face-to-face experience, participants in the Delphi study tend to be much more open to changing their minds and revising their statements.

The following are the steps needed to conduct a Delphi study:

1. Identify the issue at hand and the areas of expertise that are required for a meaningful and effective process.
2. Identify and invite stakeholder participants who represent those identified areas of expertise. Participants could also be nominated by other experts or individuals to serve on the Delphi panel. In addition to their knowledge, participants should also be willing to share their information with a large group and be willing to commit the time to the process. Ideally thirty to fifty individuals should serve on the panel so as to be able to see patterns among the responses but not overwhelm the facilitators who must synthesize the information. Typically members of the Delphi study are anonymous to one another, even after the completion of the study. This is important as it reduces personal biases, allows the free expression of ideas and critiques, and prevents participants from being intimidated by someone else's perceived expertise or reputation.

---

* For more information see Linstone, H. A. and M. Turoff (1975). *Delphi Method: Techniques and Applications*. Reading, MA, Addison Wesley.

3. Prepare and distribute the initial questionnaire asking for answers to different questions and justifications for the responses. Qualitative and/or quantitative questions can be used for the survey.
4. Analyze the first wave of responses.
5. Prepare and distribute the second questionnaire. The questionnaire should include an anonymous summary of the responses to the first survey, as well as the rationales for their responses. Common and conflicting viewpoints may be identified here in the survey. The facilitator should try to maintain the integrity of the responses but can filter out inappropriate responses. Stakeholders are encouraged to revise their first answers based on the aggregated responses of the stakeholders and to respond to the responses of others. Typically what happens is that the responses begin to converge toward just a few "best" responses during the second wave.
6. Collect and review the second wave of responses.
7. Prepare and distribute the third questionnaire following the guidelines from the second wave.
8. Analyze the third wave of responses.
9. Repeat as necessary until a consensus emerges or a stalemate has been reached.
10. Prepare and distribute a final report to all the panelists.

Although Delphi studies have traditionally been done using mail-back surveys, there are now numerous web-based applications to facilitate the Delphi study process. This not only reduces the burden on the facilitator in terms of collecting responses and preparing the waves of surveys but also allows for greater customization. For example, multiple panels could be run simultaneously on the same issue representing different groups such as experts, citizens, and policymakers.

Concentric Circles

Another simple visualization tool to help prioritize ideas is the use of concentric circles. Concentric circles are drawn on a large board and individual ideas are written on sticky notes and placed outside the circles. Each stakeholder can then move ideas forward (indicating their support) or backward (indicating their dislike) one space. Over time the most favored ideas will move to the middle, while those with the least support will be kept on the outer edges. Ideas that create a divide among the stakeholders will move forward and backward without gaining much ground. Figure 5.8 illustrates a simplified concentric circles exercise to identify public preferences for public park amenities. With large numbers of participants it may be best to include up to fifty circles to allow for greater movement and differentiation between preferences.

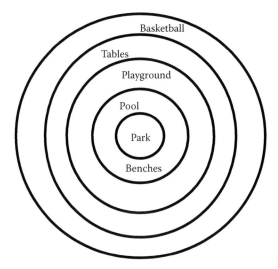

Figure 5.8   Concentric circles for public park amenities.

Risk Chart

One way to help stakeholders think about risk in public policy is to consider two dimensions: probability and impact. Risk is something that may occur, and the probability of that happening is anywhere from 0 percent (not a risk) to 100 percent (certain). Impact is the effect of the risk, perhaps in terms of cost or health or some other critical factor. A risk chart can be completed as part of a group exercise for stakeholders. The first step is to make a list of all the likely risks. Each risk is then assessed for the probability of it occurring. A simple way to assess the probability is to use a 1–10 scale, with 1 meaning a risk is very unlikely to occur and 10 meaning it is very likely to occur. The same is done for the estimated impact. Each risk is then placed on the chart shown in Figure 5.9.

The risks in the lower left-hand corner (low risk) can be ignored, while those in the top right corner (critical risk) demand immediate attention, followed by those in the medium risk categories. This chart can help prioritize actions. Figure 5.10 is an example of a risk chart highlighting the threats to Komodo dragons, an endangered species of lizard living on four islands of Indonesia. Based on the risk chart, government agencies and conservation groups can prioritize their actions, using limited funding more efficiently.

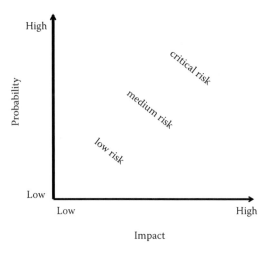

Figure 5.9   Risk chart.

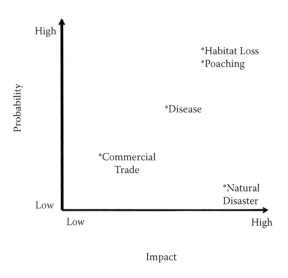

Figure 5.10   Risk chart of threats to the Komodo dragon.

Open-Ended Stories*

Open-ended stories are a tool for helping stakeholders to think creatively about issues and can also be used either as an icebreaker or to help deal with group conflict. An open-ended story has a beginning, which tells a story about the problem; a middle, which tells a story about a solution; and an end, which tells a story about an outcome. During the exercise one of those three elements is purposefully left out, and it is up to the group to discuss what might have happened. For example, if the moderator presents the beginning (problem) and the ending (desired outcome), it is up to the group to identify the solutions that would fit with the rest of the story. It can be a useful way to help stakeholders think about the outcomes of a possible solution or to identify the problems that could be solved.

This tool could also be used to engage children as stakeholders. For instance, the stories could be told using puppets and the students can either say their ideas or use the puppets themselves to act them out. Open-ended stories can also be useful to engage stakeholders with low levels of literacy or communities that have a rich oral storytelling tradition.

In order to be successful, the entire story needs to be designed in advance, so that the part that is left out fits with the complete story. The moderator must be able to both tell the story and listen to and facilitate the stakeholder discussion. A second facilitator can be involved in documenting the discussion, or videotaping may be necessary.

Advisory Committee

An advisory committee is a group of stakeholders who meet on a regular basis to share ideas and provide feedback on initiatives and performance. Advisory committees can provide ongoing external expertise and help governments think constructively about the impacts of public policies.

Unlike a board of directors, an advisory committee does not have formal authority or power; their role is simply to advise as needed. They also do not have legal responsibilities, so they are exempt from needing insurance coverage to protect them from liability exposure. It is up to the organization to decide how much private information is shared with the advisory committee, particularly in terms of financial details. The degree of formality is dependent on the needs and culture of the organization. An advisory board may operate as informally as the occasional breakfast meeting, or it may be structured and formal with regular working meetings with an agenda and formal minutes.

---

* For more information see Case, D. A. D. (1990). *The Community's Toolbox: The Idea, Methods and Tools for Participatory Assessment, Monitoring and Evaluation in Community Forestry.* Rome, Food and Agriculture Organization of the United Nations.

Before formation of the advisory committee, it is important to identify the purpose of the group. Is it to provide support and advice? Is it to solicit honest (positive and negative) feedback? Is it to generate new program ideas? Whatever the purpose is it should be clear and concise so it can be shared with the members of the committee. In addition, it is important to decide how often the committee will meet, where those meetings will take place, what the organization expects from members outside of meeting times, and the terms of service including term lengths, reappointment policies, and term limits. Most advisory committees use a three-year term of service on a staggered basis so that only one-third of the members are replaced each year.

The next task is to decide the membership of the committee. Factors to take into account may include gender, race and ethnicity, age, education, socioeconomic status, skill set, and stakeholder interests. A diverse group will be more likely to provide varied feedback. During the recruitment of the members it is important to find out whether any special accommodations are required by members in terms of either scheduling or special needs.

Once the members have been identified and recruited the first meeting is important to setting the tone for the work of the committee. Members should have the opportunity to get to know one another and should become familiar with the broader organization and the roles and expectations of the advisory committee.

Advisory committees should be evaluated on a regular basis. One of the challenges for advisory committees is that there is often a disconnect between the expectations of the committee and the agency. New members should be made aware of the role and responsibility of being a member. So as not to disappointment members, agencies should be careful to accurately state the importance of the committee to attract and retain members.

Residents' Panel

A residents' panel is a long-term initiative to engage local citizens in ongoing decision making in government affairs. Panel members volunteer to serve for a period of years (typically two years) and agree to participate in consultation activities dealing with a range of subjects and policy issues.

Panels should reflect the local demographics in terms of gender, age, and ethnicity. In some cases, it may be necessary to do active, targeted recruiting of particular demographic groups to ensure representation. In some communities, a random sample of 1,000–2,000 residents is sent recruiting letters inviting them to participate, although newspaper ads, social media posts, and the like may suffice.

Panel members may be asked to answer online questionnaires, participate in focus groups, or engage in many of the other tools presented in this chapter. Panels are most successful when there is rolling membership to ensure a balance of newcomers and members with more experience and when members can see that their participation actually makes a difference. The panel can be used to encourage regular community input on policy, strategy, and priority setting, foster closer relationships with citizens, facilitate more transparent decision making, and increase trust. It should be assumed that the panel members will share their experiences with family and friends (so confidential items should not be shared with panel members); however, such sharing promotes an information exchange that can help to inform and educate a broader segment of the community than just the members of the panel. As a result, panels can have a ripple effect throughout the community.

In order to encourage participation of panel members, participants must feel valued and that their participation matters. Simple things like a thank-you e-mail after completing a panel task, an ad in the local paper identifying and acknowledging panel members, refreshments at in-person events, or coupons/discounts to local retailers are simple ways to help people feel appreciated and to encourage their ongoing participation.

SWOT Analysis*

The Strength, Weaknesses, Opportunities, and Threat (SWOT) analysis can be an effective stakeholder engagement tool to help stakeholders think analytically about a problem, agency, or policy. This approach is based on assessing a particular situation and developing proposals based on a series of strategic and analytical questions: how can we capitalize on strengths, compensate for weaknesses, take advantage of opportunities, and mitigate threats?

Strengths are internal attributes that can be used to achieve particular objectives, for example, resources and capabilities. Weaknesses are those internal attributes that are potentially harmful to achieving objectives, internal dynamics that could be improved, or processes that are done poorly. The absence of certain strengths may also be viewed as a weakness. Opportunities are external conditions that are helpful to achieving objectives or that can be used or exploited to further a mission or expand into new areas. Opportunities may include new and emerging trends, untapped revenue sources, potential partnerships, or funding opportunities. Threats are external conditions that stand in the way of achieving objectives but may also include new trends looming on the horizon such as budget cuts, changes in the external environment, or competitors. From a stakeholder engagement perspective, a SWOT analysis encourages participants to think beyond simply pursuing the most lucrative/cost-effective or easiest opportunity and emphasizes a broader strategic approach.

The SWOT assessment should start with a specific objective—for example, to improve an organization or to test a new idea. The next step is to identify the

---

* For more information see Orr, S. K. (2011). "The Private Sector on Public Land: Policy Implications of a SWOT Analysis of Banff National Park." *Journal of Natural Resources Policy Research* 3(4): 341–354.

Table 5.7   SWOT Strategies

	Strengths	*Weaknesses*
Opportunities	S-O strategies	W-O strategies
Threats	S-T strategies	W-T strategies

strengths, weaknesses, opportunities, and threats using one of the tools in this book, such as brainstorming, and then asking the following questions:

- How can we use each strength?
- How can we stop each weakness?
- How can we exploit each opportunity?
- How can we defend against each threat?

The next step is to take the results of the SWOT analysis and develop recommendations. The matrix in Table 5.7 uses the SWOT profile to develop strategic policies to help plan for the future.

S-O strategies are intended to pursue opportunities that are a good fit with the strengths. W-O strategies overcome weaknesses to pursue opportunities. S-T strategies identify ways in which strengths can be used to reduce vulnerability to external threats. And lastly, W-T strategies are a defensive plan to prevent weaknesses from making one highly susceptible to external threats.

The SWOT analysis is not without its critics. Most SWOT analyses stop after identifying the strengths, weaknesses, opportunities, and threats, thereby failing to take it to the next level of planning. For a SWOT exercise to be useful, there must be an implementation or action plan developed alongside the analysis. Prioritizing strategies is important to facilitate use.

*Brainstorming**

Brainstorming is a technique used in writing and decision making that promotes the free flow of ideas. This technique is helpful when trying to expand on an idea, identify solutions, or narrow down options. When brainstorming, all thoughts and ideas are welcome, no matter how outrageous or creative they may be. Brainstorming can be a useful tool for promoting compromise by bringing new options to the table. Represented in both written and visual form, there are many different types and styles of brainstorms.

Traditional brainstorming involves the free flow of ideas within a group for a specific amount of time without discussion or critique. Quality is not as important

---

* For more information see Rawlinson, J. G. (1981). *Creative Thinking and Brainstorming.* New York, Wiley.

as the ability of the group to eliminate their internal critics and just engage in an open exchange of ideas.

A similar brainstorming technique is called *free writing* where individuals in a group are allotted a set amount of time to write in response to a question or problem. The individual does not censor or criticize his or her writing; it is just an outpouring of ideas. The writing can then be read or distributed to the group. This can be a useful tool for developing goals, identifying problems and concerns, or coming up with new ideas.

A group can also look at their topic in different ways using the *three perspectives* form of brainstorming. Stakeholders in this exercise answer questions from three perspectives. The questions require the group to (1) describe the topic, (2) trace it (e.g., history), and (3) map it (e.g., related ideas, influences). This process is helpful to discover any information forgotten in the previous idea.

Cubing is another technique that also stems from this question-answer form of brainstorming by looking at a topic from six different directions. In this process the group is asked to answer six questions about the topic:

- Describe
- Compare
- Associate
- Analyze
- Apply
- Argue for and against it

In addition to oral or written brainstorms the brainstorming process can be represented visually as well. With *mapping*, terms are randomly written on a larger piece of paper and then connected using lines and shapes to determine relationships. For example, potential impacts of a policy decision could be mapped out in this way.

Starburst brainstorming is a technique to help group members think more coherently about an issue or a problem by coming up with questions and then answers. The starburst format directs stakeholders to think about an issue in a focused manner.

The starburst technique begins with a six-sided star, or six circles radiating from the center as shown in Figure 5.11 with the topic/idea/problem in the middle. On each point of the star the words *who, what, where, when, why,* and *how* are written. Participants are then challenged to come up with *questions* relating to each star point. For example, the following questions might fall under the star point of *who*: "Who will benefit from this program?" "Who will be negatively impacted by this program?" "Who needs to be notified?" There is no limit to how many questions are listed under each star point. Once all the questions have been asked, the group returns to the questions to address all of the answers.

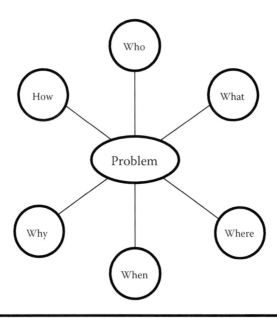

Figure 5.11   Starburst brainstorming.

Rolestorming is a technique that encourages group members to take on other people's identities while brainstorming. For instance, stakeholders may take on the identity of those with the opposite position on an issue, different background, or different job. The opportunity to be creative while also exploring other perspectives can be a nonthreatening way to help work through areas of conflict.

Regardless of what type of brainstorming is used, the setting should be comfortable with minimal distractions. One person should be responsible for recording the ideas; depending on the setting this could be done on a flip chart, whiteboard, blackboard, or computer with data projectors or via a shared online document such as Google Docs.

Participants need to feel that their ideas will be respected rather than ridiculed and that all participants can speak without the group being dominated by a few louder participants. The goal is to create an enthusiastic and uncritical attitude among the group members. If some members are not participating, then perhaps switch to a more structured process such as going around the room and having people share ideas in turn. It is key that participants refrain from criticizing or evaluating ideas during the brainstorming process, as criticism will shut down the free flow of ideas and limit creativity. It may be necessary to take breaks so that people can concentrate throughout the entire task. If the group seems stuck on a particular train of thought, the facilitator should not hesitate to pose questions about other areas or issues that have not yet been considered to try to reenergize the brainstorming.

Education

Public Exhibition

Public exhibitions can be used to inform the general public about a project, decision, or public participation program. The display can be staffed by someone to answer questions or simply be a stand-alone display. Public exhibitions can be a way to reach members of the public who do not have the time to participate in more formal activities such as public meetings. Ideal locations for public displays include shopping centers, libraries, grocery stores, municipal offices, local fairs, or other gathering spots. To be effective, displays should provide an overview of the issue highlighting the most important points and be attractive yet simple to read from a distance. Unstaffed displays should be checked on a regular basis for vandalism or to restock brochures.

Speakers' Bureau

A speakers' bureau is another tool to share new policy initiatives or programs or to identify community concerns. A speakers' bureau is a group of highly engaged, well-respected stakeholders who are tasked with going out and sharing information with other community organizations, the general public, or their peers. The speakers are recruited and brought together for an information session where they are given the materials they need to make presentations or talking points for more informal interactions. They should be made aware of the expectations in terms of message, length of presentation, compensation (if any), dress, and tips for handling difficult questions. In some cases it may be appropriate to have speakers do practice talks as a quality check. Each speaker submits an outreach plan of the groups/individuals they plan to meet, when those meetings will take place, and where they will occur to ensure broad coverage and limit duplication. The speakers should check in weekly with updates about their efforts and to convey concerns that they may have heard, as well as to share any best practices that they have developed. Afterward, a group debriefing can be arranged so that the speakers can discuss their experiences. The Atlanta Regional Commission's Family of Partners worked with nearly 800 volunteers to run meetings with local groups and neighborhoods in a concentrated public involvement initiative to bring agency planning to the grassroots level.

The advantage of the speakers' bureau tool is that it enables agencies to reach out to more people in a more personal way. The major disadvantage is that the agency must give up some measure of control over the message. Significant thought should be put into choosing stakeholders to participate, as they will be trusted to share the message, listen to others, and represent the agency. The speakers should be qualified and feel comfortable speaking; those who also have firsthand policy experience and personal stories (appropriate to share) related to the issue may be an asset. By doing speaking engagements on the organization's behalf, the speakers will be perceived as delegates of the government/organization; thus it is important to recruit people who will be positive representatives. Recruitment is key here, and a solid training program is important to ensure that all of the stakeholders understand the message. Agency members may also want to attend some of the public presentations in order to monitor their work.

The speakers' bureau can be a powerful way to raise public awareness and understanding, outreach to others, and increase the visibility of the organization and the issues. Multilingual speakers or representatives from different minority groups may also be able to reach a target audience inaccessible to government staff.

The speakers may go out to speak to business groups, service organizations, religious groups such as church congregations, working groups, political groups, businesses, social groups, or schools and universities. Speakers' bureaus can also operate more informally; instead of formal presentations they are tasked to talk to their friends, neighbors, and colleagues. In this way they function more as ambassadors of an issue or program, posting updates on social media such as Facebook and Twitter and being engaged with the topic in a more informal manner.

Website

While most likely insufficient on its own, a well-thought-out website is still an important tool for stakeholder engagement as a gateway for stakeholders to get information and begin participation. Prior to beginning the design process, the agency should engage in a reflective exercise to determine what the purpose of the website will be. A website can be designed to inform, engage, educate, entertain, or some combination of all of these. The purpose should then be the driver of the design elements. Spending time surfing the web and identifying both design elements and structural features that are appealing can help the web designer to capture what the agency is trying to achieve with a website. Promoting the new website can be done as part of a media campaign, through an e-mail blast to stakeholders, and using social media such as Facebook or Twitter.

The website should include basic information about the agency and policy issues, how to get involved, key contacts, upcoming event dates, and frequently asked questions. The website should also include tools for further engagement—for example, links to the Facebook page and Twitter feed of the organization. People visit a website when they have a specific reason (e.g., to search for information), but they do not casually check government websites to see if there is anything new and of interest. People do, however, use Facebook and Twitter in that way. This differentiation is key to the website design process. Expecting stakeholders to check the website regularly for updates and announcements is problematic, unless such reminders are regularly shared on social media.

The website should be visually pleasing with outreach materials making use of visualization techniques that include infographics and photos, rather than just downloadable print documents. While it may be useful to have some background documents loaded on the page as PDF files, most casual visitors to the page will not be interested in downloading reports. Including interactive elements such as polls, workbooks, and games can help people to be more engaged in the site.

One way to create awareness of the page is by providing a link with an automatic tweet or Facebook wall post when a user completes an exercise on the website such as a poll or posts a comment, to encourage their friends/followers to participate as well. A moderated discussion forum can be set up to solicit feedback and ideas, although a forum with very low levels of activity does not reflect well on the organization and should be removed.

Storefront

As used quite successfully by the Banff–Bow Valley Study in Banff, Alberta (Canada), a public engagement storefront can be a way to bring policy decisions directly to citizen stakeholders. Storefronts are temporary headquarters set up in high-traffic public areas such as shopping centers or main streets to improve public outreach in a more long-term fashion than many of the other tools presented in this book. Storefronts are typically filled with display materials, take-home materials, and interactive displays and are staffed by project personnel to answer questions. People can drop in at their convenience to get information or meet with others. The storefront can also host events such as public meetings and workshops or be used in conjunction with many of the other tools presented in this book.

The storefront should be welcoming and in a central location, and signage should be clear to attract visitors. Accessibility should also be a major setup consideration; making the venue accessible to those with disabilities, children, and those who speak other languages can be key for a successful operation. The staff or volunteers should have strong customer service skills, as well as knowledge of both the project/policy and participatory processes so that they will engage with visitors in different ways. Take-home materials should be available in a number of different formats and languages as appropriate. Complimentary refreshments, seating, and children's activities will all help to attract visitors and encourage them to stay.

Ongoing evaluations of the storefront can help staff to make changes based on visitor feedback. As the storefront is intended to be a longer-term initiative (from a few weeks to a few months), it makes sense to do extensive evaluation from the beginning rather than waiting for the end when it is too late to make changes. Tracking information such as numbers of visitors per hour and day can help to determine staffing needs. The needs of a storefront may also change over time. In a small community visitation may have an initial surge and then taper off; introducing special events and new services after the initial surge may help to bring people back multiple times.

Deliberative Polling

Deliberative Polling* is an initiative pioneered by James Fishkin at Stanford University's Center for Deliberative Democracy. Deliberative Polling was conceived as a way to see how public opinion changes once people are given the opportunity to become informed and engaged by the issues. In Deliberative Polling a random sample of citizens from a defined geographical area is called and given a set of screening questions. A representative sample of those respondents is invited to attend a citizen deliberation event, often with the offer of a paid stipend in appreciation. Those who agree to attend are sent a set of materials to read prior to the event, representing a balanced viewpoint on the issues to be discussed. At the event, participants are divided into small, moderated groups to discuss the issues. There may also be a panel of experts or other types of presentation during the day on the issues. Each group may prepare a series of questions, which are then used as a starting point for discussion with experts, panelists, and each other. At the end of the event the participants are given another survey, and the responses are compared to the initial screening questions to determine if opinions changed as a result of the event. The results are indicative of what the public would think if they were more informed and engaged with that issue.

Deliberative Polling can be instrumental for decision makers to get a baseline sense of general public knowledge and understanding about a particular issue and to see if additional information causes them to change their minds. It is also a way to get feedback on policies and the direction of government. While conventional polling provides just a snapshot of what people think regardless of how much they know, Deliberative Polling provides greater feedback on levels of support with greater information than may be typically available or accessed by the public.

Workshop

A workshop is an educational seminar or series of small group meetings for interactive planning. Many of the guidelines listed in the public forum section are appropriate for workshops as well. The difference between a public forum and a workshop is that a workshop tends to be a smaller group, and the emphasis is on interaction and the exchange of information. A workshop might be an intensive educational experience or a forum for strategic thinking. The workshop is not a lecture; there may be one or more presentations, but these should be accompanied by one or more of the following: discussions, demonstrations, brainstorming, active learning, group exercises, or any of the other small-group tools in this section.

---

* Deliberative Polling is a registered trademark. Additional information can be found at The Center for Deliberative Democracy at Stanford University, http://cdd.stanford.edu/.

Conference

Much like a workshop, a conference can be used to educate stakeholders about technical issues, policy, or best practices or to present different perspectives. The conference format is highly flexible and might include any combination of the following: panel presentations, keynote address, lectures, discussion groups, poster displays, field trips, or any of the other tools presented in this book. Conference proceedings, essentially a collection of the presentations, can be distributed to participants for record keeping. Conferences tend to be larger than workshops and less interactive.

Social media and app technology can create a more interactive conference experience. With the prevalence of social media and smartphones, conference organizers can use a polling app (such as Poll Everywhere) to post questions, which participants can respond to by texting a response. Similarly, a conference hashtag can be used to encourage participants and organizers to communicate over Twitter, and a Flickr tag or group can create an online photo stream. Presentations and events can also be streamed online to encourage virtual participation, and a YouTube channel can be set up as a video archive of the events.

Technical Reports

Technical reports, written either in-house or by stakeholders or commissioned to an outside research organization, can be a way to report and disseminate research or policy findings to stakeholders. The report can be posted online, shared via social media, made available at public libraries, and disseminated electronically directly to stakeholders. A technical report may be used to ensure that stakeholders all have sufficient background knowledge about an issue and may include a summary of recommendations or projections. A technical report rarely goes through a rigorous peer review process, although it should be read and vetted as part of an internal review process prior to publication. If technical reports will be a regular feature of an organization, they can be organized into a formal series with a common identifier (e.g., standard layout and serial numbers). In some cases, an agency may invite a series of stakeholders to prepare technical reports reflecting either their different areas of expertise or their different perspectives. These can be compiled into a larger stakeholder report and distributed to the broader group of stakeholders for reference and education.

Press Conference

For large initiatives a press conference can be one way to engage with the media and help get information out to the general public. While press releases or advisories about the press conference are typically sent to print/TV/radio media, influential social media representatives are increasingly invited as well. A press conference can include any of the following: a statement, a question-and-answer period, and/or a photo opportunity. Press conferences can be held almost anywhere, although it is important to think about the visual backdrop of the event for photos and news clips. The location chosen for the press conference should either help to illustrate the relevant issue (e.g., a park to discuss new policy decisions related to visitor use) or to highlight the organization/agency, such as in front of a sign or podium with a plaque identifying the agency.

Radio/Talk Shows

Radio or television talk shows are another way to reach out to public stakeholders and to inform and educate people about proposals or activities. Radio can be a way to interact with those who cannot read or write and can also be a way to reach out to people speaking different languages through cultural radio channels or shows. These shows may also be interactive, allowing the public to call in or post on social media during the show to engage in more two-way communication.

An alternative format for a talk show is a podcast, typically a prerecorded audio broadcast that can be downloaded onto a mobile device or streamed online. A podcast should be an engaging and interesting recording of topical interest to listeners. Enhanced podcasts include images with the audio, and a video podcast (or vodcast) includes video clips. Recording a podcast is very easy using free software such as Audacity or Garageband on Mac. Using the software, creating a podcast is as simple as talking into a computer microphone after clicking on the record button. A podcast can be shared via social media or posted on a website.

Telephone Hotline[*]

A telephone hotline can be used to either provide prerecorded information or contact with a staff member who can answer questions. Telephone hotlines are a cost-effective way to facilitate two-way communication with stakeholders as it requires low effort on the part of the stakeholders and has a high degree of accessibility. A hotline can be used to give callers information, provide counseling, or make referrals to other resources. Because hotlines can be anonymous, hotlines are also ideal for questions that may be difficult to ask in a face-to-face context. Hotlines can also help government agencies identify common problems of concern or trends, which can be addressed through additional means such as new policies, a public forum, or mailouts to residents. Hotlines can be an opportunity for dialogue with stakeholders. Hotlines can also be a way to ensure that stakeholders receive the most-up-to-date information.

---

[*] For more information see Stratten, K. and R. Ainslie (2003). *Field Guide: Setting Up a Hotline.* Baltimore, Johns Hopkins Bloomberg School of Public Health/Center for Communication Programs.

A few unique planning questions to consider when planning a hotline include the following: What is the purpose of the hotline? How heavy is the anticipated call load? Is there a need for multilingual service? What hours will it be staffed? Will there be monitoring of call quality? Having the hotline set up as a mobile phone increases accessibility as stakeholders can communicate via text, and answering the hotline can be transferred among staff members as needed. Depending on anticipated call load, staff can have other primary duties and answer the hotline as needed.

A successful hotline requires a publicity plan. The means to publicize a hotline might include social media, press releases, an e-mail blast to stakeholders, posters, billboards, and brochures sent to agencies or organizations that may refer callers.

Hotlines do have limitations, most importantly the lack of follow-up to determine if the information was helpful and/or implemented. Staff must also be trained to ensure that the appropriate information is passed on and to improve their customer service skills. Staff must be available to answer the calls that come in or to return text and voicemail messages promptly.

Brochure

A brochure is a one-way communication tool that can be used to convey information about policy issues and stakeholder activities. Typically printed on paper folded in half or into thirds, a brochure is a written introduction. Unlike a newsletter, the limited space of a brochure makes it difficult to provide in-depth coverage. Brochures can be a way to direct readers to other resources such as websites, blogs, information kiosks, or a telephone hotline.

Agency Open House

An agency open house can be organized to familiarize stakeholders with the office and staff and could include short information sessions, tours, access to resources, and a social opportunity to meet/network with other stakeholders. An open house can also allow for one-on-one interaction between government and stakeholders. The event can be formal or informal depending on the goals. An open house could include a tour of the site, information displays, opportunities to talk with staff, and interactive activities. Depending on the topic and target audience, having a kids' area with activities will allow parents to attend and interact with the open house.

Mailouts

Mailouts are a way to disseminate information to a large number of people by sending information packets by post. The advantage of a mailout is that you can be reasonably assured that those who need the information will receive it, and mailouts can be saved and read later or shared with others. However, with the overwhelming amount of advertisements and marketing messages that people now receive, it is important to plan thoughtfully for a successful mailout campaign.

The first step is to think about the function of the mailout and the goals of doing a mass mailing. The design and writing of the mailout should follow from the purpose and the target audience. Thinking about the target audience before beginning the design stage will ensure that issues of language and accessibility will be taken into account. Graphics and color that support the message and text will demonstrate professionalism and also increase the likelihood that the mailout is read and remembered. Designing a mailout that is postcard sized can be cost effective; however, the trade-off is that there is less space for information and graphics. Bill stuffing involves communication through bills such as utilities or property tax notices to take advantage of community-wide mailing lists.

Public Speaking

Public speaking at meetings of social/civic organizations such as League of Women Voters and Rotary can be beneficial during the problem definition and agenda setting stages, as well as to inform people about new policies. Much like the speakers' bureau, however, in this case agency staff members go out and personally make the presentations. While it is more challenging to reach as many members of the community with agency staff, there is a higher degree of credibility and accountability by doing so. Presumably agency staff would be in a better position to answer questions as well.

Featured Media Stories

Featured stories in the media can be an excellent way to disseminate information about a policy issue, publicize the agency or initiative, and increase the perceived legitimacy of a project. Press releases can ensure that the reporter has vital information at hand.

A press release is typically one page in length and written in plain accessible language without technical jargon. A successful press release will have short paragraphs and a catchy and engaging introduction. It is also good practice to include several quotes/statements from one or more key individuals associated with the project. Contact details should be provided as well. Table 5.8 is a guide to writing a press release.

Inserts and Advertisements in Newspapers

Inserts in the local newspaper can be a way to reach a large number of people and still control the message. With the opportunity to provide more information and detail than an ad or a feature story, an insert can provide policy information as well

Table 5.8   Writing a Press Release

Writing a Press Release
FOR IMMEDIATE RELEASE: These words should appear in caps in the upper right-hand or left-hand corner, just under the agency letterhead.
Contact Information: Contact information should be listed, left justified in the left-hand side under the release statement. This should include the name, cell phone number, and e-mail of the primary contact person who will be available to answer questions right up until publication.
Headline: The headline should go two lines after the contact information in all upper case and in boldface type. The title should be ten words or less and should accurately summarize the press release, but should be interesting and engaging in order to grab the attention of the editor.
Dateline: This should be the city your press release is issued from and the date you are mailing your release.
Lead Paragraph: The introductory paragraph of a press release is the most important. The most important points should be included in the first few sentences, including the traditional five W's (who, what, when, where, why). This paragraph should summarize the press release, with the following paragraphs providing additional details.
Text: The main body of the press release provides additional detail on the story. A quote can help to add interest to your press release and adds support to what you are trying to convey. The text should be written following the "inverted pyramid" format, with the most important information and quotes first, so that an editor can cut the last paragraphs without losing critical information. The entire press release should be written as if it was the actual news story, because in some cases it may be used in that way. The press release should be no longer than one to two pages; shorter is better so it has a better chance of fitting into the publishing space.
Closing: Three ###'s indicate the end of the press release text. Repeat the contact information and indicate availability for interviews below the symbols.

as listings of opportunities for stakeholders to become involved. While inserts can be effective, they are of course limited to readers of the newspaper.

Paid advertisements in newspapers (or on radio) can be a way to disseminate information and in particular alert people to policy changes. Although there is usually a limit to how much information can be conveyed in this manner, it may be appropriate in some cases. Paid advertisements, or legal notices, are often a legal requirement in environmental assessment processes. The advertisement should be clear and written for a general audience, avoiding the use of lingo or scientific terms.

Newsletters

Newsletters can be an excellent way to disseminate information to stakeholders, particularly if an agency has a large number of stakeholders who are interested in the issues but do not have the time to participate actively. This can be a way to acknowledge those who have worked on collaboration activities and to keep others updated as to the status of projects and opportunities for participation. A newsletter can be an effective way to promote an agency as well and to reassure stakeholders that valuable work is taking place. A newsletter should be interesting and engaging; stakeholders should have a clear reason to read the newsletter when it arrives. Providing information that stakeholders can use, beyond simply reporting updates and news, will increase the value of the newsletter for readers.

The downside of a newsletter is the time and expensive involved. Although word processing programs such as MS Word have newsletter templates, creating a professional newsletter can be time consuming. Sending a newsletter out by e-mail and posting on the web can reduce costs but may limit readership. A newsletter should be written with the literacy skills of the target audience in mind. If the target audience has literacy or language issues, then a newsletter will not be appropriate. A newsletter or flyer can be distributed via the web, included with monthly utility bills, sent by direct mail, delivered by hand, or left in accessible public locations such as libraries.

Project Management Tools for Stakeholder Collaboration

Meeting Planning Tools

One of the most basic challenges of face-to-face or real-time collaboration is *scheduling*. Free online tools such as Doodle can simplify the process and eliminate the confusing and tedious flurry of e-mails from participants about availability. Using Doodle as an example, the facilitator goes to www.doodle.com and creates a new event. Fields such as title, location, description, facilitator name, and e-mail address are entered, followed by possible dates and times. Once participants are invited to view the event they can simply click on the link sent to their e-mail and confirm their preferred dates and times. This simple tool reduces the e-mail burden for participants and also simplifies keeping track of availability for the facilitator.

Taking good notes during a meeting can mean the difference between getting work done outside of the meeting and accomplishing nothing. Taking *action notes* rather than minutes can help to avoid the all-too-common case of participants "forgetting" what they had volunteered to do or spending the entire meeting discussing ideas with no concrete plans for action.

Table 5.9　Action Notes Template

Date:				
Meeting Purpose:				
Facilitator/Chair:				
Participants:				
Issue				
Action				
Stakeholder				
Time Frame				

Ideally the person taking the action notes should not also be a major participant, as it is difficult to do both tasks well. Action notes are not meant to be a verbatim record of a meeting; rather they are an outline of the proceedings with a focus on recording the topics that are being discussed, the decisions that have been taken, and actions that have been assigned to participants rather than the details of who said what. As the meeting goes on, action items should be recorded into the template shown in Table 5.9, rather than trying to pull them from notes later on to ensure accuracy. At the end of the meeting, everyone should review the table to ensure that all stakeholders are aware of their responsibilities. The table also helps to foster some measure of public accountability as well.

Project Scope Chart

As shown in Table 5.10 a project scope chart can be invaluable for identifying some of the key characteristics of a project. The project scope chart is not a detailed plan of action but rather a summary of the objectives, deliverables, outcomes, milestones, technical requirements, and limits and exclusions. In cases where there are multiple projects running simultaneously, a display of project scopes can be a simple way for people to keep track of projects and dates to limit the risk of duplication.

Gantt Chart

A Gantt chart is a graphical depiction of tasks over time. A Gantt chart can be used to determine how long a project should take from start to finish, as well as to assign priority or responsibility. It also helps to identify the dependencies between tasks—for example, the order in which tasks need to be completed. If a project falls

Table 5.10   Project Scope Chart

Public Sewers Project
Project Objective
To work with stakeholders to identify solutions to reduce dumping of waste into public sewers.
Project Manager
Annie Jasper
Deliverables
10-page report summarizing findings
Outcome
Implementation of best solutions to be completed no later than September 7
Milestones
Project plan approved July 1
Stakeholder focus groups completed July 15
Surveys of other municipalities completed August 1
Final Report completed August 15
Report to Stakeholders completed August 20
Begin implementation August 25
Project completed and press notified September 7
Technical Requirements
Survey designed, distributed, and analyzed by Project Manager
Design and publication of reports by Communications Director
Limits and Exclusions
Stakeholder focus groups limited to those living or working within town limits
Survey is limited to municipalities in Ohio

Table 5.11   Basic Gantt Chart with Prioritizing

Task	May 1	May 2	May 3	May 4	May 5	May 6	May 7
Book facilities	****						
Publicity		*	*	***	****		
Write agenda		**	****				
Prepare notes							
Event day							
Write report							****

* Low priority.
**** High priority.

behind, the Gantt chart can also be used to pull it back on course by identifying what has and has not been accomplished, as well as the priorities and dependencies.

The Gantt chart can be easily created using a table in a word processing document as shown in Tables 5.11 and 5.12, or more extensive charts can be created using any number of websites. The first step is to identify all of the tasks that need to be accomplished and place them into the first column of the table in chronological order. The dates of the project are added as the top row. The next step is to identify the span of time each task will take, which is marked in some way on the table, such as by shading. Symbols such as asterisks (*) can be used to rank priorities, and staffing can be added as well.

Table 5.12   Gantt Chart with Assigned Tasks

Task	May 1	May 2	May 3	May 4	May 5	May 6	May 7
Book facilities	Joshua						
Publicity		Brandon					
Write agenda		Nicholas					
Prepare notes				Isabella			
Event day						ALL	
Write report							Anthony

Logical Framework*

A logical framework is a way to think strategically about programs. While often used in evaluation, it can also be integrated into program planning to ensure a more effective design. As illustrated in Table 5.13 the logical framework is based on if-then ideas. If the resources are available, then activities can be implemented. If the activities are implemented, then certain outputs and outcomes can be expected as a result. In Table 5.14 the logical framework is shown as a way to develop a stakeholder collaboration program for a local watershed.

Table 5.13 The Logical Framework

Inputs	Activities	Outputs	Outcomes/ Impacts
Resources (e.g., money, staff)	The activities of the program	What is produced as a result of the activities	The changes or benefits as a result of the program

Table 5.14 Logical Framework for Stakeholder Collaboration in Local Watershed Issues

Inputs	Activities	Outputs	Outcomes/ Impacts
Two staff members working ten hours per week Funding to rent public forum space Funding for advertising in local newspaper Funding for room rental and refreshments for focus groups	Public forum Three focus groups	100 people engaged Report summarizing comments	Increased support by stakeholders Improved management of the watershed Fewer conflicts over water rights

---

* For more information see Team Technologies (n.d.). *The LogFrame Handbook*. Washington, D.C., The World Bank.

Communication and Teamwork Tools

Communication Needs Assessment

Not every stakeholder has the same communication needs, and Table 5.15 outlines a way to think about communication needs in terms of the interests of the stakeholders and the power they hold. Those with low interest, for instance, should not necessarily be expected to engage actively in two-way communication, such as responding to e-mails or participating actively in social media. Stakeholders with high levels of interest are more likely to be responsive and engaged and should be given opportunities as such.

Active Listening

A facilitator who can both listen well and foster an environment of listening can help everyone to do their best thinking, planning, and discussing. One of the challenges for a facilitator is to stay focused on the task at hand and to actively listen to what is being said by others. Table 5.16 provides details on active listening techniques. It should be noted that silence can also be a useful technique for letting people gather their thoughts, reenergize, and reflect on what has been said.

Stakeholder Introductions

Before beginning any type of small-group work, it is important for stakeholders to get to know one another and for the facilitator to convey expectations. A well-designed and thoughtfully facilitated icebreaker can make stakeholders feel more comfortable with each other and the facilitator and start off engaged in the proceedings.

Icebreakers should have two goals: for everyone to get to know each other and to set the tone for the proceedings.

The choice of an icebreaker will depend on how well people already know each other, whether people come from different backgrounds, the size of the group, and any special communication needs. A good icebreaker should be focused on the meeting objectives and appropriate for the group of people involved. The first

Table 5.15   Communication Needs of Stakeholders

	Low Interest	*High Interest*
High Power	Keep informed and provide easy opportunities for responding	Work with very closely
Low Power	Ensure that they know where to get information if they desire	Keep informed as to progress

Table 5.16 Active Listening Techniques

Techniques	Purpose	Approach	Language
Encouraging	To convey interest To keep the person talking	Avoid agreeing or disagreeing with the speaker Use noncommittal words with a positive tone of voice	I see That's interesting Tell me more about … Go on
Restating	To show that you are listening and understanding To help the speaker grasp the facts	Restate the speaker's basic ideas Put it in your words	If I understand, your idea is… In other words, your decision is…
Reflecting	To show you are listening and understanding To let the speaker know that you understand how he/she feels	Reflect the speaker's basic feelings Put in your own words	You feel that… You were pretty upset that… You believe that…
Attending	To be present in the discussion	Maintain eye contact, attentive posture	I see… I didn't know that…
Clarifying	Bringing vague ideas into focus	Ask question Restate and confirm accuracy	Let me check to make sure I'm following what you said…
Defer judgment	To allow the speaker to finish thoughts completely	Avoid interrupting	(Silence)

(Continued)

Table 5.16   Active Listening Techniques (Continued)

Techniques	Purpose	Approach	Language
Summarizing	To pull important ideas and facts together To establish a basis for further discussion To review progress	Restate, reflect, and summarize major ideas and feelings	These seem to be the key ideas expressed… If I understand you, you feel this way about this situation…

Source: Decker, B. (1988). *The Art of Communication.* Menlo Park, CA, Crisp Publications; Office of Quality Improvement (2007). *Facilitator Tool Kit.* Madison, University of Wisconsin–Madison.

step is to think about the objectives of the icebreaker. Possible objectives include learning people's names and backgrounds, establishing a productive working environment, creating an open "safe" space for the sharing of ideas, getting everyone comfortable with participating on an equal basis, and creating a common sense of purpose.

The following are some examples of icebreakers:

■ *Introduction*—A basic introduction of names and positions. This is a very simple and straightforward exercise, although it can serve to highlight differences in job status.

■ *The little-known fact*—The participants state their name and a "little-known fact" about themselves. This can serve to lighten up the introduction and takes the focus away from job titles.

■ *Problem solving*—Each small group is given a simple problem or puzzle to work through for a short amount of time. Afterward each group is asked to introduce themselves and present their solution to the larger group. This creates a sense of productivity for the group and gives a sense of accomplishment in the first few minutes. It also takes the emphasis away from status, interests, and differences.

■ *Word association*—The facilitator says a word related to the topic at hand (e.g., wildlife) and, in turn, participants state their name and any words and phrases that come to mind. This can be a way to introduce the themes of the meeting and begin creative thinking.

■ *Burning questions*—Participants state their name and then ask a key question that they hope will be answered during the meeting.

- *Brainstorming*—Starting a session off with introductions and then brainstorming can get the group moving quickly into the topics at hand. The only issue is that some people may not feel as comfortable participating so quickly in a larger group and can be overshadowed by others who are more outspoken.

Team-Building Exercises

While there are countless team-building exercises available on the web, these are a select few that can help to develop positive group relationships and improve communication skills. These exercises each have a specific team-building component to them and should end with a debriefing discussion by the group to go over the experience and discuss what was learned.

- *Survival planning*—The group of stakeholders is broken into small groups and instructed that they have just been in a plane crash into the ocean. As a group they can bring just twelve items with them onto the lifeboat to help them survive on a deserted island. After the groups have presented their lists of items, have them discuss how they came to their decision. Did everyone feel heard? Did one person take the lead? Was there conflict? The purpose of this scenario is to help the group think about communication and leadership in a meaningful way, before taking on their work.
- *Back-to-back drawing*—The group is divided into pairs, and each pair sits back-to-back. One person is given a picture of a shape and gives verbal directions to the other person on how to draw it, without identifying the shape by name. After the drawing is finished the pair should compare the original with the drawing and discuss the following questions: How well did the first person describe the shape? How well did the second person listen to the instructions? What were the issues that arose with the sending and receiving aspects of communication? This exercise is another tool to help participants think about communication and to work on improving their own skills. In particular, this can help multicultural groups to start thinking about different communication styles and issues.
- *Unified story*—The group is broken down into smaller groups of five or six. Each member is given a picture cut from a magazine related to the policy issue at hand; ideally this would be related to the group purpose. For example, a group that has been formed to address the spread of the pine beetle might be given pictures related to forests, wildlife, and recreation. Working as a group they must arrange the pictures and sketch out a unified story without actually showing each other their pictures. This is an exercise in listening to the ideas of others, patience, and creative problem solving.
- *Choose your own activity*—Groups are challenged to each come up with a challenging small-group activity. The catch is that it has to be something that their group can do better than the other groups. Each group earns two points

if no other group is able to beat them at their own activity, and one point for each other activity that they win. The activities must be group oriented and not based on the abilities of just one person. This is a good icebreaker to create an atmosphere of creativity and openness. Groups are challenged to try new things and collaborate as a group in a number of different ways. In the debriefing, the larger group can discuss issues relating to risk taking, communication, and being open to new ideas.

■ *Fear in a hat*—People write anonymously their personal fears on a slip of paper and put it in a hat. Each person randomly picks a slip and reads aloud the fear and shares a few thoughts about how that person might feel. The reader does not make suggestions about how to deal with the fear but simply expresses empathy. This is a very good opportunity for a group to set up an environment of sharing and openness. Instead of fears, participants could also write their hopes for the stakeholder process, their vision of the future, a happy memory, or a personal goal.

■ *Things in common*—Each group of four to five people is tasked with identifying ten things they all have in common, which cannot include body parts or clothing. This is a good exercise to help build the notion of shared interests, particularly for groups that have been brought together because they represent very different perspectives on a particular issue. In the debriefing session the participants can discuss how difficult or easy the task was and any patterns that arose from the activity.

Conclusion

The purpose of this chapter has been to provide agency decision makers with practical tools that can be used to facilitate stakeholder collaboration at every stage of the policy process. Collaboration can fail for a number of reasons: lack of commitment, personality conflicts, irresolvable problems, power struggles, differences in cultural and personal values, unrealistic goals, and poor planning are just a few common complaints. The previous suggestions can be roughly summarized as follows:

■ *Be clear about expectations.* Groups need a sense of direction, and they also need to know what is expected of them in terms of participation, discussion, confidentiality, and expected contribution. First impressions are important; early meetings will set the tone for the future. It is important to emphasize the idea of coming together and working as a team to solve problems, rather than focus on adversarial relationships.

■ *Choose participants wisely.* Participants should be chosen because of the importance of their participation and their potential to contribute to a successful process. Identifying and using the unique skills sets and interests of participants is key; some people may enjoy doing outreach activities, while others may prefer to do things like research and writing. Understanding stakeholders' interests and abilities allows government to tap into expertise and the strengths of each individual.

■ *Be respectful of the participants.* People respond to positive incentives: positive feedback, recognition, and reward are all important to helping stakeholders to feel appreciated and respected.

■ *Be flexible.* Plans may fall apart, conflict happens, people may fail to show up, and things will go wrong. These cases should be seen not as failures but rather as opportunities and learning experiences.

■ *Create a sense of ownership.* Facilitators should make it clear that the group shares responsibility for duties, decisions, meeting goals, failures, and successes. Stakeholder collaboration is not easy, but it is worthwhile.

References

Bamberger, M., J. Rugh, et al. (2012). *RealWorld Evaluation: Working under Budget, Time, Data, and Political Constraints.* Thousand Oaks, CA, Sage.

Beck, C. (1997). *Introduction of a Participatory and Integrated Development Process (PIDEP) in Kalomo District, Zambia, Volume 1.* Weikersheim, Margraf Verlag.

Bryan, F. (2003). *Real Democracy: The New England Town Meeting and How It Works.* Chicago, University of Chicago Press.

Bryson, J. M. (2003). *What to Do When Stakeholders Matter: A Guide to Stakeholder Identification and Analysis Techniques.* London, London School of Economics and Political Science.

Case, D. A. D. (1990). *The Community's Toolbox: The Idea, Methods and Tools for Participatory Assessment, Monitoring and Evaluation in Community Forestry.* Rome, Food and Agriculture Organization of the United Nations.

Decker, B. (1988). *The Art of Communication.* Menlo Park, CA, Crisp.

Economic and Social Commission for Asia and the Pacific (2001). *Guidelines for Stakeholders Participation in Strategic Environmental Management.* New York, United Nations.

Guijt, I. and J. Woodhill (2002). *Managing for Impact in Rural Development: A Guide for Project M & E.* Rome, Italy: International Fund for Agricultural Development.

Hartslief, O. (2005). "The South African Presidential Participation Programme (Presidential Imbizo): Engaging Communities for a Better Life." International Conference on Engaging Communities. Queensland, Australia.

Kirby, E. G. (2006). "A Comparative Analysis of Stakeholder Power in the Mexican and U.S. Health Care Systems." *Journal of Health & Social Policy* 22(2): 13–29.

Krueger, R. A. (1994). *Focus Groups: A Practical Guide for Applied Research.* New York, Sage.

Lewin, K. (1943). "Defining the 'Field at a Given Time.'" *Psychological Review* 50: 292–310.

Lindsey, G., J. A. Todd, et al. (2009). *A Handbook for Planning and Conducting Charrettes for High Performance Projects.* Washington, DC, National Renewable Energy Laboratory.

Linstone, H. A. and M. Turoff (1975). *Delphi Method: Techniques and Applications.* Reading, MA, Addison Wesley.

Lusk, J. L. and J. Shogren (2007). *Experimental Auctions: Methods and Applications in Economic and Marketing Research.* Cambridge, Cambridge University Press.

Office of Quality Improvement (2007). *Facilitator Tool Kit.* Madison, University of Wisconsin–Madison.

Orr, S. K. (2011). "The Private Sector on Public Land: Policy Implications of a SWOT Analysis of Banff National Park." *Journal of Natural Resources Policy Research* 3(4): 341–354.

Rawlinson, J. G. (1981). *Creative Thinking and Brainstorming.* New York, Wiley.

Smith, J. and P. E. D. Love (2004). "Stakeholder Management during Project Inception: Strategic Needs Analysis." *Journal of Architectural Engineering* 10(1): 22–33.

Stratten, K. and R. Ainslie (2003). *Field Guide: Setting Up a Hotline.* Baltimore, Johns Hopkins Bloomberg School of Public Health/Center for Communication Programs.

Team Technologies (n.d.). *The LogFrame Handbook.* Washington, DC, The World Bank.

The World Bank. (2009). "Participation at Project, Program & Policy Level." Retrieved April 1, 2013, from http://go.worldbank.org/1S57LH08E0.

West, J. J. and T. W. Clark (2006). "Mapping Stakeholder Capacity in the La Amistad Biosphere Initiative." *Journal of Sustainable Forestry* 22(1/2): 35–48.

Index

A

ACF, *see* Advocacy coalition framework
Action notes, 176, 177
Active listening, 67, 124, 181
    attending, 182
    clarifying, 182
    defer judgment, 182
    encouraging, 182
    reflecting, 182
    restating, 182
    summarizing, 183
    techniques, 182–183
Administrative Dispute Resolution Act of 1996, 72
Administrative Procedure Act, 8, 99
ADR, *see* Alternative dispute resolution
Advisory committee, 121, 161–162
Advocacy coalition framework (ACF), 22, 25
Agency favoritism, 61
Agency open house, 123, 173
Agriculture, stakeholders in, 45
Air Force, 60
All-party monitoring, 49
Alternative dispute resolution (ADR), 72
American Association of Variable Star Observers, 82
American Land Rights Association, 5
American Red Cross, 41
ANWR, *see* Arctic National Wildlife Refuge
Aransas National Wildlife Refuge (Gulf Coast of Texas), 11
Arctic National Wildlife Refuge (ANWR), 50

B

Back-to-back drawing, 184

Banff–Bow Valley Task Force (Ministry of Canadian Heritage), 15
BAT, *see* Best Available Technology
Benefit-sharing agreements, 103
Best Available Technology (BAT), 99
Blogs, 149
Blue Ribbon Coalition, 5
Brainstorming, 121, 164–166, 184
    cubing, 165
    free writing, 165
    mapping, 165
    questions, 165
    rolestorming, 166
    starburst, 165
    three perspectives form, 165
    traditional, 164
    usefulness, 164
Brochure, 123, 173
Budget(ing)
    cutbacks (national parks), 101
    development, 112
    participatory, 61, 62
Bureau of Indian Affairs, 10
Bureau of Land Management, 3
Burning questions, 183

C

Capacity building, 77
Case study (Yellowstone National Park), 91–110
    battlegrounds, 91
    bear management, 93–96
        bear jams, 93
        closure of open-pit garbage dumps, 94
        education programs, 95
        grizzly bear mortality, 95
        Grizzly Bear Recovery Plan, 94
        habituated wildlife, 93

official record keeping of incidents, 93
policy background, 93–95
policy and stakeholder analysis, 95–96
rural development, 95
visitor education addressing garbage
removal, 94
bioprospecting and benefits sharing,
101–105
benefit-sharing agreements, 103
budget cutbacks, 101
commercial use of derived enzymes, 103
discoveries, 103
DNA extraction kits, 105
example of policy cycle in action, 105
financial agreement, 105
Freedom of Information Act lawsuit, 104
knowledge derived from research, 103
Old Faithful Symposium, 103, 105
policy background, 101–105
policy and stakeholder analysis, 105
technology transfer, 105
enhancement of national park experience,
91
law, 91
National Park Service, 92
snowmobiles, 98–101
adaptive management, 100
coalition of environmental
organizations, 100
court opinion, 101
joint lawsuit, 99
policy background, 98–101
policy and stakeholder analysis, 101
Record of Decision, 99
winter use policy history, 102–103
stakeholders and national park policy in
Yellowstone, 108–109
wildfires, 105–107
childhood notions, 107
disconnect between stakeholders and
policymakers, 107
fire suppression, consequences of, 106
media coverage, 106
policy background, 105–106
policy and stakeholder analysis, 107
public outcry, 106
wolf reintroduction, 96–98
coyote populations, 96, 97
Draft Environmental Impact Statement,
96
early disagreement, 96
experimental classification, 97

experimental non-essential population,
96
opponents, 97
park-sanctioned predator elimination
programs, 96
policy background, 96–97
policy and stakeholder analysis, 97–98
response, 97
resumption of hunting, 97
vigilante policymaking, 98
Wyoming Farm Bureau Federation, 98
Yellowstone National Park, 92–93
International Biosphere Reserve, 92–93
Old Faithful geyser, 92
range of stakeholders, 93
United Nations World Heritage Site, 93
Challenge.gov, 59, 60
Charette, 119, 151–152
Citizen Corps, 41
Citizen jury, 118, 144–145
Citizen Report Card and Community
Scorecard, 120, 156–157
Citizen science, 82–83
Citizen Volunteer Liability Guide, 41
Clean Water Act, 9
Collaboration tools, *see* Stakeholder
collaboration tools
Communication, 75–79
capacity building, 77
common language, 77
culturally appropriate, 66
data transparency, 76
dealing with threats, 76–77
gatekeepers to policy process, 76
importance of inclusivity, 76
instant communication, 75
managing relations, 77
managing technical complexity, 77–79
method of presentation, 75
moral superiority, 76
needs assessment, 124, 181
one-way, 150
position statements, 77
reinforcement of message, 75
scientific areas, 78
technical issues, 78
trust, fostering of, 77
Communication and teamwork tools, 124,
181–185
active listening, 181, 182–183
communication needs assessment, 181
icebreakers, 183

stakeholder introductions, 181–184
team-building exercises, 184–185
Community-directed visual images, 117,
    140–141
Concentric circles, 120, 158
Conference, 122, 171
Conflict management, 69–72
    administrator challenge, 72
    alternative dispute resolution, 72
    consensus building, 71
    higher-level interventions, 71
    inappropriate intervention, 70
    intervention, 70–72
    lacking interaction with stakeholders, 69
    low-level intervention, 71
    medium-level intervention, 71
    neutral third party, 72
    perception of control, 69
    reactive approach, 69
    sources of conflict, 69–70
Congress, *see also* Legislation
    committees, 19, 24
    disparate interests and, 91
    groups granted access to members of, 27
    Negotiated Rulemaking Action, 61
    policy entrepreneurs, 52
    policy legitimation, 54
    testimony by stakeholders, 53
Consensus
    assumption, 43
    -building initiatives, 8
    -building planning, preliminary step to, 35
    challenge to building, 75
    development of necessary for decision, 21
    difficulty to achieve, 85
    influence on, 71
    stakeholder conflict and, 70
    workshop, 120, 154–155
Consultation, 39
Cooperative Research and Development
    Agreement (CRADA), 104
CRADA, *see* Cooperative Research and
    Development Agreement
Criminal justice, stakeholders in, 45
C-SPAN, 58
Cubing, 165

D

Decision making, stakeholders and, 49–89
    all-party monitoring, 49
    conflict management, 69–72

    administrator challenge, 72
    alternative dispute resolution, 72
    consensus building, 71
    higher-level interventions, 71
    inappropriate intervention, 70
    intervention, 70–72
    lacking interaction with stakeholders, 69
    low-level intervention, 71
    medium-level intervention, 71
    neutral third party, 72
    perception of control, 69
    reactive approach, 69
    sources of conflict, 69–70
    fundamental tasks, 85
    importance of stakeholders for
        policymaking, 55–63
    advantages of stakeholder collaboration,
        55
    agency favoritism, 61
    anticipate reactions, 59–61
    anticipation of future problems, 60
    criticism, 58
    diverse participation, 56
    expertise and resource sharing, 56–57
    federal system, 57
    FEMA Collaboration Community, 56
    fostering innovation, 59
    government website (Challenge.gov), 59,
        60
    incomplete information, 57
    negotiated rulemaking, 60
    online petition system, 57
    participatory budgeting, 61, 62
    policy relevance, 57–58
    public distrust of government, 61
    regulatory capture, 61
    regulatory negotiation, 60
    resource sharing, 56
    social media, 58
    thinking outside the box, 59
    transparency, 61, 63
    trust and legitimacy, 61–63
    watershed management, 57
    inclusivity and working with marginalized
        groups, 65–69
    active listening, 67
    children, 67–68
    culturally appropriate communication,
        66
    helping stakeholders feel valued, 68–69
    international setting, 65
    levels of literacy, 67

lobby groups, 65
local advocacy group, 65
niche in government policymaking, 65
practical considerations, 65–68
proactive governments, 66
resources, 65
soliciting involvement, 68
theoretical considerations, 65
unfamiliar communities, 67
measuring effectiveness of stakeholder
        collaboration, 72–73
    collaborative initiatives, 72
    meeting of policy goals, 73
    monitoring programs, 73
    participants accounts, 73
    surveys, 73
open decision-making processes, 49
paradoxes, 49
promoting good communication, 75–79
    capacity building, 77
    common language, 77
    data transparency, 76
    dealing with threats, 76–77
    gatekeepers to policy process, 76
    importance of inclusivity, 76
    instant communication, 75
    managing relations, 77
    managing technical complexity, 77–79
    method of presentation, 75
    moral superiority, 76
    position statements, 77
    reinforcement of message, 75
    scientific areas, 78
    technical issues, 78
    trust, fostering of, 77
self-selection, 85–86
stakeholder and agency roles, 63–65
    agency responsibilities, 64
    complaints, 64
    false belief, 64
    meaningful participation, 65
    risk of losing personal investment, 64
    shared-responsibility relationship, 63
    stakeholder burnout, 64–65
stakeholder participation ideas in practice,
        79–84
    citizen science, 82–83
    dialogue on public involvement in EPA's
        decisions, 81–82
    dialogue sessions, 81
    Earth Summit, 79
    Facebook groups, 80

Google Maps, 83
    government-created mobile app, 84
    mobile apps, 83–84
    networks, 82
    online gaming, 83
    online viewing of negotiations, 81
    People's Summit, 81
    social media, 80
    United Nations Conference on
        Sustainable Development (Rio+20),
        79–81
stakeholders and public policymaking,
        50–55
    agency discretion, 54
    agenda setting, 51–52
    collaboration with other groups, 51
    competing problem definitions, 50
    conflicts, 55
    congressional testimony, 53
    denial, 51
    differing problem definitions, 50
    eliciting public support, 51
    evaluation, 55
    implementation, 54
    information exchange, 55
    lobbying activities, 53
    monitoring as stakeholder strategy, 53
    mutual gain solution, 54
    policy entrepreneurs, 52
    policy formulation, 52–54
    policy legitimation, 54
    problem definition, 50–51
    program beneficiaries, 55
    programmatic staff, 55
    social perception, changes in, 52
    stakeholder influence, 53
summary guidelines, 85
task of completing an agreement, 85
working with stakeholders in policymaking,
        73–75
    forming stage, 74
    information-sharing considerations, 75
    initial assessment, 73–74
    judgment, 73
    motivation to participate, 75
    normalizing stage, 74
    performing stage, 74
    stages of participation, 74–75
    stakeholders lacking information, 75
    storming stage, 74
    vision, 73
Deep core beliefs, 22

Defensive monitors, 7
DEIS, *see* Draft Environmental Impact
 Statement
Deliberative polling, 122, 170
Delphi study, 120, 157–158
Department of Energy Public Participation
 Policy, 9
Department of the Interior, 3, 92, 99
Department of Justice, 60
Diversa Corporation, 103
DNA extraction kits, 105
Doodle, 176
Dot poster, 116, 132
Draft Environmental Impact Statement (DEIS),
 96

E

Earthjustice (law firm), 100
Earth Summit, 79
Education, 167–176
 agency open house, 173
 brochure, 173
 conference, 171
 deliberative polling, 170
 featured media stories, 174
 inserts and advertisements in newspapers,
  174–175
 mailouts, 173–174
 newsletters, 176
 press conference, 171–172
 press release, writing, 175
 public exhibition, 167
 public speaking, 174
 radio/talk shows, 172
 speakers' bureau, 167–168
 stakeholders in, 45
 storefront, 169
 technical reports, 171
 telephone hotline, 172–173
 tools, 121–124
 website, 168–169
 workshop, 170
EIS, *see* Environmental Impact Study
Electoral process, 115, 130
E-mail, 17
Endangered Species Act, 5, 11, 94, 97
Engagement tools, 117–121, 140–150
 blogs, 149
 citizen jury, 144–145
 community-directed visual images, 140–141
 field trip, 144

Flickr, 149
floor plan for a public event, 146
Google Docs, 149
historical mapping, 142–143
kitchen table discussion, 143
LinkedIn, 149
Listserv, 141
mobile apps, 143–144
one-way communication, 150
online collaboration community, 149
partnership grants, 145
private forums, 150
public forum, 145–147
retreat, 141–142
road show, 140
social media, 147–150
town hall meeting, 142
wiki tools, 149
Environmental Impact Study (EIS), 99
Environmental policymaking and stakeholder
 collaboration, introduction to, 1–13
 central concepts, 3–8
  academic tactics, 4–5
  administrators, 7
  alternative energy industries, 5
  balance between competing interests, 8
  collaborative approach, 3
  consensus-building initiatives, 8
  curiosity, 7
  defensive monitors, 7
  environmental groups, factions, 4
  environmental stakeholders by interests,
   4
  fighting fires, 7
  ideological differences, 4
  learning, 7
  motivations of the media, 5
  opportunists, 7
  players, 7
  public policy, 7–8
  shared responsibility, 6
  stakeholder collaboration, results of, 6
  stakeholder participation, purpose of, 7
  stakeholders, 3–7
  twenty-four hours news cycle, 5
  would-be players, 7
 grass bank, 3
 importance of book, 2
 Malpai Borderland Group, 2
 non-governmental organizations, 3
 overview, 11–12
  closed policymaking milieus, 11

competing viewpoints, 11
study circles, 12
participatory processes, 1
stakeholder collaboration planning, 8–11
Administrative Procedure Act, 8
Bureau of Indian Affairs, 10
Department of Energy Public
Participation Policy, 9
Endangered Species Act, 10
Environmental Protection Agency, 8
unique situations, 10
United Nations action plan for
sustainable development, 9
U.S. Fish and Wildlife Service, 10
U.S. Geological Survey, 10
Whooping Crane Eastern Partnership,
10
World Bank, 10
trust, 2
Environmental Protection Agency (EPA), 8
Brownfields Economic Redevelopment
Initiative, 31
Carpet Policy Dialogue, 75
Common Sense Initiative Council's
Stakeholder Involvement Work
Group, 63
definition of alternative dispute resolution,
72
Innovations Task Force, 9
negotiated rulemaking, 60
Public Participation Policy, 81
regulatory negotiation, 60
stakeholder involvement continuum, 63
Superfund, 77
Technical Assistance Grants, 78
EPA, *see* Environmental Protection Agency
Expectant stakeholders, 23
Experimental auction, 139

F

Facebook, 17, 80, 114, 127, 168
Fear in a hat, 185
Featured media stories, 123, 174
Federal Advisory Committee Act, 113
Federal Partners for Bullying Prevention, 60
Federal Register, 9, 114, 1115
Federal system, 57
Federal Technology Transfer Act, 104
FEMA Collaboration Community, 56
Field trip, 118, 144
Fighting fires, 7

Fishbowl, 115, 129–130
Flickr, 149
Focus group, 116, 131–132
Force Field Analysis, 119, 152
Freedom of Information Act, 8, 104, 105
Free writing, 165
Fund for Animals, 99

G

Gantt chart, 124, 177–179
Girl Scouts, 41
GLOBE At Night project (NASA), 82
Good neighbor policy, 38
Google Docs, 149, 166
Google Maps, 83
Government
administration changes, 37
constitutional right to petition, 58
experiment (We the People), 57
mobile app, 84
powerful tool for, 58
proactive, 66
public distrust of, 61
website (Challenge.gov), 59
Grass bank, 3
Grassroots efforts, 27

H

Health care policy, stakeholders in, 45
Historical mapping, 118, 142–143
Humanitarian aid, stakeholders in, 45

I

Icebreakers, 183–184
brainstorming, 184
burning questions, 183
introduction, 183
little-known fact, 183
problem solving, 183
word association, 183
ICTA, *see* International Center for Technology
Assessment
Idea priority, 150
Imbizo, 116, 130–131
Impact/effort matrix, 119, 150
Information exchange, 55
Inserts and advertisements in newspapers, 124,
174–175
Institutional memory, 44

Interests (stakeholder), 31–37
    academic interest, 33, 34
    changing, 36–37
    conflict and participation, 33–36
    demographic interest, 33, 34
    economic interests, 32, 34
    geographic interest, 33, 34
    government administration changes, 37
    internal conflicts, 36
    legal interest, 33, 34
    like-minded groups, 32
    market saturation scenario, 36
    past history, 35
    personal interests, 32, 34
    policy stakes and interests, 34
    political interests, 32, 34
    professional interests, 32, 34
    satisfaction of key stakeholders, 35
    sources of conflict, 36
    sources of interests, 32–33
    symbolic/humanistic interest, 33, 34
    win-win opportunities, 35
International Center for Technology Assessment
        (ICTA), 104
International Snowmobile Manufacturers
        Association (ISMA), 99
Iron triangle, 19, 24
ISMA, *see* International Snowmobile
        Manufacturers Association
Issue network, 20, 24
Issue niches, 24

K

Kitchen table discussion, 118, 143
Knowledge derived from research, 103

L

Lawsuit
    Freedom of Information Act, 104
    Fund for Animals, 99
    ISMA, The Blue Ribbon Coalition, and
        Wyoming State Snowmobile
        Association, 99
Legislation
    Administrative Dispute Resolution Act of
        1996, 72
    Administrative Procedure Act, 8, 99
    Clean Water Act, 9
    Endangered Species Act, 5, 11, 94, 97
    Federal Advisory Committee Act, 113
    Federal Technology Transfer Act, 104
    Freedom of Information Act, 8, 104, 105
    National Environmental Policy Act, 99
    National Parks Act, 15
    National Parks Service Organic Act, 92
    Resource Conservation and Recovery Act, 9
    Safe Drinking Water Act, 9
Limited partnerships, 39
LinkedIn, 149
Listserv, 17, 117, 141
Little-known fact, 183
Lobby(ing)
    climate change, 5
    farm, 45
    twofold activities, 26, 53
    well-organized groups, 65
    would-be players, 28
Logical framework, 124, 180

M

Mailouts, 123, 173–174
Malpai Borderland Group, 2
Marginal stakeholders, 25
Market saturation scenario, 36
Media, motivations of, 5
Meeting planning tools, 124, 176–177
Message boards, 17
Mixed-blessing stakeholders, 25, 26
Mobile apps, 83–84, 118, 143–144
Mobility map, 116, 133–134
Mutual gain solution, 54

N

NASA, 60, 82
National Environmental Justice Advisory
        Council (NEJAC), 31
National Environmental Policy Act (NEPA), 99
National Institutes of Health WISER app, 84
National Parks Act, 15
National Park Service (NPS), 92
National Parks Service Organic Act, 92
Nature Conservancy, 3
Negotiated rulemaking, 60
Negotiated Rulemaking Action, 61
NEJAC, *see* National Environmental Justice
        Advisory Council
NEPA, *see* National Environmental Policy Act
Networking, 114, 115
Newsletters, 124, 176

Newspapers, inserts and advertisements in, 174–175
NGOs, *see* Non-governmental organizations
Non-governmental organizations (NGOs), 3, 30
Nonsupportive stakeholders, 25
NPS, *see* National Park Service

O

Office of Management and Budget (OMB), 59, 113
OMB, *see* Office of Management and Budget
One-way communication, 150
Online collaboration community, 149
Online gaming, 83
Online petition system, 57
Online surveys, 138
Open ended-stories, 121, 161
Opportunists, 7, 29

P

Participatory cost/benefit analysis, 116, 136–137
Partnership grants, 119, 145
People's Summit, 81
Petitions, 57
Players, 7
Policy community, 25
Policy entrepreneurs, 52
Policy issues, stakeholders in, 45
    agriculture, 45
    criminal justice, 45
    education, 45
    health care policy, 45
    humanitarian aid, 45
Policy monopoly, 25
Policy subsystem, 24
Political savvy, 23
Position statements, 77
Press conference, 122, 171–172
Press release, writing, 175
Private forums, 150
Problem tree, 120, 153
Project management tools, 124, 176–180
    action notes, 176, 177
    Doodle, 176
    Gantt chart, 177–179
    logical framework, 180
    meeting planning tools, 176–177
    project scope chart, 177, 178

scheduling, 176
Project scope chart, 124, 177, 178
Proximity and power, 115, 127–128
Public comments, 138–139
Public exhibition, 121, 167
Public forum, 119, 145–147
Public notices, 115, 125
Public policy, stakeholder models in, 24–25
    advocacy coalition, 25
    iron triangle, 24
    issue network, 24
    issue niches, 24
    policy community, 25
    policy monopoly, 25
    policy subsystem, 24
    subgovernment, 24
Public speaking, 123, 174

R

Radio/talk shows, 172
Ranking exercise, 152
Recombinant Biocatalysis Inc., 103
Record of Decision (ROD), 99
Recruitment tools, 114–127
    cluster sample, 125
    Facebook, 114, 127
    Federal Register, 114
    networking, 114
    public notices, 125
    sampling, 125
    simple random sample, 125
    snowball sampling, 114
    social media, 127
    stratified random sample, 125
    systematic sampling, 125
    Twitter, 114, 127
Regulatory capture, 61
Regulatory negotiation, 60
Resident's panel, 121, 162–163
Resource Conservation and Recovery Act, 9
Retreat, 118, 141–142
Risk chart, 120, 159
Road show, 117, 140
ROD, *see* Record of Decision
Rolestorming, 166

S

Safe Drinking Water Act, 9
Sampling, 115, 125
Scheduling, 176

Seasonal calendar, 116, 135
SEIS, *see* Supplemental Environmental Impact
    Statement
Smokey Bear app, 83
Snowball sampling, 114
Social audit, 120, 155–156
Social media, 80, 119, 127, 147–150
Sorting exercise, 153
Speakers' bureau, 121, 167–168
Stakeholder analysis, 115, 127
Stakeholder collaboration tools, 111–187
    active listening techniques, 182–183
        attending, 182
        clarifying, 182
        defer judgment, 182
        encouraging, 182
        reflecting, 182
        restating, 182
        summarizing, 183
    being clear about expectations, 185
    being flexible, 186
    being respectful of participants, 186
    brainstorming, 164–166
        cubing, 165
        free writing, 165
        mapping, 165
        questions, 165
        rolestorming, 166
        starburst, 165
        three perspectives form, 165
        traditional, 164
        usefulness, 164
    choosing participants wisely, 185–186
    communication and teamwork tools,
        181–185
        active listening, 181, 182–183
        communication needs assessment, 181
        icebreakers, 183
        stakeholder introductions, 181–184
        team building exercises, 184–185
    creating a sense of ownership, 186
    education, 167–176
        agency open house, 173
        brochure, 173
        conference, 171
        deliberative polling, 170
        featured media stories, 174
        inserts and advertisements in
            newspapers, 174–175
        mailouts, 173–174
        newsletters, 176
        press conference, 171–172

        press release, writing, 175
        public exhibition, 167
        public speaking, 174
        radio/talk shows, 172
        speakers' bureau, 167–168
        storefront, 169
        technical reports, 171
        telephone hotline, 172–173
        website, 168–169
        workshop, 170
    engagement tools, 140–150
        blogs, 149
        citizen jury, 144–145
        community-directed visual images,
            140–141
        field trip, 144
        Flickr, 149
        floor plan for a public event, 146
        Google Docs, 149
        historical mapping, 142–143
        kitchen table discussion, 143
        LinkedIn, 149
        Listserv, 141
        mobile apps, 143–144
        one-way communication, 150
        online collaboration community, 149
        partnership grants, 145
        private forums, 150
        public forum, 145–147
        retreat, 141–142
        road show, 140
        social media, 147–150
        town hall meeting, 142
        wiki tools, 149
    icebreakers, 183–184
        brainstorming, 184
        burning questions, 183
        introduction, 183
        little-known fact, 183
        problem solving, 183
        word association, 183
    identifying stakeholder interests, 127–139
        dot poster, 132
        electoral process, 130
        experimental auction, 139
        fishbowl, 129–130
        focus group, 131–132
        Imbizo, 130–131
        mobility map, 133–134
        online surveys, 138
        open-ended questions, 137

participatory cost/benefit analysis,
  136–137
proximity and power diagram, 127–128
public comments, 138–139
seasonal calendar, 135
stakeholder analysis, 127
stakeholder importance, 128
surveys, 137–138
Vickrey auction, 139
village walk, 134
investment up-front, 111
multi-stakeholder environment, 111
planning, 111–114
  budget and timeline development, 112
  choosing of stakeholder collaboration
    tool, 112
  evaluation, 113
  implementation, 113
  output and outcomes, 112
  purpose of stakeholder collaboration
    process, 111
  qualitative assessments, 114
  quantitative data, 113
  questions to consider when choosing a
    collaboration tool, 126–127
  recruitment plan, 113
  statutory or regulatory requirements, 113
problem solving, 185
project management tools for stakeholder
    collaboration, 176–180
  action notes, 176, 177
  Doodle, 176
  Gantt chart, 177–179
  logical framework, 180
  meeting planning tools, 176–177
  project scope chart, 177, 178
  scheduling, 176
recruitment tools, 114–127
  cluster sample, 125
  Facebook, 114, 127
  Federal Register, 114
  networking, 114
  public notices, 125
  sampling, 125
  simple random sample, 125
  snowball sampling, 114
  social media, 127
  stratified random sample, 125
  systematic sampling, 125
  Twitter, 114, 127
stakeholder tools summary, 115–125
  active listening, 124

advisory committee, 121
agency open house, 123
brainstorming, 121
brochure, 123
Charette, 119
citizen jury, 118
Citizen Report Card/Community
    Scorecard, 120
communications needs assessment, 124
communication and teamwork tools,
    124
community-directed visual images, 117
concentric circles, 120
conference, 122
consensus workshop, 120
deliberative polling, 122
Delphi study, 120
dot poster, 116
education tools, 121–124
electoral process, 115
engagement tools, 117–121
featured media stories, 123
Federal Register, 115
field trip, 118
fishbowl, 115
focus group, 116
Force Field Analysis, 119
Gantt chart, 124
historical mapping, 118
Imbizo, 116
impact/effort matrix, 119
inserts and advertisements in
    newspapers, 124
kitchen table discussion, 118
Listserv, 117
logical framework, 124
mailouts, 123
meeting planning tools, 124
mobile apps, 118
mobility map, 116
networking, 115
newsletters, 124
open ended-stories, 121
participatory cost/benefit analysis, 116
partnership grants, 119
press conference, 122
problem tree, 120
project management tools, 124
project scope chart, 124
proximity and power, 115
public exhibition, 121
public forum, 119

public notices, 115
public speaking, 123
ranking and sorting, 120
recruitment tools, 115–117
resident's panel, 121
retreat, 118
risk chart, 120
road show, 117
sampling, 115
seasonal calendar, 116
social audit, 120
social media, 119
speakers' bureau, 121
stakeholder analyses, 15
stakeholder introductions, 124
storefront, 122
surveys, 116
SWOT analysis, 121
team-building exercises, 125
technical report, 122
telephone hotline, 123
town hall meeting, 118
village walk, 116
website, 122
workshop, 122
strategic thinking tools, 150–166
advisory committee, 161–162
brainstorming, 164–166
Charrette, 151–152
Citizen Report Card and Community
Scorecard, 156–157
concentric circles, 158
consensus workshop, 154–155
cubing, 165
Delphi study, 157–158
Force Field Analysis, 152
free writing, 165
idea priority, 150
impact/effort matrix, 150
open-ended stories, 161
problem tree, 153
ranking and sorting, 152–153
residents' panel, 162–163
risk chart, 159
social audit, 155–156
SWOT analysis, 163–164
three perspectives form of
brainstorming, 165
team-building exercises, 184–185
back-to-back drawing, 184
choose your own activity, 184–185
fear in a hat, 185

survival planning, 184
things in common, 185
unified story, 184
Stakeholder introductions, 124, 181–184
Stakeholders, decision making and, 49–89
all-party monitoring, 49
conflict management, 69–72
administrator challenge, 72
alternative dispute resolution, 72
consensus building, 71
higher-level interventions, 71
inappropriate intervention, 70
intervention, 70–72
lacking interaction with stakeholders, 69
low-level intervention, 71
medium-level intervention, 71
neutral third party, 72
perception of control, 69
reactive approach, 69
sources of conflict, 69–70
fundamental tasks, 85
importance of stakeholders for
policymaking, 55–63
advantages of stakeholder collaboration,
55
agency favoritism, 61
anticipate reactions, 59–61
criticism, 58
diverse participation, 56
expertise and resource sharing, 56–57
federal system, 57
FEMA Collaboration Community, 56
fostering innovation, 59
government website (Challenge.gov), 59,
60
incomplete information, 57
negotiated rulemaking, 60
online petition system, 57
participatory budgeting, 61, 62
policy relevance, 57–58
public distrust of government, 61
regulatory capture, 61
regulatory negotiation, 60
resource sharing, 56
social media, 58
thinking outside the box, 59
transparency, 61, 63
trust and legitimacy, 61–63
watershed management, 57
inclusivity and working with marginalized
groups, 65–69
active listening, 67

children, 67–68
culturally appropriate communication,
  66
helping stakeholders feel valued, 68–69
international setting, 65
levels of literacy, 67
lobby groups, 65
local advocacy group, 65
niche in government policymaking, 65
practical considerations, 65–68
proactive governments, 66
resources, 65
soliciting involvement, 68
theoretical considerations, 65
unfamiliar communities, 67
measuring effectiveness of stakeholder
    collaboration, 72–73
collaborative initiatives, 72
meeting of policy goals, 73
monitoring programs, 73
participants accounts, 73
surveys, 73
open decision-making processes, 49
paradoxes, 49
promoting good communication, 75–79
capacity building, 77
common language, 77
data transparency, 76
dealing with threats, 76–77
gatekeepers to policy process, 76
importance of inclusivity, 76
instant communication, 75
managing relations, 77
managing technical complexity, 77–79
method of presentation, 75
moral superiority, 76
position statements, 77
reinforcement of message, 75
scientific areas, 78
technical issues, 78
trust, fostering of, 77
self-selection, 85–86
stakeholder and agency roles, 63–65
agency responsibilities, 64
complaints, 64
false belief, 64
meaningful participation, 65
risk of losing personal investment, 64
shared-responsibility relationship, 63
stakeholder burnout, 64–65
stakeholder participation ideas in practice,
    79–84

citizen science, 82–83
dialogue on public involvement in EPA's
    decisions, 81–82
Earth Summit, 79
Facebook groups, 80
Google Maps, 83
government-created mobile app, 84
mobile apps, 83–84
networks, 82
online gaming, 83
online viewing of negotiations, 81
People's Summit, 81
social media, 80
United Nations Conference on
    Sustainable Development (Rio+20),
    79–81
stakeholders and public policymaking,
    50–55
agency discretion, 54
agenda setting, 51–52
collaboration with other groups, 51
competing problem definitions, 50
conflicts, 55
congressional testimony, 53
denial, 51
differing problem definitions, 50
eliciting public support, 51
evaluation, 55
implementation, 54
information exchange, 55
lobbying activities, 53
monitoring as stakeholder strategy, 53
mutual gain solution, 54
policy entrepreneurs, 52
policy formulation, 52–54
policy legitimation, 54
problem definition, 50–51
program beneficiaries, 55
programmatic staff, 55
social perception, changes in, 52
stakeholder influence, 53
summary guidelines, 85
task of completing an agreement, 85
working with stakeholders in policymaking,
    73–75
forming stage, 74
information-sharing considerations, 75
initial assessment, 73–74
judgment, 73
motivation to participate, 75
normalizing stage, 74
performing stage, 74

stages of participation, 74–75
stakeholders lacking information, 75
storming stage, 74
vision, 73
Stakeholders, theoretical foundations, 15–48
    accountability in policymaking, 46
    counterarguments to participation, 41–44
        common thinking, 42
        compromise, 42
        cultural contexts, 43
        false assumption, 42
        fear of conflicts, 42
        historical conditions, 41–42
        priorities, 43
        reason for failure, 43
        resource constraints, 42
        too many stakeholders, 42
    disenfranchisement, feelings of, 44
    evolving interests, 44
    identifying stakeholders, 29–31
        communication, 31
        demographic method, 31
        focal organization approach, 31
        imperative approach, 31
        opinion-leadership approach, 31
        particular personality style, 31
        reputational approach, 31
        social-participation approach, 31
    institutional memory, 44
    interest-based typology, 26–29
        barriers to participation in
            policymaking, 27
        genuine concern for policy issue, 26
        grassroots efforts, 27
        lobbying activities, 26
        monitors, 29
        opportunists, 29
        self-interest, 29
        stakeholder typology, 28
        would-be players, 27
    interests, 31–37
        academic interest, 33, 34
        changing, 36–37
        conflict and participation, 33–36
        demographic interest, 33, 34
        economic interests, 32, 34
        geographic interest, 33, 34
        government administration changes, 37
        internal conflicts, 36
        legal interest, 33, 34
        like-minded groups, 32
        market saturation scenario, 36

past history, 35
personal interests, 32, 34
policy stakes and interests, 34
political interests, 32, 34
professional interests, 32, 34
satisfaction of key stakeholders, 35
sources of conflict, 36
sources of interests, 32–33
symbolic/humanistic interest, 33, 34
win-win opportunities, 35
participation, 37–41
    citizen involvement, 40
    consultation, 39
    disenchanted stakeholders, 38
    elements of successful collaboration, 40
    forums, 37
    goal, 37
    good neighbor policy, 38
    leadership, 40
    levels of stakeholder involvement, 38–39
    limited partnerships, 39
    nonparticipation, 37–38
    open decision making, 40
    passive participation, 38
    person stonewalling a decision, 40
    review and comment, 39
    smart practices, 41
    stakeholder liaison officer, 40
    successful collaboration, 39 –41
    token involvement, 37
    whole community planning, 41
stakeholders in key policy issues, 45
task force, 15
theories, 18–26
    active dissemination of information, 19
    advocacy coalition framework, 22
    approaches to stakeholder analysis,
        23–26
    competitive subsystem, 22
    deep core beliefs, 22
    definitions, 18–19
    disintegrated subsystems, 22
    dominant subsystems, 21
    dormant actors, 23
    expectant stakeholders, 23
    government advisory group, 16
    iron triangle, 19
    issue network, 20
    legitimacy, 23
    Listserv discussions, 16
    marginalized groups, 18
    marginal stakeholders, 25

mixed-blessing stakeholders, 25, 26
nonsupportive stakeholders, 25
participatory measures, 17
policy core beliefs, 22
policy subsystems, 20
policy theory, 19–23
political savvy, 23
pooling of knowledge from experts, 20
public involvement plan, 16
round table meetings, 16
secondary aspects of belief system, 23
self-identification of stakeholders, 17
stakeholder models in public policy,
    24–25
study objectives, 16
subsystem diversity, 21
supportive stakeholders, 25
trend in environmental policy, 19
watershed cooperation model, 19
Storefront, 122, 169
Strategic thinking tools, 150–166
advisory committee, 161–162
brainstorming, 164–166
Charrette, 151–152
Citizen Report Card and Community
    Scorecard, 156–157
concentric circles, 158
consensus workshop, 154–155
cubing, 165
Delphi study, 157–158
Force Field Analysis, 152
free writing, 165
idea priority, 150
impact/effort matrix, 150
open-ended stories, 161
problem tree, 153
ranking exercise, 152
residents' panel, 162–163
risk chart, 159
social audit, 155–156
sorting exercise, 153
SWOT analysis, 163–164
three perspectives form of brainstorming,
    165
Subgovernment, 24
Superfund, 77
Supplemental Environmental Impact Statement
    (SEIS), 99
Supportive stakeholders, 25
Surveys, 116, 137–138
Survival planning, 184
SWOT analysis, 121, 163–164

T

TAGs, *see* Technical Assistance Grants
TBNEP, *see* Tillamook Bay National Estuary
    Project
TckTckTck (environmental group), 80
Team-building exercises, 125, 184–185
back-to-back drawing, 184
choose your own activity, 184–185
fear in a hat, 185
survival planning, 184
things in common, 185
unified story, 184
Technical Assistance Grants (TAGs), 78
Technical reports, 122, 171
Telephone hotline, 123, 172–173
Texting, 17
The Nature Conservancy (TNC), 30
Things in common, 185
Thinking outside the box, 59
Three perspectives form of brainstorming, 165
Tillamook Bay National Estuary Project
    (TBNEP), 78
TNC, *see* The Nature Conservancy
Town hall meeting, 118, 142
Twenty-four hours news cycle, 5
Twitter, 17, 83, 114, 127, 168

U

UNCED, *see* United Nations Conference on
    Environment and Development
Unified story, 184
United Nations
climate change treaty negotiations, 6
Conference on Environment and
    Development (UNCED), 79
Conference on Sustainable Development
    (Rio+20), 79–81
World Heritage Site, 93
U.S. Fish and Wildlife Service, 10, 11, 97
U.S. General Services Administration, 59
U.S. Geological Survey, 11

V

Vickrey auction, 139
Vigilante policymaking, 98
Village walk, 116, 134
VOC emissions, *see* Volatile organic compound
    emissions

Volatile organic compound (VOC) emissions, 75

W

Watershed cooperation model, 19
Watershed management, 57
Weather conditions, industries dependent on, 5
Web conferences, 17
Website, 122, 168–169
Web traffic, 58
We the People, 57
Whole community planning, 41

Whooping Crane Eastern Partnership, 10
Wiki tools, 149
Win-win opportunities, 35
WISER app, 84
Word association, 183
Workshop, 122, 170
World Bank, 10
Would-be players, 7, 27

Y

Yellowstone National Park, *see* Case study (Yellowstone National Park)
YouTube, 83, 148